The Return of the Russian Leviathan

New Russian Thought

The publication of this series was made possible with the support of the Zimin Foundation

Maxim Trudolyubov, *The Tragedy of Property*
Sergei Medvedev, *The Return of the Russian Leviathan*

The Return of the Russian Leviathan

Sergei Medvedev

Translated by Stephen Dalziel

polity

First published in Russian as Парк Крымского периода. Хроники третьего срока Copyright © Bookmate 2017
Reprinted: 2019, 2020 (THREE TIMES), 2021

This English edition © Polity Press 2020

The translation of this work was funded by the Zimin Foundation.

Polity Press
65 Bridge Street
Cambridge CB2 1UR, UK

Polity Press
101 Station Landing
Suite 300
Medford, MA 02155, USA

ISBN-13: 978-1-5095-3604-7
ISBN-13: 978-1-5095-3605-4 (pb)

A catalogue record for this book is available from the British Library.

Library of Congress Cataloging-in-Publication Data
Names: Medvedev, Sergei, author.
Title: The return of the Russian leviathan / Sergei Medvedev.
Other titles: Park Krymskogo perioda. English
Description: English edition. | Cambridge, UK ; Medford, MA : Polity Press, [2019] | Translation of: Park Krymskogo perioda : khroniki tret'ego sroka. | Includes bibliographical references and index. | Summary: "In this lively and well-informed book, the Russian sociologist and political scientist Sergei Medvedev sets out to explain Russia's apparent relapse into aggressive imperialism and militarism during Putin's third term in office, from 2012 to 2018"-- Provided by publisher.
Identifiers: LCCN 2019017512 (print) | LCCN 2019980220 (ebook) | ISBN 9781509536047 (hardback) | ISBN 9781509536054 (paperback) | ISBN 9781509536061 (epub)
Subjects: LCSH: Russia (Federation)--Politics and government--1991- | Russia (Federation)--Social conditions--1991- | Russia (Federation)--Civilization--21st century. | Russia (Federation)--Intellectual life--21st century. | Russia (Federation)--Social life and customs.
Classification: LCC DK510.763 .M4213 2019 (print) | LCC DK510.763 (ebook) | DDC 947.086/4--dc23
LC record available at https://lccn.loc.gov/2019017512
LC ebook record available at https://lccn.loc.gov/2019980220

Typeset in 10.5 on 12pt Sabon
by Fakenham Prepress Solutions, Fakenham, Norfolk, NR21 8NL
Printed and bound in the United States by LSC Communications

For further information on Polity, visit our website:
politybooks.com

CONTENTS

PREFACE TO THE ENGLISH EDITION

On 23 February 2014, President Vladimir Putin stood on the podium of the Fisht Olympic Stadium in Sochi and presided over the closing ceremony of the Winter Olympic Games. For the first time in many years, Russia had won, coming top of the unofficial medal table. The world had yet to learn of the doping scam that was behind the triumph in Sochi; at that moment it was Putin's personal victory. He had shown the world the Russia that he had built, with its pretence at global leadership, its vertical of power, its skyscrapers in the Moscow City business area, its victories on both the sporting and the gas fronts, and its fabulously expensive Winter Olympiad, which had been put on in a subtropical region.

That very same morning, 23 February, the decision was taken in the Kremlin to annex Crimea from Ukraine. Russian special forces, *spetsnaz*, wearing unmarked uniforms, began to land in Crimea and seize strategic points. They were referred to as 'little green men'. Within a month, on 17 March, Crimea declared its independence, and the next day it was incorporated into Russia. Russia fell into a spectacular downward spiral from its Olympic heights. It went from being a triumphant country and member of the G8, to being an outcast, a country that flew in the face of international law and the world order, one by one ripping out the threads that had tied it to the outside world, destroying all the structures of normality and globalization which Russia had built up in the quarter of a century since the collapse of the Soviet Union.

Today, almost five years later, there is no end in sight to this freefall. On 18 March 2018, on the fourth anniversary of the annexation of Crimea, Vladimir Putin was re-elected president by an overwhelming majority of the population for a further six-year term up to 2024.

He has built his rhetoric on nationalism, militarism and an aggressive confrontation with the West. Russia has become a rogue state, constantly raising the stakes in its symbolic confrontation with the West, and turning its own population into the hostages of its geopolitical ambitions. But the start of this deadly spiral was laid down on that day in February 2014 with the decision to annex Crimea. Now we are all living in a post-Crimea world.

When I say 'we', I include also the readers of the English-language edition of this book. The toxicity of this new Russian regime instantly crossed the borders of Russia and Ukraine. As early as 17 July 2014, during a military operation started by pro-Russian separatists in the east of Ukraine, a Malaysian Airlines Boeing aircraft, flight MH17, was shot down by a 'BUK' air defence system brought in from Russia. All 298 passengers and crew, from ten different countries, perished. Then we had the interference by Russian hackers in elections in the USA and Europe; an attempt to bring about a *coup d'état* in Montenegro; intervention in the civil war in Syria and the barbaric bombardment of Aleppo and other towns, with subsequent huge loss of life. Next, in March 2018 in the English city of Salisbury, there was the poisoning and attempted murder of the former Russian spy, Sergei Skripal, and his daughter, Julia, using a nerve agent. You couldn't find a better (or perhaps that should be a worse) metaphor for the toxicity of the Russian regime.

This book is an attempt to understand where this regime appeared from and how it got a grip on power. Is it simply a logical continuation of the post-Soviet transition; or is it a sharp break with the script, thanks to the will of one man? Is it a deeply Russian invention; or is it the Russian version of a global trend towards de-globalization and a return to the idea of the nation-state, with its old grievances and unfulfilled ambitions, part of which was the 'Brexit' vote and the election of Donald Trump as President of the USA?

Undoubtedly, Vladimir Putin has become the harbinger and the personification of the global return of the state. But on top of this he turned to the Russian tradition of autocracy, which goes back some 600 years, to the time when the state of Muscovy was established as the successor to the Golden Horde. As a historian, this has been fascinating to observe. I have watched as the traditional forms of power and slavery have returned; totalitarian discourses combined with Soviet figures of speech; the practice of state distribution and the rituals of class in society; and all of this linking together the Brezhnev period, Stalinism, serfdom, and practices from the time of Ivan the

Terrible. The whole history of Russia is being played out before us once again, repeating most of the social, political and economic matrices that we have known; and it seems as if Russia is once again sliding back into its old historic rut.

Under Putin, the first decade of the twenty-first century was a time when the state returned in all its former glory: the elite enjoyed their privileges while elections were repressed; the law and the ordinary citizen were regarded with disdain; there was the rhetoric of a great state along with wars for an imperial heritage. The key period was Vladimir Putin's third term as president, from 2012 to 2018. This was the time when we saw the repression of the people's protests which had occurred in the winter of 2011–12, the passing of dreadful repressive laws (such as banning foreigners from adopting Russian children, or the outlawing of 'homosexual propaganda'), the annexation of Crimea, wars in Ukraine and Syria and the waging of an undeclared 'hybrid war' against the West. In short, the portal into the past opened up, and the political arena was taken over by the dinosaurs of autocracy and imperialism.

And it was in these years of Putin's third term, alongside the establishment of this revanchist, repressive regime in Russia, that I wrote the essays which make up this book. These are pages from the modern history of Russia, variations on the main theme: the return of the state and its war against different areas of civil, territorial and symbolic autonomy. This is a chronicle of the state's attack on the individual, the assertion of its sovereign rights on our territory, our body and our memory.

The book is divided into four parts, each of which describes one of the 'wars' being waged by the state:

1 *The War for Space*: from the battles for Moscow's squares and boulevards taking place between the authorities and the protest movement, to the symbolic actions of the 'gathering in' of Russian territory, such as plans to militarize the Arctic; from the post-imperial adventures in Crimea and the Donbass to the neocolonial war in Syria.

2 *The War for Symbols*: the battle for symbolic dominance through various locations, signs, rituals and performances by the authorities: the Kremlin and Red Square portrayed as sacred sites; military parades and patriotic parks as sanctuaries of sovereignty. Russian strategic nuclear missiles have become one of the main symbols of power: paraded through the streets of Moscow; pictured on popular tee-shirts; threatening the West from giant screens during

Putin's pre-election speech in March 2018. They have become the symbolic basis for the new Russian self-awareness.

3 *The War for the Body*: this is a new area of state regulation, which has been particularly noticeable in the second decade of the century. It refers to the practice dubbed 'biopolitics' by Michel Foucault – state interference in the private lives of citizens, from their consumer habits to their sexual and reproductive practices. In this category we have the battles with gay propaganda and foreign adoptions; religious education in schools; and the destruction of Western food products that came under Russian sanctions. The authorities are poking their noses into places that were previously considered the domains of our private lives: the bathroom, the bedroom, the kitchen – even looking inside the fridge – and trying to regulate our bodily functions, disguising this as a battle for demographics and a claim of a sort of Russian 'sexual sovereignty'.

4 *The War for Memory*: this includes the active historic and memorial policy of the state, from the publication of a single history textbook for schools, to the cult of Victory Day on 9 May; from the creeping rehabilitation of Stalin to the battle against the 'falsifiers of history'. Having become desperate to build the future, the state now lives on dreams about an heroic past, creating the myth about Russian history being an unbroken line of victories, while being terrified to acknowledge failures and mistakes and repressing traumatic memories.

The common denominator of these four wars is the battle for 'sovereignty', under which the Kremlin understands maintaining unlimited state power and defending its independence against any outside influence. The authorities wish to control the geographical and symbolic territory of Russia; the collective body and the collective memory of the nation. Over all these battles hangs the figure of the sovereign: President Putin. And it is no coincidence that throughout this book the name of the main theorist of sovereignty in the twentieth century, the German jurist and political theorist, Carl Schmitt, keeps cropping up. 'The Crown Jurist of the Third Reich' is very popular among pro-Kremlin political scientists.

But it would not be entirely accurate to link the return of the state with Putin alone; rather, he himself became an iconic figure, who embodied and designated a great historical cycle: the eternal return of the Russian Leviathan. It is not Putin who has resurrected the traditional model of Russian history, it is that Russian history itself in the twenty-first century has become embodied in the figure of Putin, who has become the 'national idea of Russia' (to use the highly accurate words of the Russian fiction writer, Victor Pelevin).

Should we be afraid of Putin's post-Crimea Russia? Hegel wrote that history repeats itself twice: the first time as a tragedy, the second as a farce. Despite all the tragic individual crimes of this regime, like unleashing the war in Ukraine, or the shooting down of MH17, the Russian Empire has entered a final, tired, imitative period of its history. Many of the passages in this book talk about fakes, about simulacra, about historical reconstruction. The new Russian approach to sovereignty may at times be deadly, but on the whole these are now phantom pains, the wars of an outdated Empire that is already past its sell-by date, that has exhausted its resources and that is now fighting a rearguard action on an inexorably declining territory. At times, it is terrifying to witness these battles; at times it is edifying. But more often than not it is simply funny. This book is written at the point where historical intuition meets comical intonation, and tragedy meets farce.

Moscow, May 2018

TRANSLATOR'S NOTE

A number of concepts referred to in the text may be unfamiliar to the non-Russian reader. These are explained in both endnotes and a glossary provided by the translator. The endnotes also include references to a number of original sources. The reader should be aware that many of these sources are in Russian only.

PART I: THE WAR FOR SPACE[1]

SOVEREIGN TERRITORY ...
WITH NO ROADS

There's only one thing more dreadful than Russian roads: Russian roadworks. Recently I had the misfortune to witness one of these local catastrophes, when I was driving from Moscow to Tartu, in Estonia, along the M9 'Baltiya' federal highway. It has to be said that this road, which passes through the Tver and Pskov Oblasts, was never renowned for its smooth carriageway, which was why those in the know would travel to the Baltic region via the Minsk highway. But on this occasion, I came across something extraordinary even by the standards of Russian roads: 250 kilometres from the capital, the asphalt ran out. We're not talking about somewhere east of Lake Baikal, or somewhere in the distant reaches of Siberia; right in the heart of European Russia, a federal highway had become a dirt-track, with holes of epic proportions, covered with a metre-thick layer of slushy muck. Trucks were trying to crawl through it, making drunken patterns. Some bashed into each other, others disappeared into ditches. Coming in the other direction were mud-spattered cars with Moscow number plates; I exchanged ironic smiles with their drivers. Occasionally I came across a few cars with foreign number plates. I saw one Toyota carrying a group of Portuguese, who were enthusiastically taking photos out of every window; this would be something to tell the grandchildren.

It took me four hours to cover 100 kilometres of this asphalt-free highway, during which time I didn't see a single roadworker; not one police car; no equipment for repairing the road; no signs saying how long the roadworks would last or indicating any diversion. There was just the long-extinct road-bed. At the petrol station they told me that the roadworkers had dug up the surface at the beginning of autumn and then disappeared without saying when they'd be back. For the fourth month in a row, the road looks as it did after the aerial bombardment at the end of 1941, when battles were raging with the Germans around Rzhev and Velikiye Luki. At the same petrol station, they told me about the French long-distance lorry driver who came

3

and pleaded with them: 'I got lost on these roads; how do I find the main road again?' This, they told him, is it. This is the main road from Europe to Moscow.

It was on this road that I came to understand two important things. First, we have entered a new stage: one of absolute impunity. Even five years ago it would have been difficult to imagine something like this in Russia. Yes, people stole from the state, but there was nonetheless the obligation at least to give the impression of doing something. Now, anything goes, and no one is held accountable. Hot on the heels of what was simply theft has come total indifference. What the practice of the past few years has shown is that in Russia now no one ever answers for anything – not for stolen billions, not for satellites which crash, not for the unleashing of wars.

But that's only half the trouble. What's even more frightening is something else: we're losing the country. I've been driving along this road to Estonia for almost ten years; exactly the same period of time that, the propagandists tell us, Russia has been steadily 'picking itself up off its knees'. And what I see with every passing year is that just 100 kilometres from Moscow this landscape is falling apart before my eyes. The M9 highway is constantly being repaired, but it simply gets worse and worse. All around there are ever more dead villages; at night you can travel for dozens of kilometres and you don't see a single light on anywhere. The people you come across are increasingly wretched. They wander aimlessly along the roadside with their sledges, or they try with a look of hopelessness on their face to wave down a car. (Incidentally, I didn't see any local buses, either.) With the exception of a few petrol stations, services along the road are miserable. There are a few dodgy-looking cafés – even the thought of stopping at them is scary – and there's the odd stall with spare parts for lorries. Just as in the sixteenth century, locals flog by the roadside whatever they've gathered in the forest: dried mushrooms, frozen berries, coarse fur clothing. And the forests themselves are gradually claiming back the space that civilization has left behind: the abandoned fields and villages are overgrown with shrubs and bushes, and the trees are creeping ever closer to the road. And if in the past you could be ambushed along the road by the traffic police with their speed radars, this time I didn't see a single one. The authorities, infra-structure, people – everything is dissolving into oblivion ...

But the problem is much wider than just this road. What we're talking about here is the very structure of the Russian state: how it relates to the area it governs and the territorial sovereignty of Russia. And even as the Ministry of Justice and the State Duma do battle

4

with 'foreign agents' and revolutions in neighbouring countries, and Deputy Prime Minister Dmitry Rogozin tells us that Russia is defending its sovereignty in the battle for Syria – all this time we've already lost our sovereignty on the M9 highway. There are two sides to sovereignty: formal power and control. You can still see some symbols of power along that road. For example, in the town of Zubtsov, right next to the Boverli Hill Hotel, you can see the building of the local administration, flying the Russian flag. And on the road into the town of Nelidovo there's a concrete booth adorned with the slogan 'Forward, Russia!' But effective control over this area has already been lost. Here, there is no state, no infrastructure, no institutions; in short, no life.

Another decade of such decay and no one will be travelling along this road to go to Pushkin Hills; or Karevo, birthplace of the composer Modest Mussorgsky; or to Ostrov, with its unique skiing tracks; or to ancient Izborsk; or to the white stone walls of the Pskov Kremlin. And after another ten years, all that will be left of Russia will be twenty large cities; showpiece infrastructure projects like Olympic Sochi; a ring road around Moscow; and stadiums built for the 2018 football World Cup. In between them will be just emptiness, with sparse forests and neglected roads. Russia is turning into a moth-eaten blanket – one with ever more holes and ever less fabric. We defended our sovereignty in the bloody battles around Rzhev and Vyazma in the winter of 1941; but we've lost it on the roads going through those same places.

THE SMOKE OF THE FATHERLAND

Dulcis fumus patriae, as the ancient Romans used to say: 'The smoke of the Fatherland smells sweet'. In Russia we breathe in this smoke each springtime: the country is enveloped in fire. As soon as the snow melts and last year's grass dries out, people go out into the countryside and set fire to their rubbish, the grass, stubble, reeds and cane. According to Greenpeace, every year hundreds of thousands of acres of fields and forests are burnt. Some five or six thousand homes burn down; old country estate houses and nature reserves are destroyed; people are killed; cattle are burnt alive. Irreparable damage is done to nature, the soil, vegetation and the creatures that live in the grass and the forests. As the spring creeps up from the south to the north of Russia, for a month or more the whole country plunges into a mad frenzy of self-destruction, until the rains come and the first greenery appears.

The most dangerous time of the year is when the spring holidays occur. Last year, tragedy struck at Easter when on just one day, 12 April, Khakassia burst into flames all at once in a number of different places. And just around the corner lay an even greater ecological disaster: the May holidays, from 1 May until Victory Day on the 9th.[2] This is when millions of Russians answer the call of the wild, and go to meet it with their barbecues and buckets full of meat to skewer; with music and various forms of transport. Off-road vehicles and quad-bikes go charging all over the soft earth, churning up the fresh grass shoots; cars are lined up all along the banks of the rivers and the waterways; songs blare out; you can't get away from pop music; tree branches begin to crack; the air is heavy with smoke from the meat; and the May twilight is lit up by the first piles of rubbish. A substantial proportion of the Russian population long ago established that they're firmly at odds with their surroundings, thus reducing it to a state of chaos. The burning grasses are just one part of a huge problem, which is summed up by the fundamental anti-ecological nature of our existence.

Why do people in Russia burn grass? Anthropologists talk about the genes that have been handed down from the slash-and-burn agriculture practised by our ancestors in the forests of Eastern Europe, chopping down and burning the forest so as to fertilize with ash the poor clay soil. Cultural historians describe the archaic rituals of spring and the belief in the cleansing power of fire. And representatives of the Emergency Situations Ministry just call it blatant hooliganism. In fact, the idea that burning the grass warms up the soil and enriches it with ash, which helps new grass to grow, has long since been irrevocably exposed as a myth. Soil doesn't warm up significantly from a fast-moving grass fire; but what does happen is that buds and grass seeds on the surface perish, as do useful micro-organisms and tiny creatures. Birds' nests and eggs are destroyed; newly born hares die, as do hedgehogs and their babies, frogs, insects, larvae, cocoons and worms. Weeds such as burdock and cow-parsnip, which are more resistant to fire, grow up in place of different grasses; and after cane has been burnt down, more cane grows to take its place.

There is one other popular explanation: the great desire to burn off the grass before your neighbours burn it from the other side; you want to be the first to do it. The idea that you don't actually have to burn off the grass, it seems, doesn't occur to the inhabitants of the neighbouring villages. This sort of 'war of all against all' is typical of societies that are totally fragmented and socially dysfunctional.

The philosopher Maxim Goryunov sees in the fires the metaphysics of the Russian world: 'The Russians, like their Finno-Ugric predecessors, who burnt the primeval forests in order to plant turnips and swedes, burn the cultural and political landscape around themselves for the sake of their gas pipelines and their multi-storey prefabricated towns.'[3] Likewise, the 'Russian Spring', as they have called the separatist movement of Russian-speaking Eastern Ukraine, has turned out to be a Russian conflagration and a Russian pogrom, as experienced first hand by the inhabitants of the Donbass, which has become an area of total social catastrophe.

But the main way to explain the grass fires is the irrational Russian phrase, 'Let it all burn with a blue flame!'. In other words, 'To hell with it all!'. The Russians are inexplicably drawn to demonstrative and exuberant self-destruction. 'It burns beautifully!', they think, as they set fire to the outskirts of the village, which leads to the torching of the field, the forest, the village and ultimately of themselves. In the fires on the steppe we see Pushkin's idea of the Russian *bunt* or riot, which he described in *The Captain's Daughter*, as well as shades of

7

the 'worldwide conflagration drenched in blood', about which the poet Alexander Blok wrote in his poem 'The Twelve', for which he was attacked. Fellow poet, Vladimir Mayakovsky, recalled how, in the first days of the Revolution, he was walking past the thin, bent figure of Blok warming himself by a fire in front of the Winter Palace in Petrograd. 'Do you like it?' asked Mayakovsky. 'It's good', replied Blok; but then added, 'They burnt down the library in my village.'[4]

The metaphysics of the Russian conflagration can be found in the secret dreams of the 'underground man' in Dostoevsky's *Notes from Underground*, in the desire to destroy harmony in the world and live according to your own 'stupid will'. The cultural theorist Mikhail Epstein locates the underpinnings of post-2014 Russian politics specifically in the wounded pride of the 'underground man'. Today, Russia is voluntarily torching all that was created over a quarter of a century of reform and change – bourgeois comfort and a fragile post-Soviet sense of well-being; openness to the outside world and a system of relations with the West – all for the sake of crazy geopolitical gestures done for effect. Russia is pouring oil on the fires of civil wars in Ukraine and Syria, and threatening the West with a nuclear holocaust. But at the root of this suicidal policy is the very same irrational passion for self-destruction and for wiping out their own habitat which drives the anonymous fire-raisers. And just as the television presenter Dmitry Kiselyov in a live broadcast was threatening the USA with 'radioactive ash' from a Russian nuclear strike, so the whole of southern Siberia was being covered in genuine ash from fires that had been started by ordinary Russian citizens. As the writer Viktor Pelevin said: 'There is undoubtedly an anti-Russian plot; the only problem is that the whole adult population of Russia is complicit in it.'[5]

SACRED ICE

On 16 September 2013, Russia brilliantly carried out a small victorious war.[6] In the Kara Sea the Russian Federal Security Service (FSB) forcibly seized the Greenpeace vessel *Arctic Sunrise*. Greenpeace activists had been trying to carry out a peaceful protest on the Prirazlomnaya drilling platform in the Pechora Sea. People armed with automatic weapons landed by helicopter. In the course of the operation warning shots were fired from an AK-74 Kalashnikov rifle and from the gun of a coastal patrol vessel. Then the eco-warriors' icebreaker was towed into Murmansk, where thirty activists were sentenced by the court to two months' imprisonment and the Prosecutor's Office opened a case under article 227 of the Criminal Code of the Russian Federation, 'For Piracy', which carries a prison sentence of up to fifteen years.

No one was bothered by the disproportionate nature of the proposed sentence for the crime. If a year earlier three girls from Pussy Riot could each receive two years in prison for singing a punk-prayer in the Cathedral of Christ the Saviour in Moscow, then in this case the ecologists had encroached on something far more sacred than a church: a gas platform belonging to Gazprom! This was a clear case of blasphemy! Never mind that the Prirazlomnaya platform was a decommissioned Norwegian platform, had faulty equipment, and was infected with radionuclides; or that they hadn't been able to use it for two years because of safety violations or its general unprofitability: none of that mattered at all. In the eyes of the *siloviki*[7] and patriots, the oil platform was a national treasure, a symbol of energy security, of the sovereignty of the state and a forward post in the battle for the resources of the Arctic. This is what explains the cruel actions of the *siloviki*, the patriotic hysteria whipped up in the press and the typically Russian conspiracy theories which claimed that Greenpeace was acting in the interests of Russia's Western competitors for the Arctic's oil.

A resources war has been under way in the Arctic for decades: over the oil and gas deposits on the Shelf, over fishing grounds and over commercial shipping routes. As global warming increases and the Arctic ice continues to melt, the appetites of both states and corporations are being sharpened. The pinnacle for territorial claims so far has been the triumphal planting of a titanium flag of the Russian Federation on the bottom of the Northern Ice Ocean, on the Lomonosov Ridge, to lay claim to Russia's part of the continental shelf.

The problem is that the biggest loser in this war is Russia itself, irrespective of the volume of Arctic waters it manages to appropriate. The threat to Russia's future comes not in the territorial claims of competitors, but in the ecological disaster happening right now in the Arctic. If mass industrial mining of hydrocarbons begins there, along with busy commercial shipping, this disaster will quickly turn into a total catastrophe, which will affect Russia most of all because of its extensive Arctic coastline and its reliance on the Arctic 'air-conditioning'. Oil exploration is the dirtiest sector in Russia (principally because of gas-flaring), and were there to be an accident the tragedy would be many times greater than the explosion that took place on the oil platform in the Gulf of Mexico in 2010: in the Arctic waters, it would be possible to collect no more than 10 per cent of the oil which would be spilt.

What's more, the proven reserves of 'black gold' on the Arctic Shelf will last for no more than three to five years. In the Barents Sea, for example, proven reserves are five times less than Russian companies currently produce annually. The oil on the Shelf is 'heavy', of inferior quality, and its production cost is significantly higher than oil produced on land. If the global oil price falls lower than one hundred dollars a barrel, then drilling for oil in the Arctic becomes unprofitable.

The real reason for the pursuit of oil in the Arctic, and the way in which this is defended by helicopters and coastal protection vessels, has nothing to do with sovereignty or Russia's national interests; instead, it is all about the mercenary aims of the oil corporations. The entire Arctic infrastructure, including ice-breakers, exploratory drilling and auxiliary vessels, is paid for out of the state budget. In the same way, tax relief is given for the mining and export of natural resources. Russian people never see any of the oil, since it goes straight from the well-head for export; nor do they see any benefits from the tax deductions from the almost zero profitability of the product.

When questions of the Arctic and the incident with Greenpeace are raised, there's often talk about sovereignty, about the sacred borders

10

of Russia, about the generations of Polar explorers, about victories and sacrifices. The point is that you can't put sovereignty into your pocket. Russia can seize huge Arctic territories, but expanding economic activity there simply for the good of a few individual corporations could prove exceedingly costly to the country. Sovereignty means not simply having judicial control over a territory, but having the ability to use it in a rational manner, nurture it and pass it on to future generations. In this understanding of the term, Russia has already lost sovereignty over hundreds of thousands of square kilometres of territory, which is saturated with oil, or polluted by radiation or the results of all manner of economic or military activity. Furthermore, as is well known, the fragile nature in the Arctic takes centuries, not years, to recover. Take Novaya Zemlya, with its high background radiation levels; or Wrangel Island, where lie hundreds of thousands of empty fuel barrels that have been spilt over the years. These are shown on the map as Russian territory; but in reality, for the foreseeable future, they have been lost not just to Russia but to all mankind. These sovereign territories have suffered an ecological catastrophe on a global scale.

Beyond the territorial waters of a few individual states, the Arctic is the property of all mankind. A global movement has already existed for several years calling for the Arctic to be regarded as international territory with special conservation status, with economic and military activity prohibited and only science or tourism allowed. Greenpeace's 'Save the Arctic' petition has been signed by more than eight million people. There is already a precedent for this in international law: the 1959 Antarctic Agreement, and the Convention on the Conservation of Antarctic Marine Living Resources (CCAMLR), from 1982. For the preservation of Planet Earth and of the future of Russia, it would be worth extending such a regime to the Arctic.

We're not talking here about states giving up their sovereignty within the confines of existing borders or territorial waters. And we're not talking only about Russia, but about all the countries bordering the Arctic. We do mean the possibility of giving up exclusive economic zones and, in general, military activity; about stopping mining for natural resources; about industrial fishing and the transit of commercial shipping. It's one thing to consider using the Northern Sea Route at present rates and for present tasks, such as supplying Arctic ports or supporting scientific activity. But it would be a completely different matter if, even as the ice continues to melt, a commercial route were to be established through the Arctic from the Atlantic to the Pacific Ocean, providing a waterway for container

11

ships and supertankers, thus turning the Northern Ice Ocean into a busy transport highway with all the high risks this brings for shipping. This must not happen. Like the Antarctic, the Arctic must be turned into an international nature reserve.

Right now, this call sounds like a kind of utopia, especially considering the tangle of historical, economic and geopolitical problems connected with the Arctic: modern civilization developed in the Northern Hemisphere, and the Arctic has been an arena for a centuries-long confrontation. It is highly unlikely that states – especially Russia as it 'gets up off its knees' (according to the propaganda slogan) – will be prepared to give up their appetites for sovereignty or their economic ambitions. But when the global campaign to save the Antarctic began, that too seemed no less utopian. Now it's the turn of the Arctic.

Ultimately, Russia's national interests consist not in sticking titanium flags on the bottom of the sea, nor in illusions of territorial acquisitions; not in new military bases, nor in 'energy security' (which, in fact, simply defends the interests of the oil corporations); but in the ecological security of the country and its sustainable development. For Russia, the Arctic represents an ecologically vulnerable zone, and in such a situation our interests are defended not by Gazprom and Rosneft, not by Arctic troops, nor by coastal patrol vessels, but by a bunch of gutsy Greenpeace activists. But it's difficult for the country to understand this when it's been blinded by the mirage of sovereignty and myths about inexhaustible resources.

CRIMEA AS A TERRITORY
OF THE SUBCONSCIOUS

How funny it all was at the start: we had the 'Cat Stomping Law' (the nickname given to the Law on Silence that forbids loud noises during the night and was adopted in St Petersburg)[8] and the return of school uniform – State Duma deputies Vitaly Milonov and Elena Mizulina comically battling away for morality; and the creation of the Theology Department of the National Research Nuclear University (MEPhI – Moscow Engineering Physics Institute), the country's leading university in the sphere of the natural sciences. At first this all seemed absurd, grotesque, like trolling: Cossack patrols, the blessing of space rockets, the banning of exhibitions and shows by demand of the Orthodox community. In 2012, things began to look rather more serious, when the court case against Pussy Riot began; and the 'Dima Yakovlev Law' was passed, forbidding foreigners from adopting Russian orphans. And then came the law banning gay propaganda. There was still the hope that this resistance to change was just the result of political games; that it was propaganda for internal consumption, just an attempt to scare people after the protests that took place in Moscow in the winter of 2011–12.

Observed from outside, Russia was just another authoritarian state which habitually put pressure on the media and on dissenters but played according to global rules – carrying out IPOs; attracting investment; preparing for the Winter Olympics in Sochi and for the chairmanship of the G8; speaking at the Council of Europe and in the UN Security Council. There was some criticism of Moscow on human rights issues, but it was still possible to reach agreement with the Kremlin when it came to international affairs, Syria being a case in point. Pragmatism was the watchword in politics, and Putin gave the impression that he was a man 'who'd backed the right horse'. Domestic policy and foreign policy were separate. At home, there were 'spiritual bonds' – the name that Vladimir Putin gave to traditional values – while abroad, there were credit ratings, the NordStream gas pipeline and his good friends Gerhard and Silvio.[9]

And suddenly the dam burst, and the murky waters of Russian internal policy gushed abroad, dragging Russia into the Crimean gamble, taking it beyond the boundaries of international law and starting a new Cold War with the West. The 'spiritual bonds' of the internal Russian product became the basis for foreign policy. The Eurasian fantasies of the philosopher Alexander Dugin, the patriotic kitsch coming from the pen of Alexander Prokhanov, the primitive geopolitics coming out of the military academies, led by retired generals: this intellectual rubbish suddenly became mainstream, resulting in an actual war, intervention in Ukraine and nuclear threats made to the West by the Deputy Prime Minister, Dmitry Rogozin, and the television presenter, Dmitry Kiselyov. The sound of the anecdotal stomping of cats became the clank of caterpillar tracks. In the three weeks separating the Winter Olympics in Sochi from the referendum on the status of Crimea on 16 March 2014, Russia went from being the victorious and hospitable host of the Olympic Games to an aggressor state, putting on the line its own reputation and international stability for the sake of a rocky peninsula in the Black Sea. On 16 March, Russia changed the situation at a single stroke, at the same time ending the twenty-five-year project of normalization and adaptation to the global world that had been going on since 1989, the year when Soviet troops pulled out of Afghanistan and the Berlin Wall fell. Russia found itself in this new world with an annexed territory – but with no rules, guarantees or norms of international law. The unexpectedness, sheer scale and possible consequences of this stunning transformation all put it on a par with the collapse of the USSR.

There's no point in looking for any rational basis, or for any systemic boundaries in this revolution; the wheels have come off and it's not clear what else it will destroy. To try to understand this you don't need the geopolitical specialists Kissinger or Brzezinski; you need the Russian philosophers and writers, Fyodor Dostoevsky and Nikolai Danilevsky. Russian policy has been grabbed now not by the Gazprom manager with the villa in Antibes (who's flying off on his private jet to save his shares), but by an Orthodox *Chekist*[10] with a slim volume by Ivan Ilyin, an émigré philosopher and monarchist. For too long, we ignored the revanchist rhetoric of 'the Russian world'; and now that world has come to us in armoured personnel carriers.

Russian politics has passed through a Jungian revolution in which the collective unconscious, the archetype and the myth have triumphed once and for all. Having begun as trolling and political technology, the irrational has gradually burrowed its way to the very core of politics and has itself become the policy, the lens through which the Kremlin sees the world. This discourse has taken hold of the subject and brought to life a new ideological and messianic form of politics. As the political scientist Alexander Morozov writes, 'the ideas of profit, trade, exchange, cooperation, institutional and traditional "politics of interests" – indeed, the whole discourse of *Realpolitik*, has given way to risk, heroism, heroic suicide and "fate". No sacrifice, nor even the final catastrophe, will convince the initiators of such a policy of how absurd it is.'[11]

Crimea became that very 'fate': the moment of truth; the focal point for all the grudges of recent years; the post-imperial resentment and the wounded pride, like in Alexei Balabanov's film *Brother 2* ('You bastards still have to answer to me for Sevastopol!', screams the hero at a group of Ukrainians); the thirst for revenge and the search for 'fascists' in the neighbouring countries; the inferiority complex ('America can, so why can't we?'); and the global ambitions. Crimea was where the mix of complexes and fears was satiated and proved to be the crystallization of the new Russian regime. And at one and the same time, the territorialization of the collective subconscious, which found a launchpad for itself, deep in the heroic myth of Sevastopol.

Today in the hero-city[12] there's a carnival: the main figures of this new Russian discourse strut their stuff, such as Duma deputy Vitaly Milonov, and the leader of the patriotic bikers, Alexander 'the Surgeon' Zaldostanov, along with Cossacks and war veterans. Alexander Prokhanov praises the Russian President to the skies as 'Putin Taurida',[13] and ecstatic commentators talk about 'the beginning of new Russian conquests'. Inspired by the success of the Sochi Olympics and charged with a messianic role, Russia decided to rewrite the global rules of the game and reconsider the whole global architecture built after 1991 – and even what came out of Yalta in 1945. Sensing the West's impotency and disunity, the crisis of leadership in America and the weakness of the European Union, Moscow decided to stake everything and throw down the gauntlet to the modern world order. At first, Russia simply criticized the West for its moral degradation, and built up its own protective barrier against homosexuals and liberals. Now, Russia has decided to spread the borders of the empire, doing so, what's more, on the same conservative and moralistic foundations it has used to create order at home.

Will this new Russian crusade be successful? In the final analysis, it is based on a romantic myth, not on sober calculations. At its root is an irrational impulse, just like the German *Blut und Boden*, 'blood and soil', which today has brought millions of Russians out in solidarity with Crimea, but which has very few resources or institutional foundations. In contrast to Stalin's USSR, today's Russia does not have the army, nor the technology, nor – and this is crucial – an attractive ideology to present to the outside world, which was the case with socialism. Analogies with Iran in 1979 don't hold water, either. Putin is not Khomeini, Patriarch Kirill is not Khamenei, and Moscow's Orthodoxy does not have the mobilizing potential of Shiite Islam. It's just as impossible to create Holy Rus' in secularized, urban Russia as it is to create 'the Russian world' on bayonets, or to unite Orthodox civilization according to Samuel Huntington's principle[14] – if, of course, you don't count as such the gathering of the 'age-old Russian lands' of Crimea, Trans-Dniester, Abkhazia and Ossetia.

History repeats itself twice. What is happening today in Crimea is the final act of Russia's imperial drama, which in a tragi-comic way is eliminating its Soviet legacy. It is somewhat frightening to observe this exorcism, when the Kremlin has breathed the cold of the grave and the spirit of the past has arisen. But this is just a wild and unrealistic chimera, shadows, a superficial simulacrum, be it of rusty Cossacks or Orthodox bikers. Right now in Russia it is nighttime; we simply have to wait for the cock to crow for the third time.

DRUM SOLO

In my Moscow childhood long ago, there was a map of the world hanging in the kitchen of our flat. It hung there partly to educate me, but partly to cover up the paint that was peeling off the walls. In the upper right-hand corner, the most beautiful country in the world stood out in red. As I ate my porridge and listened to the children's radio programme, *Pioneer Dawn*,[15] I thought how unspeakably lucky I was to have been born in the happiest and biggest country in the world; what's more, in its capital city! And I dreamt about the future, when we would grow even bigger and stronger, and we'd probably incorporate Mongolia, Bulgaria, perhaps Romania and Hungary as well (after all, they were brotherly countries); then we could take in Afghanistan, and Alaska … Outside the window dawn had not yet broken, and huge snowflakes were falling, the kind you get only in childhood; clear children's voices were delivering a Pioneer song on the radio, and the future looked wonderful.

Forty years have passed since then. The country creaked when it made a final imperial charge to the south,[16] began to crack up on the Berlin Wall and finally crumbled in a cloud of dust. We Soviet citizens became used to living with new borders; we built our own states and began to visit each other. We learnt the new global rules of the game, engaged in talks about disarmament, set up new rules and institutions for ourselves, gained access to new countries and joined new markets, and opened up for ourselves a world that was much more complicated, colourful and interdependent. It seemed that we had begun to appreciate that great powers are determined not by their size, not by having hundreds of warheads and millions of square kilometres of territory, but by their GDP per capita, the openness of their society and the attractiveness of the country. It seemed as if we had cast aside our childish geopolitical romanticism and messianic dreams and were becoming a grown-up country.

But today, looking at the masses rejoicing over the annexation of Crimea, seeing the flags on the balconies and the celebratory fireworks over Moscow (as if this were May 1944, as if Sevastopol had been liberated from actual – rather than imaginary – fascists); and watching how the *Politika* talk show on Channel One finishes with a collective rendition of the Russian national anthem, I once again hear the theme tune to *Pioneer Dawn*. And when I read the note which the leader of the Liberal Democratic Party of Russia,[17] Vladimir Zhirinovsky, sent to the Polish foreign ministry suggesting that Russia and Poland should divide Ukraine between them, and I see the plan he drew up for the suggested occupation of Ukraine, showing Russia extending across the whole of the Black Sea coast from Adzharia in the east to Bessarabia in the west (and the jester, as everyone knows, comes out with things that the king would never dare say out loud), I once again see the red map of my childhood on the wall and remember the joke about the Soviet schoolchild who went into a shop and asked for a globe of the Soviet Union.

All this reminds me of the novel by Günter Grass, *The Tin Drum* (and the superb film of the book, directed by Volker Schlöndorff). The hero of the story is a small boy, Oskar Matzerath, who is living in Danzig in the 1930s. Oskar is appalled by the adult world around him and decides not to grow up. It is only thanks to the cheap tin drum which his mother has given him that he is able to cope with reality. The little lad beats his drum day and night as he watches the storm clouds of history gather, and the adults around him turn into heartless children, smashing up the Jews' shops and greeting the nascent fascism, as the Third Reich annexes the Free City of Danzig and the Second World War begins.

This phenomenon might be dubbed the mass infantilization of public consciousness, when childish romantic dreams burst forth along with ideas of historical justice. People want some sort of gift *here and now*. The adult world, with all its ideas of norms and laws and procedures, seems unbearably boring and dull, and those who constantly bang on about the need to observe the rules are *so* irritating. Why do we need routine when it's springtime and we're enjoying a holiday? When the drum beats and history is being created?

The infantilism of the Russian consciousness has been treated at length by the Soviet Georgian philosopher, Merab Mamardashvili, who understood it to mean the weakness of both individuals and social institutions; avoidance of accepted behaviour; the intrinsic nature of Russian culture and Orthodoxy as a whole. His wise voice resounds today as a warning:

As for anger, this is linked to the underdevelopment of the social fabric of the country; it is linked to infantilism. This is a powder keg. We have no intellective tradition that would afford us an awareness of our own states of being, that would enable us to ponder lucidly: What are my feelings? Why do I hate? Why do I suffer? And failing to understand this, we create imaginary enemies. In a word, this anger arises in large measure from infantilism.[18]

For a quarter of a century we have attempted to integrate ourselves into an adult world, where there are limits on the individual's desires; a world where we must learn to overcome childish traumas and fears, reworking them into politics, philosophy, culture and art. This is what Germans have done for half a century, sitting at their school desks and agonizingly working their way through their neuroses. (*The Tin Drum* itself reopened many unhealed wounds. Günter Grass was hounded, accused of being unpatriotic and of indulging in pornography.) Now all our efforts have gone down the drain. The teenage complexes of the 'Russian boys', as Dostoevsky called them, have slipped out from behind their desks and are raising hell. The adults have gone out, so the boys can smoke, swear, scoff unlimited amounts of ice-cream, and steal the long-coveted bicycle from the boy next door. The Russian spirit is taking a holiday, and, having pulled up our pants, we're ready to chase after the Komsomol,[19] wave our flags, and march in step.

Until the parents come back.

JIHAD IN DONETSK

At the end of 2014, Russia could be congratulated on a foreign policy victory: in the wake of *Forbes* magazine naming Vladimir Putin 'the most influential man in the world', the *Foreign Policy* journal included him in its list of 'The One Hundred Global Thinkers', under the category 'Agitators'. In a footnote to the list of nominees, the journal explained that, for Putin, 'Russia' is defined not by its present-day borders, but by the common culture, language and history of the Russian people. And that the manifest destiny of the state is to unite all these people, even if that means spitting on the territorial sovereignty of other countries.

However, the joy of receiving this award was somewhat overshadowed by the fact that the Russian President shared it with some rather dubious characters: the pro-Eurasian philosopher, Alexander Dugin ('for expounding the ideology of Russia's expansion'); the political strategist and former prime minister of the so-called Donetsk People's Republic (DPR),[20] Alexander Borodai; the leader of ISIS, Abū Bakr al-Baghdadi; the leader of the Boko Haram sect, Abubakar Shekau; the British Islamist known by the nickname of 'Jihadi John', who was 'famous' for a video put out by ISIS in which he is seen beheading an American journalist; and two Kuwaiti citizens who organized the funding of ISIS and units of Al-Qaeda. So here we have an alternative G8: three Russians and five Islamists, who in the previous year had sent out a challenge to the existing world order.

Did Vladimir Putin dream about achieving such status on 11 September 2001, when he telephoned George Bush to offer him his support in the battle against the world's evil? Now the American President [at the time of writing, Barack Obama] officially names Russia on the list of the three greatest threats to the security of the USA, along with ISIS and the Ebola virus. Separatists in Eastern Ukraine who are supported by Russia are put on a par with Islamic terrorists. And the President of Lithuania, Dalia Grybauskaitė, has publicly labelled Russia 'a terrorist state'.

One could, of course, simply say that such comparisons are tendentious and provocative; just another part of the West's information war against Russia. But the real problem is that the 'hybrid war' which has been unleashed in Eastern Ukraine with Russia's active participation has demonstrated just the sort of social chaos, uncontrolled violence and archaic practices that are in many ways similar to the actions of Islamic fundamentalists in Syria, Iraq, Nigeria and other countries in Africa and the Middle East.

Maybe in Donetsk there haven't yet been manifest executions such as the theatrical punishments carried out by ISIS, where, in the middle of the desert, hostages with orange hoods over their heads have had their throats cut. But 'people's' courts and military field courts are already held in the Donbass, in which, with no due judicial process, death sentences are handed down to alleged rapists and looters. Lynch mobbings happen, such as the one against Irina Dovgan, a resident of the Donetsk Oblast who was accused of having links with the Ukrainian Army. She was tied up for hours in the centre of Donetsk and subjected to beatings and insults from passers-by. Then there's the infamous Donetsk 'Pit' (in the military prison of the former Ukrainian Security Service), where mass torture and rape are carried out. Maybe the Donetsk militias haven't forbidden children to go to school, or kidnapped more than two hundred schoolgirls, as militants from Boko Haram did in Chibok, Nigeria, in April 2014; but in the Lugansk People's Republic (LPR), by order of the field commander Alexei Mozgovoi, women are forbidden from going to clubs, cafés and restaurants, because they should 'sit at home and sew cross-stitch'. Mozgovoi declared: 'She should sit at home, cook pies and celebrate 8 March.[21] It's time that she remembered that she's Russian! It's time that she remembered her spirituality!' At the same time, there's a video on the Internet showing a Cossack beating a girl who has apparently broken this ban.

On the territories controlled by the separatists, total de-modernization has taken place. Archaic tribal practices rule; the strong hold all the rights; there's the law of the Kalashnikov – indeed, all the characteristics that we have come to associate with conflict zones in Africa. It's not surprising that the Lugansk and Donetsk Peoples' Republics have together earned the nickname on the Internet of 'Luganda'. Vladimir Maksakov, a journalist for the website Colta, who spent twenty-two days in the Donetsk People's Republic as a volunteer, and was then locked up in 'the Pit', witnessed the primitive behaviour in Donetsk in 2014:

21

Sunday was one of the main holidays in Donetsk, 'Miners' Day'. That evening we saw two men by the lift. One of them had been brutally beaten, the other was lying on a stretcher and had been shot in the legs. I took them for Ukrainian prisoners of war. But no: they were miners who had carried on celebrating after the curfew came into effect.

One of the militia came in. He had a broken nose and a battered and bruised face. He told us what had happened. He was seeing a girl home when he saw some guys on the staircase doing something with the switchboard. He took them for fighters and opened fire on them. It turned out that they were from the Internet provider; but he understood that too late.[22]

The militarized regimes in Donetsk and Lugansk try to hide behind a fig leaf of legitimacy and democracy by holding elections and referenda. In reality, these pirate republics have far less in common with modern states than with the free lands of the Cossacks, to which runaway peasants and convicts fled from all over Russia, because 'the Don doesn't give up escapees'. They are like the bands of robber Cossacks who gathered around Stepan Razin in the seventeenth century, and Yemelyan Pugachev in the eighteenth;[23] like the insurrections of Nestor Makhno and Alexander Antonov during the Civil War of 1919–21.[24] The separatism which Russia encouraged in the depressed region of the Donbass brought to the fore the archaic strata of the Russian psyche, which, it seemed, had already been destroyed by Soviet modernization. Few even guessed that it existed, apart from the ingenious screenwriters of the 1990s, Pyotr Lutsik and Alexei Samoyardov in their films, *Children of Iron Gods* and *The Outskirts*, who touched on these chthonic depths, as well as the blood and soil of the 'Wild East'. The prophet of Putin's Russia, the film director Alexei Balabanov, also worked with these archaic strata, predicting the annexation of Crimea, war with the West and Russian fascism.

And if we look further afield, then one can compare the DPR and the LPR with the partisan republics in Latin America, such as the narco-guerrillas of the FARC in Colombia; the Maoist 'Sendero Luminoso' (Shining Path) and 'Túpac Amaru' in Peru; the Túpac Katari guerrilla army in Bolivia; and the Red Sun in Ecuador (the Communist Party, also known as Puka Inti). All these groups also love left-wing rhetoric, 'people's justice' and racketeering under the guise of 'revolutionary justice'; and they have a passion for black balaclava masks. And it is no coincidence that one of the heroes of the 'Russian spring', the field commander Arseny Pavlov, who went under the nickname of Motorola, used to wear a bracelet with a portrait of Che Guevara.[25]

What do the fighters of the FARC, ISIS and the DPR have in common? First and foremost, traditionalist anti-globalist ideas. Their ideologues are inspired by examples from the past, be it Islamist theocracy in the Middle East; the bizarre mix of Maoism, Trotskyism and Bolivarianism in Latin America; or the crazy cocktail of monarchism, Stalinism and 'Orthodox civilization' in the minds of the separatists in Eastern Ukraine. Their enemy is not governments, but contemporary society itself, with its free market, the emancipation of women, its temptations and permissiveness, and its social inequality, liberal values and domination by America. They proclaim the armed struggle under the flag of national, territorial or religious liberation; but in reality they are fighting against the anonymous tide of globalization, which erodes everything. They are trying to put up dams, having taken the local population hostage.

Twenty-five years ago, at the start of the 1990s, when the whole world was expecting 'the end of history' as predicted by Francis Fukuyama, the American political theorist Benjamin Barber wrote a book called *Jihad vs. McWorld*. In it, he foresaw the basic type of conflicts that would follow the fall of the Berlin Wall: fundamentalists rising up against globalization. And under the term 'jihad', he meant not only the Islamist movement for the purity of the faith, but the wider protests by the remnants of traditional society against the global tide, from Osama bin Laden to Subcomandante Marcos. In this sense, the leaders of Donetsk and Lugansk also have their own local jihad. These are depressed industrial regions with high levels of unemployment and a poorly reformed mining sector with barbaric mining technology (including mines that they have dug out themselves), which does not fit the post-industrial world. Under the banner of Orthodox sharia law, these leaders are standing up to the advance of Western civilization and its agents, 'the Kiev junta'. This is why, in its listing of 'Agitators', *Foreign Policy* puts these men on a par with the Islamic terrorists of ISIS and Boko Haram.

What unites all these phenomena is that in Nigeria, Syria and Iraq, as well as in Donetsk and Lugansk, similar zones have emerged where there is uncontrolled violence. They are examples of what the British sociologist, Mary Kaldor, has called 'new wars'. These are new types of organized violence, in which the boundaries are wiped away between the traditional type of war, in which states and armies take part, and organized crime, terrorism and the systematic violation of human rights. 'New wars' are like whirlpools that suck in people, territory and resources. Their existence is fuelled both by external military and humanitarian aid, as well as by their own 'economy of violence', based on robbery and murder as well as trade in arms, humanitarian aid and people. For the local 'entrepreneurs of violence' (field commanders and political leaders), violence is a profitable business that demands constant new investment. Many economists who examine modern wars see them not as 'ethnic conflicts', 'struggles for national liberation' or 'decolonization', but simply as a type of organized crime.

The 'hybrid war' in Eastern Ukraine, of which Russian military theoreticians are so proud, has become another of the 'new wars' as defined by Kaldor. Donetsk and Lugansk today remind one of Chechnya between 1996 and 1999: a bandit state, a 'black hole' of violence, contraband and terrorism, which almost pulled in the whole of the North Caucasus. It is no coincidence that among the ranks of the militia bands in the Donbass there are Chechen battalions. These are not simply warriors sent by the Chechen President, Ramzan Kadyrov; they are also fighters for the purity of the faith against the hated West. The paradox of this situation is that Vladimir Putin, who came to power and gained popularity at the peak of the struggle against terrorism, blood and money that fuelled the hotbed of terrorism in Chechnya, has now created with his own hands a second Chechnya even closer to the centre of Russia, right on the border with the Rostov Oblast. All sorts of mercenaries are undergoing a military baptism, and the mad 're-enactors' of historic battles are living out their bloody fantasies. Here we have yet another similarity with ISIS, which attracts fanatics and scumbags from all over the world. Some 15,000 foreigners are fighting in their ranks, including up to 2,000 citizens from Western Europe, such as 'Jihadi John', who beheaded journalists and became one of the 'heroes' on *Foreign Policy*'s list.

A social and humanitarian catastrophe is unfolding in the Donbass, and violence is becoming a way of life. This violence cannot be contained within the region's borders. More and more frequently, it is bursting out into the outside world, as happened with the destruction of flight MH17. The global community has already shown that Russia was responsible, having provided the separatist fighters with modern weaponry. This violence is already being felt in Russia itself, as shown by an incident that happened on 3 November 2014, when four drunken militia fighters from the DPR who were taking a break in the Moscow region and celebrating election day in Donetsk, shot up a traffic police patrol in the Solnechnogorsky District. Three of them got away. Apparently, they were all from the 'Ghost' (*Prizrak*) brigade led by the Lugansk commander, Alexei Mozgovoi. Mozgovoi himself is given huge support in Russia, where he holds meetings with leaders of the parliamentary parties – the Liberal Democratic Party of Russia and A Just Russia – and travels around Moscow in a four-by-four with number plates decorated with the Novorossiya symbol. As he himself acknowledges, if traffic police inspectors stop him and recognize him, they wave him on his way, wishing him well.

According to rumours, the brains behind these pirate republics meet not in the frozen wastes of Donetsk or Lugansk, but in Moscow, in a separate room in the 'Kofemaniya' café on Bolshoi Cherkassky Lane,[26] exactly halfway between the FSB building on Lubyanka Square and the Presidential Administration headquarters on Staraya Square. Alexander Borodai, ministers from the DPR and senior representatives of the Presidential Administration have been spotted there. It seems that these 'global thinkers' of the twenty-first century, the postmodernists, can slip away from their cosy Moscow offices to bless the jihad with military Orthodoxy and modern weaponry. They have not yet managed to build their 'Russian world'; but they have succeeded in tearing Russia away from developments going on around the world, just as their like-minded thinkers who cannot cope with globalization have done in Nigeria, Colombia, Iraq and elsewhere.

GLOBAL BIRYULYOVO

The Russian media came up with another reason to laugh at Europe. In October 2013 in Paris there were mass demonstrations and strikes at the *lycées* in protest at the extradition from France of two migrant schoolchildren, a fifteen-year-old gypsy girl from Kosovo and a nineteen-year-old Armenian lad. The students demanded the resignation of the Minister of the Interior, Manuel Valls. Once again, Russian propaganda talked about 'the extremes of tolerance' and 'the dominance of migrants'. It would simply be impossible to imagine such a scenario in Russia.

Two vital factors are missing from any Russian discussion about migrants. The first is the human dimension (hardly surprising in a country where social Darwinism has triumphed). The migrant problem is examined from a variety of viewpoints: economics, corruption, the labour market, national security, street crime, society's adaptability, Russia's cultural immunity. It is looked at using biological terms such as 'fresh blood' and mechanical terms such as the 'assimilative machine', as the conservative economist and politician Maxim Sokolov describes it. But hardly anyone talks about the most basic fact: this is first and foremost about people who have lived side by side with us for years, decades even; people with their own joys, heartaches and rights. And not just the legal rights of entry, residence and work, but the standard human rights to life; freedom from slavery, hunger and oppression; the right to shelter and to justice.

This is very difficult to explain to Russians, who have become so hardened and neglected over the past twenty-five years that they are constantly creating their own outcasts: the elderly, the homeless, drug addicts, AIDS sufferers. You could even add to that list stray dogs, which in Russia are looked on as biological rubbish, not as living creatures with their own inalienable rights. Migrants (or 'animals' to use the slang of Russian neofascists) are effectively on a par with those stray dogs. Society can regulate their usefulness and their population

26

at its own discretion. Some can be trapped and sterilized; others can be poisoned; a third group can be sent to shelters. *Gastarbeiter* (guest workers) are looked upon merely as biomass. All that needs to be agreed is how many there are, the correct way in which they can be used, and the regulation of their social and cultural hygiene.

Not surprisingly, over the last few years Russian society has adopted the most primitive form of racism. One can recall the pathetic posters of the nationalist 'Russian March' (which now takes place in the depressed Moscow suburb of Biryulyovo), with their slogan, 'For the sake of the white children's future'; against a background of a field of wheat there's a dyed blonde woman holding a fair-haired child. Or the ultraliberal journalist Yulia Latynina, who writes in the opposition newspaper *Novaya Gazeta* about the 'slave subculture', with its 'traditional culture of despotism, oppression and Islam'. There's even the respected opposition figure, Vladimir Ashurkov, a graduate of the prestigious Moscow Institute of Physics and Technology and the Wharton Business School at the University of Pennsylvania, who presented the classic civilizing argument in the business newspaper, *Vedomosti*:

> What is closer to me is the theory of the progressive development of mankind, according to which – from the point of view of social evolution – society can be on different levels of civilization ... The gradual transformation of non-Europeans into Europeans is a long, difficult and painful process; but from the point of view of the development of society and the country, there is no alternative to this.[27]

Progressive thinkers in the late nineteenth century could argue this way, as when Kipling wrote about 'the white man's burden' and the Count de Gobineau spoke of racial superiority; when non-Europeans were touted around the world in cages and put on display in circuses; and when the English advertisement for Pears soap suggested that it could wash clean black skin. It is impossible to imagine such ideas being put forward now in Western newspapers or at Wharton; but in Russia in the second decade of the twenty-first century it is still considered a normal level of discussion.

The key misconception of Russian advocates of racial purity is the idea that there is a certain understanding of what is 'our' identity; 'our' city, in which 'we' are the 'landlords' and 'they' are simply 'tenants'. This is an ideological statement, but does not represent social reality. Russia – and Moscow, what's more – is a veritable cauldron of life, in which the process of ethnic integration has been operating for longer and more successfully than in the most tolerant of European countries; we simply stubbornly refuse to acknowledge this fact. As a Eurasian civilization, Russia stands at the junction of various cultures. Aliens who were conquerors (Tatars) or the conquered (from the Caucasus) were easily assimilated. Russia has never been a 'pure' nation, but an eternal colonial frontier, with its Slav-Ugric genes, its soul from the steppes, and its elite, made up of descendants of Tatar mirzas (royal princes), Baltic barons and Caucasian princes. And the main melting pot of this *potpourri* was Moscow, which for more than six hundred years has been mixing together these human tides, races and religions.

Even the names of streets in Moscow speak of this multicultural heritage: Ordynka was the road to the Golden Horde; on the Arbat stood the Tatars with their carts called arbas; then there are also Great Tatar Street and Little Tatar Street, with its mosque, within walking distance of the Kremlin; there's Armenian (Armyansky) Lane near Lubyanka Square; Georgian (Gruzinsky) Streets, both Large and Small, just off Tverskaya; Maroseyka Street, a short form of Malorossiki, or 'Little Russians', where the 'Little Russians' – as the Ukrainians were known – settled.

It is true, though, that Russia was never a haven of tolerance. In our ethnopolitical history there are plenty of classic examples of colonialism, barbarism and violent russification: the Pale of Settlement and the Black Hundreds; pogroms and uprooting of whole peoples. But this was, after all, an empire. The empire could accommodate different peoples and they could serve the empire. And Moscow, unlike St Petersburg, was always a giant marketplace, a massive transit hub; and in the age of globalization the capital's role as a giant valve for the transfer of resources – be they raw materials, finance or people – has only grown.

And here we have the second blunder of modern Russian nationalism: in their search for 'blood and soil', the nationalists are turning away from Russia's massive imperial heritage, from the breadth of a great power and its ability to live with Others. It is surprising that the nationalists cannot see this as they march under their black and yellow banners of the Russian Empire in the 'Russian March' in Biryulyovo. They are unaware that Russia has an imperial, not a Russian, ethnos; that it was the empire which gave Russia its great history, but at the same time replaced the Russian nation. By demanding that the city should be cleansed of migrants, that the Caucasus should be cut off from Russia or that visa regimes should be established for the Central Asian states, the nationalists want to turn the Russian Federation once and for all from the successor state of the empire into just another provincial country.

This is the main difference between Russia and other former empires, such as France, Britain or the Netherlands. In the postcolonial era, they have managed to transform their experience of empire into a sense of responsibility for the peoples whom they oppressed for centuries, into a proactive policy of immigration, assimilation and tolerance. In recognition of their moral responsibility for colonialism, the great nations have demonstrated generosity, having no fear for their gene pool and cultural immunity. If Russia wants to be a global player, if it wants to influence events in Syria and in the Balkans, to hold talks on a par with the USA and China, it must accept its responsibility for the centuries of colonialism, for 'its' Tajiks and Dagestanis, for their markets and their ethnic quarters, for the builders and cleaners from these regions, for the mosques and the doner-kebab kiosks. This is normal; this is the legacy of empire. And today, holding 'great nation' status includes being welcoming.

Unfortunately, the word 'welcoming' does not come into the Russian political lexicon. With its discordant 'Russian March', with its pretend Cossacks, its Nazis, its heathens and its football fanatics, Russia is turning away from an empire and becoming a mere province; as is evident in the distant Moscow suburb of Biryulyovo.

SEDUCED BY GEOPOLITICS

Political scientists have always had a hard time in Russia. It's a country where there have never been free universities; where independent political thought has led to prison sentences; and where critical thinking has remained the stuff of dreams. This is a country where political science has been simply a timid servant, at the beck and call of those in power, and where you could count genuine political scientists on the fingers of one hand.

There is, however, one sphere of knowledge in which political thought in the Fatherland has been allowed to develop fully: the secretive and mystical discipline known as 'geopolitics'. One hundred years ago, at the time of the fathers of geopolitics, Rudolf Kjellén and Friedrich Ratzel, the concept was infused with a particular intellectual freshness; but in the past fifty years it has grown considerably stale, and in Western political science it has been kicked into a far-off corner of a cupboard as one of the guises of the theory of political realism. It has become the destiny of veterans of the Cold War, such as Zbigniew Brzezinski or John Mearsheimer, whose article in *Foreign Affairs* in July 2014, talking about how the West had 'missed its chance' with Russia, was greeted with delight by Russian experts.

On the contrary, in post-Soviet Russia, with its virginal political thought, geopolitics became the queen of the sciences. Provincial teachers of Marxism, military philosophers in military uniform and mere charlatans flocked to it, covering up their lack of knowledge of the humanities with this deceptively thin theory, which, to the kind Russian heart, looked like a conspiracy containing pretty words such as 'Eurasia', 'heartland' and 'Atlantic civilization'. In Russia, for the ruling class geopolitics removed the need for a critical outlook on the wider world, suggesting instead messianic myths and simulacra such as 'national interests' and 'the struggle for resources'.

In the Russian understanding of geopolitics, the world consists of unitary states, all of which have their own 'interests' and political will and which exist in a Darwinian battle for resources. Vladimir

Nabokov beautifully described this view of the world in his novel *The Gift*, using as an example a Russian émigré, Colonel Shchyogolev, who analyses the world from his couch:

> Like many unpaid windbags, he thought that he could combine the reports he read in the papers by paid windbags into an orderly scheme ... France was AFRAID of something or other, and therefore would never ALLOW it. England was AIMING at something. This statesman CRAVED a rapprochement, while that one wanted to increase his PRESTIGE. Someone was PLOTTING and someone was STRIVING for something. In short, the world Shchyogolev created came out as some kind of collection of limited, humourless, faceless and abstract bullies, and the more brains cunning and circumspection he found in their mutual activities the more stupid, vulgar and simple his world became.[28]

In reality, of course, everything is much more complicated than this. There is no unified 'West', or 'Russia' or 'America'; nor are there any abstract 'national interests'. There are the interests of Vladimir Putin and Igor Sechin (the President of the oil company, Rosneft); the interests of Putin's friends, the Kovalchuk brothers and the Rotenberg brothers; the corporate interests of the Federal Security Service (FSB) and the External Intelligence Service (SVR). There are the interests of the White House and the Pentagon; the interests of NATO, and of the [then] President of Ukraine, Petro Poroshenko. Then there are the interests of corporations such as Siemens and Shell. In other words, there is a complicated multilayered configuration of strategies, institutions, bureaucracies, selfish intentions and fatal errors, all pulling in different directions. And there is no single point where these interests coincide, however much the lovers of these narrow theories might wish for it to be so. 'Geopolitics' in today's Russia is simply an ideology that justifies imperial ambitions and the state's priority over the individual in the allegedly eternal confrontation between Russia and the West in the battle for resources.

In actual fact, there is no competition for 'Russian resources'; Russia is merely flattering itself thinking that there is. There is simply a normal concern that our country, like the Saudis, regularly produces oil, buys its iPhones and its cars from the West, and doesn't interfere in the internal affairs of the West. Back home, as far as the West cares, Russians can carry out exorcisms or light the bonfires of the Inquisition. In the West, they gave up caring long ago about the state of democracy or human rights in Russia. And when a single 'petrol pump which pretends to be a country' (in the very apt words of Senator John McCain) suddenly starts to kick up a fuss by saying it has been insulted, and takes out its offence on those around it, the West simply sees it as a fire or health hazard and puts it into quarantine.

The fiasco in Ukraine is a good example of how Russia, acting upon its geopolitical fears and myths (a fear of strategic encirclement, Ukraine joining NATO or the European Union), rather than on a rational assessment of the risks and advantages, has forced itself into a trap. Moscow turned its fears into self-fulfilling prophecies: by annexing Crimea and starting a war with Ukraine it simply pushed Ukraine into the embrace of the EU and NATO, wrenching away from itself and embittering a formerly fraternal people. Russia has shot itself in the foot, leaving the West simply to look on in amazement at what Russia is doing, and then gave itself a headache about what to do with this Ukraine that has suddenly fallen into its hands. All this is the result of an erroneous assessment of Russia's 'national interests' and the false conclusion that they lie in a battle with the West for Ukraine in the geopolitical space of Eurasia.

If we look at this closely, we see that Russia is not facing any sort of 'challenge from the West'. There is the challenge of globalization and of the post-industrial society, and the West and Russia must both face up to that. After 1991 Russia was offered the chance to play by the general rules of the game, perhaps not as a world leader but certainly as a regional player. Over the course of twenty or so years, a unique architecture for mutually advantageous cooperation was constructed, in which Russian resources were exchanged for Western investment, technology and institutions. A Westernized consumer society was created in Russia which, in the words of the American political scientist Daniel Treisman, turned Russia into a 'normal country'. By the start of the twenty-first century, the West had given up on the idea of a democratic transition in Russia and gave Putin licence to maintain internal stability. At the same time, no one promised Russia a role in resolving global issues simply because of its past merits and victories. Today such a role is guaranteed only by deep structural changes and the construction of a competitive economy and responsible foreign policy, as in China.

A decade and a half ago, in the year 2000 (which now seems so far away that it is hard to imagine that it ever existed), on the eve of his first election, the young and progressive Tsar Vladimir, answering the question of his confidants as to what was meant by the national idea in Russia, answered briefly: 'being competitive'. Much water has flowed under the bridge since then – and now much blood, too – but if we take that as the definition of national interests, then everything in Russia has been turned on its head. It seemed that at last national interests would include investment and technology, the strengthening of human capital, available education and healthcare, working institutions, freedom of speech and association and free and fair elections. These were the slogans with which the liberal opposition took to the streets; and it is they who today still represent the genuine – and not the false – national interests of Russia.

On the other side are those who are committing acts of aggression against a neighbouring state; who have unleashed a dirty war right under their very noses; who send Russian soldiers to be slaughtered and try to cover up this crime; who have torn up the whole system of links with the West, from arms control to investment and financial instruments; who have turned Russia into an international outcast; who are destroying the very capability for economic growth and modernisation. These are the people who are destroying Russia's national interests.

Today Russia does not need geopolitical myths that lead us to war and mobilization, but a programme of national demobilization and a lowering of the temperature of hatred and confrontation with the West. The Cold War is over; it's time to build our house and bring up our children, not send them to the slaughterhouse. We are faced by a multitude of small wars – with the Islamic State, with drugs, poverty, cancer, the Ebola virus – and in these wars the West is our ally. We need to take back the concept of 'national ideas' from paranoid people and charlatans, and forbid them by law from using the term 'geopolitics' as a false science, on a par with conspiracy and astrology.

PROFESSION: INVADER

In Russia, they love jokes about invading other countries. After Prague in 1968, there was a joke doing the rounds about who uses which mode of transport: the Frenchman said that he goes to work on a moped, on holiday in a Renault, and abroad by aeroplane. The German goes to work on a bicycle, on holiday in a Mercedes, and abroad by ship. The Soviet citizen answered that he goes to work on the tram, on holiday by train, and abroad in a tank.

In the well-fed, post-Soviet era, there's a popular joke about the Russian tourist who is being questioned at the border on arrival in a Western country:

'Nationality?'

'Russian.'

'Occupation?'

'No, just visiting.'

Now the jokes have been turned around. On the anniversary of the annexation of Crimea, a video, called 'I Am a Russian Invader', went viral across the Russian Internet. Created in the infamous studio, My Duck's Vision, the film is an apologia for Russian colonialism and gives a list of the blessings that the 'invader by birthright' has brought to the occupied territory. Yury Degtyarev, the studio's general director, who is known for his links to the pro-Kremlin youth movement *Nashi* ('Our people'), acknowledged that the video was ordered by people close to the state. The film has been translated into ten languages, including Polish and Chinese. It should be noted that, curiously, the link to it was placed on the Facebook page of the Russian Embassy in Finland, which caused quite a stir in the Finnish press.

The video itself is not worthy of attention. My Duck's Vision has already produced a string of trashy film clips, from the 'scandalous truth' about McDonald's and Apple to one where the hero grabs the breasts of thousands of girls and then, with the same paw, shakes hands with Putin at a youth gathering at Lake Seliger in the

Tver Oblast. The point is the avalanche of popularity achieved by 'Invader'. In the first week it was watched on YouTube nearly five million times and received six times more 'likes' than 'dislikes'. When such a viral video explodes on the Internet, it causes an even deeper virus within the Russian subconscious: it helps create a false impression of superiority, confidence in our infallibility and a painful nostalgia for the empire.

The droning voice of the presenter stresses the advantages of civilization that Russia has brought to its conquered lands, creating an almost Kipling-like impression of the 'Russian man's burden'. Look, in Siberia, where previously 'they sold women for a bundle of sable pelts', we have begun to extract oil, gas and aluminium, and we have built cities with nurseries and hospitals. Farmsteads in the Baltic States have been turned into electricity stations and factories producing radio technology and cars. And, guess what, in the steppes of Central Asia, we constructed cosmodromes and stadiums, and we grew wheat and cotton.

The voice forgets to say that the advantages of the modern era, which were imposed upon the native peoples of the North, destroyed their traditional way of life, took away the feeding grounds for their reindeer and soaked these grounds with oil, tore children away from their nomadic families and stuck them in boarding schools, killed off shamans and healers, destroyed the knowledge of pre-European civilizations and brought with them the main exterminator of the aboriginal peoples: vodka. The voice forgets to say that cotton became the curse of Central Asia, drying up the Amu Darya and Syr Darya Rivers for the sake of irrigation, turning the Aral Sea into a desert, and every year forcing the men, women and children of Uzbekistan to take part in the compulsory harvesting of this 'white gold'. And in any case, Uzbek cotton cannot compete on global markets: it is much poorer in quality than Egyptian cotton. Equally uncompetitive were the RAF minibuses and Rigonda radiograms made in Latvia. These clumsy creations of the Soviet automobile and radio industries were in demand only in the semi-closed socialist camp; they had no chance on the world market against 'Toyota' or 'Sony'. And the Baltic peoples could remember much more besides: their occupation by the Red Army and the deportation of tens of thousands of people to Siberia, the destruction of farmsteads and their enforced replacement with collective farms, and the ecological disasters they suffered. The apocalyptic scenery of the Zone in Andrei Tarkovsky's film *Stalker* was shot at a disused electricity station near Tallinn.

The Russian Empire and then later the USSR behaved towards their outlying districts in the classic manner of an agent of modernization, smashing the traditional way of life with the iron fist of industrialization, creating modern infrastructure but, at the same time, destroying the natural environment and reshaping the map of the nations. Over the course of hundreds of years, Russia expropriated neighbouring territories, reaching out in what the historian Paul Kennedy called 'imperial overstretch'. But by the end of the twentieth century this gigantic territorial project had run its course and collapsed under the weight of its own ambitions and responsibilities. It is enough today to compare the standard of living on the Karelian Isthmus in the Leningrad Oblast, which was occupied by the USSR during the Soviet-Finnish War of 1939–40, with the standard of living in neighbouring Finland. Travelling by train or car from Helsinki to Vyborg is an existential act. It seems that when you cross the Russo-Finnish border the very quality of the space around you changes. The houses are dilapidated; the roads get worse and worse; there are neglected forests and abandoned fields, in which lies a huge amount of scrap metal: rusting rails, old car bodies, severed cables – the remains of a great dream of modernization, long-forgotten. The 'Russian invader' may have been able to conquer territory ('at what price?' is a separate question), but he was not very capable of making it fit for habitation.

From an historical perspective, the Russian colonization of Eurasia was simply a part of the Age of Exploration of the early capitalist and imperialist time. Russia was caught up in the Age of Modernity; like England, France and Holland, Russia widened the borders of the known world. They conquered foreigners using cold steel, gunpowder and the cross, incorporating new lands and creating one of the largest empires ever known. But here the similarities end. After the fall of the French and British Empires and the turbulent social changes of the 1960s, the discourse of postcolonialism was established in the West. This was linked to Edward Said's 1979 book *Orientalism*, in which he describes how the West dreamt up the East as an object of study, to be disciplined and colonized; and with the works of Gayatri Spivak, which in the 1980s posed the radical question, 'Can the subaltern speak?'

The postcolonial theory has never gained popularity in the academic community in Russia, and is regarded with the same disdain as the Western ideas of tolerance and political correctness. Intellectually, Russia is half a century, if not a century, behind, back in the times of Kipling, with its ignorant sense of pure racism and colonialism and its naive certainty of the superiority of the white man. In reality, Russia always lags behind by about fifty to a hundred years. This was the case with the gunpowder revolution, with socialism, with liberalism ... and it is only now that we are reaching the most painful phase of coming to terms with the collapse of our colonialism (Putin described the collapse of the USSR as, 'the greatest geopolitical catastrophe'), which the West went through half a century ago.

The popularity of a video about the Russian invader is based on the same dense arrogance – on the myths of the advantages of Soviet civilization and of the superiority of the fictional 'Russian world'. The annexation of Crimea and the war in the Donbass demonstrate the same 'invader's syndrome'. From the Belovezha Accords in 1991,[29] which signalled the end of the USSR, Russia had a contemptuous attitude to Ukrainian independence. The very word *'nezalezhnost'* (Ukrainian for 'independence') is spoken by Russians with irony. Russia does not consider Ukraine as a state but as an ethnography, merely a Cossack in his baggy trousers, standing in the doorway of one of the chain of 'Taras Bulba' Ukrainian restaurants; for them, Ukraine is simply a sort of lesser Russia. Just as two hundred years ago, at the time of the Monroe Doctrine, the Latin American countries were looked on by the USA as 'banana republics', so Ukraine is now regarded by the Russian chauvinist in the same way: it is the 'pork fat republic', named after a typical Ukrainian product (and Belarus is the 'potato republic'), and it does not have the right to political sovereignty.

This is why the first Ukrainian revolution of 2004, and particularly the second of 2013–14, were such a blow to Russian pride. The declaration about their own values and priorities was a clear demonstration that Ukrainians did not want to be simply 'the little brother'. And Crimea and the Donbass were the 'Russian world's' answer to the Maidan, as the Ukrainian revolution has been called.[30] This was not simply a geopolitical takeover, but a demonstration of the superiority of one civilization over another; the idea that, under Russia, Crimea and Eastern Ukraine will have a happier and richer life.

What happened as a result, though, is well known. Crimea is effectively living in a state of emergency. Water supplies are insufficient, and electricity is constantly being turned off. It is struggling as a holiday resort: in 2013 there were six and a half million tourists; this fell to three and a half million in 2014. Prices have risen by 50 per cent, and there has been a mass seizure of private businesses under the guise of 'nationalization'. The peninsula has been turned into a huge military base, with the abuse of the rights of civil activists and repression of Crimean Tatars. Dozens of people have been tortured or simply disappeared without trace, and thousands of refugees have fled to mainland Ukraine. The road and rail blockade of Crimea has caused increased chaos on the ferry from the Russian mainland to Kerch, only slightly lessened by the construction of a bridge. Even with this bridge, Crimea is less of a peninsula; rather, it is a besieged island.

And if the 'little green men' who invaded Crimea were nicknamed 'the polite people' (as the propaganda called the Russian special forces in their unmarked uniforms), the Russian volunteers and full-time soldiers who entered the Donbass in their hastily renumbered military vehicles with the markings scratched out were anything but polite. The result is that up to ten thousand people have been killed and a million refugees have fled. The Donbass has been destroyed and turned into a humanitarian Chernobyl,[31] an open wound of the kind that did not exist even after the collapse of the USSR. One year after the event, the results of the 'Russian invader's' actions in Ukraine have been catastrophic; but this fact does not worry those who created the viral video. The video has had an excellent effect on the internal audience, sowing chauvinism and hatred. By calling itself an 'invader by birthright', Russia is most of all occupying itself.

NOUGHTS AND CROSSES

The patriot's dream has come true: Russian SU-34s are proudly flying over far-off colonial lands and dropping smart bombs on nasty men with beards – just as American F-16s did in the skies over Kosovo and Iraq. In briefings to the General Staff, dashing officers show videos from the optics of the missiles' homing devices: the ground gets closer and closer in the crosshairs of the sight; you can see buildings, cars and people; then you see the silent cloud of the explosion and all these items have been turned to naught – just like the Americans did in Iraq! Russia is once again in the premier league of geopolitics and it can bomb whomsoever and wheresoever it likes! The country looks on, bewitched by this hi-tech show, which is so strikingly different from the blood, dirt, crying children and incinerated tank crews in the Donbass; even the colours are fashionably calming: the cloudless blue sky and the sandy-coloured desert. A collective anaesthetic is applied to the consciousness of the masses, which has been exhausted by the news from Ukraine.

I remember how it was sixteen years ago, when an ageing NATO, seeking enemies and a purpose in the wake of the Cold War, unleashed the full strength of its air forces against Serbia. The seventy-nine-day air war in Kosovo became one of the more shameful pages in the history of the North Atlantic Alliance: cities, passenger trains and buses, which in just the same way came within the crosshairs of the missile's sight, all destroyed, leaving more than five hundred civilians dead. And I remember how old Europe forgot about the values of humanity and went completely mad in a militaristic rage: in Britain, the Sky News television channel jealously counted the number of sorties flown by the Royal Air Force; in Germany the *Bild* newspaper wrote up the bombings as if it were talking about Michael Schumacher's races: 'The German Tornados are taking-off in pole-position!' Now Russia, offended by its apparent geopolitical losses, has decided to get its own back on the West by means of a virtual, telegenic and, it seems, safe postmodern war, answering the principal question of Russian life in the twenty-first century: if the Americans can do it, why can't we?

The first virtual war was described by the French philosopher, Jean Baudrillard, in his book *The Gulf War Did Not Take Place*. For him, Operation Desert Storm in January and February 1991 was not a war but a media spectacle of the aerial destruction of the Iraqi Army. Desert Storm was the first war in history formatted by the media. For example, at the request of CNN, some of the bombing missions were carried out at night – even though this increased the risk of collateral damage and even friendly fire incidents; but CNN wanted this because it produced even more spectacular television pictures. Eight years later, in Kosovo, the technology for showing war reached a new level. The homing devices in the warheads of the bombs and missiles had become television cameras. In a world where the mass media rules, the aim of the war becomes not winning but showing; not capturing territory but capturing the audience. It is likely that the day is not far off when miniature cameras in bullets will show in slow motion how they approach a person (let us say, a terrorist) and enter his body – the ratings will be sky high. And from here it is just a short step to the idea of a demonstration war, even one for fun, like the one described by the Russian fiction writer Viktor Pelevin in his anti-utopian novel, *S.N.U.F.F.* He wrote about drones equipped with both television cameras and machine guns, flown by a long-distance operator, which at one and the same time shoot the enemy's soldiers and film it for the television evening news.

The postmodern war is like a computer game. Together with the virtualization and dehumanization of the enemy, it becomes as safe as an electronic game, the aim being to have no losses for the technologically superior civilization. The death of Western military personnel becomes both an image problem and a legal problem, which they try to minimize. Already today, widows of British Army officers are filing multimillion-pound claims against the Ministry of Defence, demanding extra compensation for the death of their husbands in Iraq, as if death was not one of the professional risks an officer takes in a war zone. A hedonistic society is no longer prepared to come to terms with the death of its soldiers.

And now, inspired by the bloodless successes of 'the little green men' in Crimea, and wishing to demonstrate the technical modernization of the armed forces over the past few years, Russia has decided to stage its own exhibition war in Syria: 'Ladies and Gentlemen, we present "Patriot" on tour.' The newest name for an arm of service – the Air-Space Troops – suggests a futuristic mode: now we are going to be shown Star Wars, the battles of the future! This is exactly how the Russian media paints the operation in Syria: as an easy war, a bloodless game of noughts and crosses; a bit of fun in which these heroes with their high technology, these terminators in their hermetically sealed helmets, destroy an abstract, dehumanized, evil enemy. The reports issued by the General Staff amaze us with their attention to detail: workshops making suicide vests, warehouses with spare parts, garages housing pick-ups and armoured vehicles, headquarters and training camps – all are destroyed. All one can do is marvel at the professionalism of the Russian intelligence services, who know the enemy's territory right down to the last bush. It is as if we are being given the chance to take part in an online shooting game: from underneath the wing of the jet fighter, take aim at the houses, the sheds and the hangars from which these funny little men are running. Television reports either that these fighters are running away, shaving off their beards and putting on niqabs, or turning up by sea in Odessa in their thousands, before going on to the Donbass to fight against the pro-Russian separatists.

The decidedly game-like, cartoon nature of this information is matched by the sheer impossibility of believing it. They bombed a workshop or an empty shed, and five hundred, or maybe just fifty, people gave themselves up? Or did they just pop off to a wedding in a neighbouring village? These reports contain no pain; no blood; no information about the dozens of casualties suffered by the peaceful population – the sorts of things reported by the international media and human rights organizations every day. All we hear about is the hi-tech operation, in which a couple of dozen Russian aeroplanes jokingly sorted out the enemy who could not be defeated by an international coalition headed by the USA using hundreds of aircraft and flying some seven thousand bombing sorties over the course of a year.

The apotheosis of this show came when Russia launched twenty-six cruise missiles from ships of the Caspian Sea flotilla as a celebratory salute in honour of Vladimir Putin's birthday on 7 October 2015. They flew 1,500 kilometres over Iran and Iraq at a height of just fifty metres (and it was shown that four of them fell on Iranian territory), struck unidentified targets and made an indelible impression on the outside world, principally because their launch was totally pointless. Given that the so-called 'Islamic State' has no serious air-defence weapons, Russia could have hit the same targets using air-dropped bombs, which are infinitely cheaper than missiles, which cost one million dollars each; but, as they say, putting on a good show is priceless.

In the same celebratory tone, like in the Stalinist propaganda film *Cossacks of the Kuban*, television describes the daily life of Russian soldiers in Syria: they show ruddy-faced cooks serving up borshch and pancakes (everything made from Russian products, even the fruit juice, the correspondent stresses); prefabricated dormitories with air-conditioning; a bath-house with eucalyptus branches provided.[32] The *Zvezda* television channel of the Ministry of Defence enthusiastically describes daily life at the Russian air force base in Latakia as 'destroying Islamic State in comfort'. Once again, this reminded me of an incident during the war in Kosovo, when an American pilot of a B2 stealth bomber, which had flown from its base in Missouri to bomb Yugoslavia, said: 'The great thing about this plane is that you take off from base, carry out your mission, and return to wife, and children, and a cold beer.'

The question about the effectiveness of the military operation becomes lost behind the aesthetics of war porn and the simulacra of the virtual war. The fact was that three months of Russian bombardment did not bring about any change to the situation on the ground: but the opposition counterattacking on all fronts plainly did not tie in with the reports from the General Staff about the destruction of workshops and the Jihadists fleeing to Odessa. However, who needs military effectiveness when you have media effectiveness, and when Russia has got the whole world talking about its aircraft and cruise missiles?

Reality unexpectedly exploded upon this virtual story on 31 October 2015, with the crash of a Russian Airbus over Sinai and the death of 224 people – just as it came back to haunt America in the terrorist attacks of 11 September 2001. Jean Baudrillard wrote about all this in 2002 in his essay *The Violence of the Global*. In his opinion, the answer to the technological and information domination of the new world order is apocalyptic terrorism, as a return to physical reality. In its pursuit of illusory geopolitical bonuses and cheap media effects, Russia voluntarily stepped into a war with widespread international terrorism. Suddenly we became hostages in a game of noughts and crosses, which had seemed so far away and harmless when it was on our television screens and in the General Staff's briefings. Now it has come into our homes; and it is no longer clear who or where will be wiped out.

THE WAR WITH POKÉMON

In July 2016, on Ilyinka Square in Moscow, by the Kitai-Gorod metro station and just a stone's throw from the holiest of holies of Russian power – the complex of buildings that make up the Presidential Administration on Staraya Square – a spontaneous, unsanctioned rally occurred. Every day, especially as dusk fell, hundreds of people began to gather in the square. Sitting on the benches and on the grass, they became engrossed in their smartphones. They introduced themselves to each other, quietly chatted, and went off for a drink and a bite to eat, before once again taking up their positions. In the darkness among the trees and bushes, hundreds of screens glowed.

No, this was not an opposition rally called 'Occupy Kitai-Gorod'; it was the hunt for Pokémon. On Ilyinka Square there were four PokeStops[33] with constantly activated 'lures' (bait to catch Pokémon). The creatures were appearing roughly every couple of minutes, including rare examples, such as Vaporeon, who caused a well-publicized crush in New York's Central Park. He was chased by dozens of people, all trying to catch him on their smartphones. All night in the square a life understood only by the initiated went on; a few vehicles rushed past on Ilyinka Lane; while in the windows of the buildings of the Presidential Administration lights burned behind the white blinds, which, it seems, had remained there from the time when the buildings housed the Central Committee of the Communist Party of the Soviet Union.

Divided by a fence under the watchful eye of the Federal Protection Service, two civilizations met, two concepts of space: the world of the state and the world of Pokémon. And the question arose as to whether these two worlds could live peacefully side by side in the consciousness of the citizens and on the streets of the city. The second Pokémon invasion of Russia began in the summer of 2016 when the new Pokémon Go game, with its added realistic features, was released. (The first invasion was way back in 1996, when Pokémon for Game Boy, the first version, appeared on the scene. It was accompanied by a franchise with cards and souvenirs, and mainly captured fans of computer games and the younger members of the population.) In the new version, characters are linked to Google Maps and actual places on the planet, and players move out of the virtual space into real places: on the streets of cities, in woods and parks.

This time, as opposed to the politically innocuous year of 1996, when the very idea of bringing in legal restraints on a computer game would have seemed funny, the Russian authorities saw in Pokémon a threat to national security. Denis Voronenkov, a Duma deputy from the Communist Party,[34] asked the FSB and the Communications Ministry to ban the game in Russia; he believed that it had been developed by the US special services in order to carry out reconnaissance and gain access to places otherwise difficult to reach. The deputy was convinced that 'the USA is trying through this video game to formulate the image of the next war, which will exactly suit the aims and the interests of Washington'. Senator Franz Klintsevich agreed with the Communist deputy, suggesting that playing the game should be banned in churches, prisons, hospitals and in cemeteries and at memorials. Predictably, the Culture Minister, Vladimir Medinsky, waded in, declaring that 'culture and Pokémon have nothing in common'. He compared the game with the Langoliers – creatures from the novels of Stephen King, which destroy reality. 'There was a time when I played. I played at the start of the 1990s when "Tetris" appeared, and I immediately understood that this is evil. These are creatures that devour everything, like in Stephen King's books; they devour space and time', said Medinsky.[35]

Here, one could simply once again laugh at these Russian obscurantists, who throttle everything that is alive and progressive; or talk about this particular period of heightened paranoia in the history of Russia, when the *siloviki* have seized power and see conspiracies and threats everywhere. This would certainly be partially true; but the real piquancy of this situation is that deep down they really do feel a threat to their very existence: these amusing cartoon Pokémon characters announce the arrival of a new reality, one in which today's Russian authorities – or, indeed, any others – simply have no place.

What we are talking about here is a new cartography, which is writing new laws of sovereignty and citizenship. Historically, the modern state was defined by geographical maps. This was how it happened: it was not the state that drew the maps, but the modern epoch, with its geographical, geometrical and cartographic imagination, which gave birth to the state. The state is a geometrical entity; it arises out of Cartesian rationalism, Hobbesian empiricism and the lineal geometry of Euclid and Newton. In his fundamental book *The Power of Maps* from 1992, the American culturologist and geographer, Dennis Wood, demonstrated how, at the start of the modern age, in the sixteenth to eighteenth centuries, people began, with the help of maps, to imagine and then construct the wider world and political order. The cartographical images of the world led to the era of the Great Geographical Discoveries; and following on from that, colonialism and the ideas of state sovereignty and the nation-state. Lineal cartography gives us borders, regularity, planned and organized life, a controlled population living within the boundaries of defined territories: all the elements that make up the modern state. In fact, it is from maps that the idea arises of sovereignty as a territorial dimension of power, and the idea of citizenship as belonging to a particular territory.

At the end of the twentieth century, with the appearance of computer networks, the idea of territorial sovereignty received its first serious blow: networks became widely pervasive and trans-border; a transaction could take place remotely from the server; space lost its connection with a particular place; the so-called 'space of flows' appeared (such as the Internet, the global financial market and satellite television). But the desktop computer was still joined to a cable, a provider and an IP address, which meant it could still be controlled and registered. With the appearance of the mobile Internet, all these restrictions were removed. The individual is set free from cables, providers, coverage areas and national operators: with his smartphone and tablet, he is instantly connected to millions of other users within a global information sphere. A new cartography is born before our very eyes, one without borders, states and the usual institutions: this is Google Maps, working in real time, in which a person with his gadget (and soon this will be one and the same thing as we turn into one biotechnical item – an android), linked to an anonymous GPS satellite, becomes an anonymous point of coordinates on the global map.

And suddenly Pokémon appears like agents of this new space, and with them a new cartography of reality, which is not even tied to street names. In the Pokémon Go interface there are no street names, only nameless areas and crossroads with special places marked out by the programme. It reminds one of navigating by orientation points, as was done before maps existed: 'Go as far as the big rock; turn left and keep going until sunset.' The game does away with the rules of linear cartography of the age of reason, with its hierarchies, borders, institutions of power, territorial rules and administrative

45

regimes. Millions of people wander around the streets as if these streets don't exist; they are moving according to an alternative map, paying no attention to cars, trees, fences or law-enforcement officers. And herein lies the actual threat to the authorities. Pokémon Go is a global 'occupy' movement, a rethinking of the principles of urbanization, borders and the boundaries of the city; a radical rewriting of the social space; a desacralization of the concept of 'space'(the Holocaust Museum in Washington has forbidden the capture of Pokémon on its territory). It is a round-the-clock flash mob with no clear political goals.

Yet it is just a single step away from politics. The whole concept of the city and the city state – the cradle of politics and the object of the social contract, and the reformatting of the new cartography – is an act of politicization. Pokémon Go is a challenge to territorial splits and divisions; on the West Bank of the River Jordan, Palestinians put Pokémon on the other side of the border wall or in Israeli settlements and, in attempting to catch them, a warning appears: 'the mistake of apartheid'. I won't be at all surprised if rare Pokémon turn up in Kim Jong-un's secret bunker or in Islamic State camps. This organization may be officially banned in Russia, but not on Google Maps.

Yes, Pokémon may be just a game, a mere fad of the summer of 2016, which quietly died away with the coming of the severe winter in the Northern hemisphere. But they are, nevertheless, emissaries from the future, forerunners of an augmented reality, which, with each passing day, will take a stronger grip on our imagination, our communications, our cities and our streets in a way that has proved impossible for, say, NATO or Islamic State. What's more, no state can possibly build any barriers to defend itself against this reality. An ever-increasing number of users will make their way onto this map, outside the control of the laws of sovereignty or citizenship, and they will spend ever-increasing amounts of time in this fluid and flexible space, earning and spending money, falling in and out of love and living by their own rules. Enhanced reality will take the place ever more strongly of what is 'real' (but is it actually 'real'?). Just look already at how fans of *Game of Thrones*, disappointed by both candidates in the 2016 US presidential election, created their own political party. Soon the state itself will have to go into its own augmented reality, creating there its own virtual objects.

As a result of this, the Moscow city government is planning on creating a Russian answer to Pokémon, an app for iPhone and Android called 'Know your Moscow', where instead of cartoon characters you will be able to catch the doubles of the poet Alexander

Pushkin, the first cosmonaut Yury Gagarin, or the rock star Viktor Tsoi, and take a selfie with them. And International Memorial, the historical-educational and human rights organization, has since 2013 supported a site called 'The Topography of Terror' (the idea and the name have been borrowed from the museum of the same name in Berlin). On an interactive map of Moscow, sites are superimposed where the Soviet Terror was carried out: apartments of those who were repressed, prisons, torture chambers, sites of execution and burial. It is possible that this project could be expanded into enhanced reality in such a way that, as you walk the streets of the city, everyone would be able to see the hidden archaeology of repression, meet the ghosts and hear the voices of the victims of the Terror ... A variety of frequently contradictory realities will cross over each other in the city, users of the app will be able to migrate between them or live in a number of them all at once; and with time the state will become simply one layer of this hybrid world – what's more, far from the most interesting one.

KREMLIN FIREWALL

News from the world of Russian hi-tech sounds ever more like information reports from a battlefield. Natalya Kaspersky, the President of the InfoWatch group of companies and a co-founder of 'Kaspersky Lab', has introduced a system to record telephone conversations in the office. The police are going to use the GLONASS satellite tracking system (the Russian equivalent of GPS) to remotely turn off the engines of offenders' cars: since 2017 all cars produced on the territory of the Customs Union of Post-Soviet Countries[36] have been fitted with special modules that allow them to be tracked and controlled with the help of GLONASS. Furthermore, Russian commercial centres have welcomed the new Russian Federation law on protecting personal data, which means that they have to keep the personal information of Russians living in the country: many Western firms were forced to install special equipment in Russia in advance. Russian hi-tech is preparing for the construction of the century: the creation of a digital iron curtain, an analogue of the 'great Chinese firewall'.

Back in the far-off days of 1990s techno-optimism, we believed that the computer (in partnership with the video recorder) would bring us freedom. Russians, being masters of the grey import, flooded the country with IBM computers with AT and XT processors. The first programs were written by long-haired guys with holes in their sweaters, physics students from Phystech, the elite technical college, who had just opened their first cooperative businesses. They were the heralds of the open information society, the pioneers of the digital frontier. We greeted the successes of our native IT entrepreneurs – Ilya Segalovich, Arkady Volozh, Anatoly Karachinsky and Eugene Kaspersky – as a counterweight to raw state capitalism. The Yandex and ABBYY brands seemed to be the Russian bridges into the world of globalization; and the Facebook symbol invariably appeared on the banners of the demonstrators at the protests on Bolotnaya Square in the winter of 2011–12.[37]

Now everything has changed. The lesson has been well learned by the domestic IT industry of Pavel Durov, the creator of the social network *vKontakte* ('In Touch', considered the 'Russian Facebook'). This libertarian clashed with the FSB, had his business taken from him and ended up being chased out of the country as a digital dissident. Now those programmers – still wearing the same sweaters with holes in them – write the code for 'SORM': Operational Search Systems, a complex of measures giving the special services control over telephones, mobile and wireless networks; and they are building the new Russian panopticon, a digital prison with a system for total monitoring of the population.

The optimism of the 1990s about the liberating actions of the Internet rested on the illusions that the new technologies, which are at one and the same time personalized yet provide a network, would produce a new type of social relationship: non-hierarchical, egalitarian, participatory; and that they would create a new type of politics, which would shake up the old hierarchy of parties, elites and states, which the industrial age left us as its legacy. And indeed, in the past twenty years completely different forms of politics have appeared, based on the new technologies, from the networked campaigning of Barack Obama in 2008 and the success of the Pirate Party in Iceland, to the 'Twitter Revolutions' in the Arab world. But Obama left office, Facebook helped bring to power the populist and chauvinist Donald Trump, and Twitter in the Arab states was taken over by the Islamists. At the same time, authoritarian regimes learnt how to live with the net; not just live with it, but use it to their own advantage: personalization and customization can be turned into personal control over citizens by means of their gadgets and their social network accounts. And social media activity, it turns out, can easily be transformed into noise on the net, when different forms of civil activity on the Internet can become lightning rods, a valve for letting off steam – a substitute for political protest. And at the same time, hi-tech companies can be changed from being agents for change into agents of the state, as happened, for example, with Kaspersky Lab in Russia.

Here we see a fundamental rule of 'network neutrality': technology is neutral, not only in relation to its content and application formats, as the very term implies, but in relation to political regimes, too. The network can be used both to liberate people and also to spy on them; both to consolidate a protest and to disperse it. Technology itself is neither good nor bad, in the same way that an axe is neither good nor bad: it is simply an instrument in a person's hands. The same axe can be used to chop the wood to make a cottage or to kill someone. The network does not exist separately from society, the elite, or the state. It transmits the vast majority of social relationships, but it does not define them. For example, the Islamic State has shown itself to be very advanced technologically, combining the social and religious practices of the Middle Ages with skilled management of the media and social networks.

In Russia the interrelationship of technology and the governing regime has its own peculiarities. First, it is a question of resources. In terms of the distribution model of the economy and the skilfully manipulated paranoia about 'national information security', the IT sector becomes a vital feeder of the budget alongside other strategic sectors: atomic energy, the air and space sector and the military-industrial complex. The IT sector gives rise to a large number of go-betweens who peddle 'threats' (people such as Duma deputy Irina Yarovaya; the creator of the League for a Safe Internet, Konstantin Malofeev; or the Communications Minister, Nikolai Nikiforov, who suggested that .doc files and the Times New Roman font could undermine the Russian Federation's information sovereignty). These people dream up threats to information security to obtain resources from the budget. Storing Russians' personal data; archiving for three years the contents of telephone and Internet communications ('the Yarovaya Law'); relocating credit card transaction transfers to Russian servers; the creation of a national search engine and operation system; the transfer of state structures onto a national software system; and the possibility of creating the infrastructure for a sovereign Internet along the Chinese model: all of this gobbles up a huge slice of the budget pie, which no hi-tech company would turn away from.

Second, this is a question of the innovation culture. An engineer in Russia is a state worker. In Russian history, technology and modernization (particularly in the military-industrial context) were always first and foremost strategic priorities for the state, and only in a distant second place matters for private capital. For centuries, it was with this in mind that the state trained its engineers. As the Russian investigative journalist, Andrei Soldatov, has said:

Russian and Soviet engineers were never taught ethics and were never given normal philosophy courses. All that a Russian engineer knows is that, 'there are these chattering artists, while we ensure order'. And, of course, the idea of 'order' chimes perfectly with the state's way of thinking, because it is a hierarchy with a clearly defined structure. Many engineers have told me that if you ask an engineer with no training in the humanities to build you a defence system, he'll produce a prison, because nothing is better protected: there's one way in, one way out, and everything is controlled.[38]

Soldatov makes the comparison with Napoleon, who closed down the schools of philosophy and opened engineering schools, because he didn't need revolutionaries; and with Stalin, who created a huge number of polytechnical colleges in order to teach people technical skills but without a university education. So the problem is far from being a specifically Russian one; but it was particularly in the USSR, where technical modernization became a question of national security, that the state almost completely took responsibility for the engineering culture. This went from Stalin's *sharashki* (special camps for scientists who were carrying out strategic research), to Khrushchev's and Brezhnev's scientific-research institutes, to the 'closed towns' under the control of the military-industrial complex,[39] to the 'post boxes' – secret institutes and factories that were known only by their postcode.

From the end of the 1980s a new culture of innovation began to grow in Russia. This was based, on the one hand, on the mighty Soviet engineering potential and strong school of physics and mathematics, and, on the other, on private initiative and networks. This produced a string of unique computer programs and home-grown IT leaders with global ambitions, such as the afore-mentioned Eugene Kaspersky. But it failed to create a sphere of technological, intellectual or civil autonomy, or an innovative environment like Silicon Valley in California. All attempts to create such an environment, such as Skolkovo, were closely tied to their state patrons; and in the current conditions of the financial crisis and economic sanctions they are stagnating.[40] And in Putin's third term, when the authorities set out to clean up and nationalize the information and hi-tech sphere, they simply went back to the bosom of the authoritarian state.

It has become common to describe Putin's regime in 'hybrid' terms, and here we have yet another 'hybrid': hi-tech authoritarianism, embedded in the structures of the information society. This phenomenon was described in the anti-utopian works of Vladimir Sorokin (*Day of the Oprichnik*; *The Sugary Kremlin*; *Telluria*),[41] where a future Russia, having shut itself off from the West by a wall, and having restored the monarchy and the customs of the Middle Ages, uses artificial intelligence devices, mobile video telephones and

the advances of bionics and genetics. In this way, Russian tradition-
alism works hand in hand with the iPhone in exactly the same way
as Islamic State: the patriarchal consciousness and archaic social and
political institutions blend perfectly with postmodern technologies
that have been bought or stolen in the West or developed under the
control of the authoritarian state.

We can see, therefore, how in the modern world authoritarianism has adapted to the demands of the information society and
uses its infrastructure for its own survival. In their book, *How
Modern Dictators Survive: Cooptation, Censorship, Propaganda and
Repression*, economists Sergei Guriyev and Daniel Treisman write
about how in the past few decades a new type of authoritarianism
has arisen, better adapted to coping with a world of open borders,
global media and the knowledge economy. Illiberal regimes, from the
Peru of Alberto Fujimori to the Hungary of Victor Orbán have learnt
how to concentrate power in their hands while avoiding isolating
their countries and engaging in mass killings, and, at the same time,
working cleverly with information. Although they may resort to
violence from time to time, they hold on to power less through terror
then by manipulating society's consciousness.

The same thing is happening in Russia. On the one hand, the
regime controls the flow of information in the traditional media
and on the Internet; on the other, it tries to monopolize the hi-tech
sector, bringing it under its own interests and preparing structures
to possibly shut off the country's access to information. This is the
looking-glass of authoritarianism: namely, those areas where new
networks and civil autonomy could be born – this digital frontier
which could become the space for freedom – is being used in Russia
to create archaic means of authority. Once again in Russian history,
technology is working not to free society but to strengthen the state;
the axe is once again becoming not the carpenter's instrument but
a weapon of repression. And if Russia in the future shuts itself off
from the world with a 'Kremlin firewall' created by state-of-the-art
technology, then by its very nature this wall will still be that of the
Middle Ages.

A SOVEREIGNTY FULL OF HOLES

On 28 July 2017, Russia suffered a diplomatic embarrassment. The Deputy Prime Minister, Dmitry Rogozin – who has been put under sanctions by both the USA and the EU – flew to the Moldovan capital, Chisinau, and planned to go on from there to the region of Transnistria, which no country has recognized as a separate state. But the Romanian authorities would not allow him to fly over their territory; and the aeroplane with the Deputy Prime Minster on board returned to Minsk.

Of itself, this incident is not worthy of attention. Dmitry Rogozin is a comical figure, one moment suggesting building military bases on the Moon, the next, underwater cities in the Arctic; but this latest incident is an example of the wider problem facing modern Russia – it is rapidly losing its sovereignty in foreign policy. How can you describe it otherwise, when the government's Deputy Prime Minister cannot fulfil his mission in a country in the near abroad because the route goes either through Romania (which is taking part in the sanctions against Russia) or through Ukraine (with whom Russia is at war)?

Now to a far more serious problem: the scandal involving turbines made by Siemens, which were illegally sent to Crimea in contravention of European sanctions. The export to the peninsula of technology and equipment had been banned more than a year earlier, after the EU condemned the occupation of Crimea. What was more, Vladimir Putin had given the company's senior management his assurances that their goods would not be used in Crimea. Siemens filed a lawsuit with a demand to seize the four turbines, which were supposed to provide all the electricity to the peninsula. As a result, because of the European sanctions and Russia's clumsy attempt to circumvent them, Russia was unable to provide electricity to a part of its strategic territory; in other words, Russia's energy sovereignty was undermined.

Finally, the packet of American sanctions signed by Donald Trump on 2 August 2017. The full scale and effect of these sanctions has yet to be seen (including losing one third of exports of Russian gas to Europe); but what can be said is that they have significantly restricted Russia's foreign policy and foreign trade capabilities. If we assess the overall situation over the past three years, Russia's room for manoeuvre has been severely restricted and it has suffered political and reputational damage. It is impossible not to see that our country is steadily losing its sovereignty.

One of the recognized theoreticians on sovereignty in political science is the American, Stephen Krasner. In his textbook work from 1999, *Sovereignty: Organized Hypocrisy* (which is a clear reference to Max Weber's definition of the state as 'organized violence'), he writes that the word 'sovereignty' has four meanings: international legal sovereignty (the judicial recognition of a state within its own borders); Westphalian sovereignty (the exclusion of foreign inter-ference on the authorities of a state); domestic sovereignty (the ability of the authorities to exercise control within their own borders); and interdependent sovereignty (the ability to conduct policy regarding transborder flows of information, people, ideas, goods and threats).[42] One glance at the policy of Putin's Russia makes it clear that, for its sins, it can partially meet only these first two demands of sovereignty: the country is recognized by the United Nations (although without Crimea); and 'foreign agents' have been driven out of internal policy. At the same time, the ability of the authorities to exercise control over processes taking place within the country and, what's more, to play a role in globalization have dramatically weakened.

The problem for the Russian political class is that it lives exclu-sively in the past. It sees international policy wistfully within the framework of some sort of 'Yalta Agreement', or even 'the Congress of Vienna'; and internal policy in an even more ancient way – within the framework of the Peace of Westphalia of 1648, which brought an end to the Thirty Years' War, and for the first time recognized the state as sovereign within its own borders. The Russian elite does not want to acknowledge that 'Westphalia' ended long ago. States no longer control global flows; they share their authority with transnational organizations. It is no wonder that Krasner calls absolute sovereignty 'hypocrisy' and compares it to a Swiss cheese: full of holes.

If we take even the most basic meaning of the word 'sovereignty' from any political dictionary, it means the independence of the state in domestic and foreign policy. But what sort of independence can we talk about when Russia is dependent on Siemens to provide electricity to Crimea; on Romania for the Deputy Prime Minister to fly over Moldova; on America for all of its foreign policy; and on Ukraine for its domestic agenda? In actual fact, Russia's foreign policy is nothing more than an agonizing and deep dialogue (with overtones of Freud or Dostoevsky) with America about spheres of influence, great power status and ambitions. And it is a dialogue that turns into a monologue about wounded pride. The obsession of the Russian authorities with the US elections; the childishly naive battles with Barack Obama and Hillary Clinton; the vaudeville romance with Donald Trump; the attempts to interfere like an awkward bear in the American elections: these are all signs of the hopeless, pathological and psychological dependence of Moscow on Washington.

In the same way, Russia is dependent on a fragment of its empire, which has broken away: Ukraine. Russia has built its whole external and internal agenda on the demonizing of the Ukrainian Maidan, filling the air time on television and radio with endless talk shows about Ukraine, turning the Ukrainian agenda into an internal Russian one in such a way that, if Ukraine suddenly disappeared, Russia would be left hanging in the air and would crash to the ground. All this indicates that Russia simply does not have its own agenda or its own policy. These are just sporadic reactions to external irritating factors, an inability and a lack of desire to accept the world as it is and acknowledge its own dependence on this fact.

To understand its situation better, the Kremlin should look at those who have gone even further down the road of 'sovereignty': Iran, for example, or, even better, North Korea. Boasting about its absolute independence, North Korea finds itself in a state of total vulnerability. It lives under sanctions and under the permanent threat of a nuclear strike. The only way it can survive is by raising the stakes in a deadly game of poker; its sovereignty hangs by the narrow thread of nuclear bluff and mutual threats.

The irony of the situation is that at the root of Russia's problems today lies this very striving for sovereignty that became the basis for Putin's conservative about-turn. First, there was the YUKOS affair in 2003: the arrest of Mikhail Khodorkovsky and the state's capture of the largest oil company. Then there was the Beslan tragedy in 2004, when Chechen fighters seized a school and, thanks to the incompetence of the operation to free the hostages, more than three hundred children died. Putin suddenly blamed this terrorist act on the West, accusing them of trying to destroy Russia. Next there was Putin's famous speech in Munich in 2007, in which he effectively declared a new cold war; then the war with Georgia in 2008; and after that came Crimea, the Donbass, the battle with separatism and 'foreign agents' in Russia, the destruction of Western sanctioned goods and the construction of a sovereign Internet. But the deeper Russia dug itself into the mud of an imagined Westphalian sovereignty, the more it lost its actual sovereignty, the independence of its foreign policy, control over its economy and society and the ability to adapt to globalization.

The key mistake in all of this was the annexation of Crimea (just like the saying: 'This is worse than a crime; it's a mistake'). It seemed as if Russia was strengthening its territorial sovereignty, beginning to gather in its lands; but by this action it radically blew up the nation's independence. Four years on it is clear that Russia has lost its techno- logical sovereignty (ask the oil men who cannot drill on the sovereign Arctic Shelf without Western technology); its sovereignty in foreign policy (by going over to a regime of confrontation with the West, every subsequent step taken by Russia narrowed down its room for manoeuvre until it hit the wall of sanctions); and even its internal sovereignty. As Krasner writes, rulers often confuse authority with control; and in Russia, while there has been a formal strengthening of the vertical of power, actual control over the economic and social situation grows weaker by the day. On closer inspection, one of the main achievements of Putin's rule, which the propaganda constantly trumpets – the strengthening of sovereignty – is a myth.

The result of all this is the usual Russian story: however much you battle for sovereignty, you simply strengthen the authorities. Perhaps all the Kremlin was after was the strengthening of the authorities, and this striving for sovereignty was a mere ideological smokescreen to give the appearance of legitimacy? But this has the reverse effect: the more power the Kremlin holds, the less sovereignty Russia has. In the end we could have the situation where power lies just in the Kremlin, the Forbidden City, the emperor's palace – and the country will be left to the dictates of fate. Such a situation has already occurred in Russian history. In December 1565, Ivan the Terrible left with his court, treasury, icons and tsarist regalia for the village of Kolomenskoye, and from there for the settlement of Alexandrovsk, about one hundred kilometres from Moscow. Here he founded the *Oprichnina*, a state within a state. In reality, the Tsar took with him his authority, leaving Russia at the mercy of the Tatars and then his own *oprichniki*. And when he died, the Polish-Lithuanian forces took over, as a result of which the country's sovereignty was lost for many years, right up to the *Zemsky Sobor* of 1613, when the House of Romanov came to the throne.[43]

Sovereignty is not the tsar's wagon train laden with icons or the president's cortège; it is not Russian special forces, *spetsnaz*, in

Crimea, nor military bases in the Arctic, nor a parade of Topol-M ballistic missiles on Red Square, nor a defile of ships on Navy Day in St Petersburg. It is the constant work of the authorities to improve the country, to integrate it into the wider world and have the rest of the world acknowledge this. And in this sense, the Siemens case is a warning sign for Russia: you can take over territory, clear it of undesirables, stuff it with weaponry and hold a military parade; but without turbines and international recognition, sovereignty doesn't work. At the end of the day, Crimea ends up as that hole in the cheese which Stephen Krasner wrote about in his book.

PART II: THE WAR FOR SYMBOLS

THE STATE'S GAME RESERVE

I remember well my school-leaving 'do'. It was in Moscow in June, in the early 1980s. My classmates and I were standing on the bank of the river, opposite where they have since built Moscow-City.[1] Back then it was a run-down industrial area, with a few small factories, warehouses and chimneys. Behind them, some distance away, you could see Stalin's 'wedding cakes'.[2] We were gazing on this huge, sleeping city. The early dawn had begun to creep over this vast expanse. Everything had already been said; all the promises had been made; everything had been drunk; we stood and watched in silence as the morning broke on our new life.

Suddenly one of the girls said, 'Let's go to Red Square!' We looked at her in bewilderment, as if she had just appeared from another planet. In fact, she had come from another planet, because she had lived in Canada for many years, being the daughter of the Soviet Ambassador, and she had returned simply to finish her schooling. And she was the only one who had got the idea into her head at this significant moment in our lives to go to Red Square; to stand in the shadow of the towers of state, alongside Lenin's Mausoleum and the tombs of the Bolsheviks. We stayed where we were, on the bank of the river, listening to the dawn chorus.

I really love Moscow. I love its boulevards, and the little alleys that lead off from the streets around Nikitsky Square; the sound of music coming from the open windows of the Conservatory; the old houses in the Bauman Street District, and the monasteries along the Yauza River. But I can't bring myself to love Red Square and the Kremlin. Maybe I can enjoy the picture-postcard view you get from a distance, from the Bolshoi Kamenny Bridge; but I don't want to go there simply to marvel at the beauty, or for a bit of peace or to feel the history.

The poet, Osip Mandelstam, wrote: 'The earth is nowhere as round as on Red Square'.[3] The enormous size and the slope of the square make it suitable for parades and processions, for state executions and state funerals. Its proportions are right for intercontinental ballistic missiles, but not for people. It tries to be part of the city – all of these 'stalls' in the GUM shopping arcade with their sky-high prices, the popular ice-rinks put up by the Bosco company each winter and the concerts with military bands. But you'll hardly find any Muscovites there, just crowds of people from out of town, policemen, foreigners and actors dressed up as Lenin and Stalin, who pose for photographs with the visitors. There is nothing in this space designed for people: no cosy park with benches; no little alleyways like in Prague Castle; no cathedrals to pop into even if you don't have any special reason, just to light a candle and stand in front of the icon. The whole Kremlin is simply the embodiment of the state, the *raison d'état*. It is not a space for the individual, for the people or for a memorial: it is a space for power.

As a result, Red Square evokes the uncomfortable feeling that nothing is on a human scale. Lenin's restless corpse lies there; the shadows of the *Streltsy*, executed in 1698, are still alive;[4] and the corridors of the Kremlin, so many witnesses say, are stalked by the ghosts of Ivan the Terrible and Stalin. You can even smell the smoke of 'Herzegovina Flor', Stalin's favourite tobacco. The Spassky (or Saviour) Gates were once open for everyone. Before the Revolution, the people would pray to the icon of the Saviour, then pass through these gates into the Kremlin; having obtained their free ticket, they could then wander freely everywhere. But under Stalin the gates became the symbol of the inaccessibility of the Kremlin. Having taken over the Kremlin in March 1918, the Bolsheviks did everything to destroy its historical memory.[5] More than half the buildings inside its walls were demolished, including the Monasteries of the Miracles and of the Ascension and the Smaller Nikolaev Palace. The Kremlin was sterilized, all signs of history or humanity were done away with; it was made suitable only for the state. That is why it is so frightening to stand there on winter nights, caught in the glare of the spotlights and the icy wind of history.

There are two types of towns or cities. There's the market town, which grew up in the Middle Ages as a counter to royal power and where institutions were formed such as guilds, communal authorities and an independent third estate, which represented the 'citizen' (a word derived from 'city', originally meaning someone who dwelt in a town or a city). Then there's the fortress town, which arose in the shadow of power, is controlled by, and serves, the state. Moscow grew up around a fortress constructed at the confluence of the rivers Moskva and Neglinka and was always of the second type;

just a trading quarter in the shadow of the Kremlin. The whole planning of the city, its radial structure, pulls everything into the centre. The rings of Moscow, like the Garden and the Boulevard rings, were in fact walls built as a defence against the external enemy.

It is inconvenient to live next to a fortress, especially in the twenty-first century. Moscow's radial structure suited the Tsar's forays in the sixteenth century, but not today's million cars; hence the city's traffic problem. Most journeys in the city one way or another go through the centre, just as 70 per cent of all cargo in Russia goes through Moscow, because all the customs terminals are here. Sooner or later the fortress will be choked by this flow of resources. Living next to the centre of power pushes up the price of real estate and creates familiar problems, from the shutting off of main roads so that the country's leaders can pass by, to the closure of whole areas of the city for reasons of security. For example, on behalf of the Presidential Administration, the Federal Protection Service (FSO) demanded that a whole historic part of Kitai-Gorod alongside the Kremlin between Varvarka and Ilyinka Streets be shut off, enclosed by 'a Great Chinese Fence', thus creating in the centre of Moscow something like Beijing's Forbidden City.

When the powers-that-be decide to come closer to the people, it causes havoc, such as when the Prime Minister, Dmitry Medvedev, chose to step outside the walls of the Kremlin. When he visited the Faculty of Journalism of Moscow University, they cancelled all classes and banned students from the building. When he went to the reopening of the Bolshoi Theatre, the police stopped rehearsals that were taking place in theatres nearby, and even destroyed scenery in the neighbouring Maly Theatre. It seemed that he was going just a couple of hundred metres outside the Kremlin, but the living body of the city was torn apart by the intrusion of the state.

There is only one solution: the city and the state have to get a divorce. The state should no longer be the main idea and the mystical purpose of life in Moscow. The trading quarter has grown so much that the fortress has become a burden on it. In modern theories of governance, the state has lost its sacred origins, and power has become a mere function, just another production line, like the factories and the municipal economy. Manufacturing has today been moved outside the city boundaries, and the old factory workshops are going through a process of gentrification, being converted into museums, artists' studios and university campuses. The old industrial areas are being given back to society.

In just the same way, the implementation of the functions of state power with all its costs – the emergency flashing lights on the cars, the government cortèges, the restricted areas – should be taken outside the city boundaries. The Kremlin must be given back to the people, to the nation, to society. Ten years ago, in an interview with the *Vedomosti* newspaper, the writer Vasily Aksyonov proposed a plan to clean up the Kremlin: 'There's an unhealthy aura there', he said. 'The President and his administration shouldn't be in there. Instead, there should be a museum of the centuries, a museum of Russian history. The Kremlin should be a cultural and historical memorial area.'[6]

The Kremlin could be turned into a beautiful historic park, where all the gates are open twenty-four hours a day, like in the Old City in Jerusalem. People should be able to have romantic encounters there at nighttime; to touch the ancient walls and sit on the Red Steps, the parade entrance to the Kremlin Palace; to stroll with a friend on the raised bank above the Moskva River.

Where can state power be relocated? There are plenty of ideas, including the latest plan for expanding Moscow, according to which the state could have its own little city somewhere in the far reaches of the Moscow Region. The state could be configured in a Eurasian manner, setting up its new capital somewhere in the Orenburg Steppe, from where it would be easy for the government cortèges to switch on their flashing lights and call on brotherly Astana, the new capital of Kazakhstan. But the idea I like the best is that dreamt up by the students of the Moscow Architectural Institute, which I saw recently in a competition of student work in the Architecture Museum. It was called, 'The Mobile Government', and it was based on a sound Russian principle: wherever the leadership goes, life improves dramatically. The students suggested constructing a mobile model of the government, based on a special train. Travelling all over the country, the train would travel under its own cloud of abundance, and everywhere it went life would automatically improve.

And then there would be absolutely no need for it to return to Moscow.

THE ELITE AVENUE ... TO DEATH

Yet another routine bloody harvest occurred on Moscow's Kutuzovsky Prospekt: on the night of 2–3 October 2015, at the widest part of the road, where it crosses the third ring road, two accidents happened almost simultaneously. First, a BMW-X5 was flying down the middle of the road when the driver lost control, crossed the central lane and drove into a Range Rover and a Porsche Cayenne coming in the other direction. Then a four-by-four travelling at high speed rammed into the traffic jam that had formed after the first accident. As a result, two drivers died, three people were taken to hospital with serious injuries and three more suffered minor injuries. Witnesses reported that a lot of drivers got out of their cars and ran to look at the burning vehicles, thus preventing the ambulances from reaching the scene of the crash.

Two years earlier, in December 2013, the influential Deputy Prime Minister of Dagestan (a Russian region in the Caucasus), Gaji Makhachov, died at exactly the same spot on Kutuzovsky Prospekt. Rushing along in the central lane in his Mercedes GL four-by-four with his wife and three children he caught the edge of a plastic block around some roadworks, spun into the oncoming traffic and hit a minibus. In that accident, three people died and six others were injured. And on the night of 8 November 2014, just half a kilometre from that spot, a BMW-M5, travelling at more than two hundred kilometres per hour, also crossed the central lane into the oncoming traffic and hit a taxi, killing the driver and his female passenger. On this occasion, five people died and a further six were injured.

One can go on forever about fatal accidents on Kutuzovsky. According to both official and unofficial statistics, it is the most accident-prone stretch of road in the capital. In 2011 alone, there were eighty-six accidents there, resulting in fourteen deaths and ninety-six injuries. Various urban legends try to explain this: from its being a geopathogenic zone, to the existence of a magnetic anomaly; all the way through to the 'graveyard theory', which says that when they were laying down Kutuzovsky Prospekt in the 1950s, a number of cemeteries that lay outside the city's boundary were destroyed, and now the restless dead are taking their revenge on the living.

I grew up close to these spots, and I remember how, when my friends and I were playing in the dip that now houses the third ring road, we used to find broken slabs with indecipherable writing on them. It was only later, when I was studying old maps of Moscow, that I understood that these were tombstones from the ruined Jewish cemetery which was once situated there. But going to school in the mornings I noticed something else: how black government Chaika and Volga cars with little curtains over the rear windows would emerge from the courtyards of smart apartment blocks built in the style of Stalinist architecture. These carried the Communist Party nomenklatura who lived on Kutuzovsky and were on their way to work. In block number twenty-six on Kutuzovsky Prospekt lived two General Secretaries of the Central Committee of the Communist Party of the Soviet Union, Leonid Brezhnev and his successor, Yury Andropov. At the time we guessed this because of the rumours that were circulating and also because of the guys in identical coats who would be stamping their feet while waiting around in the courtyards; nowadays, there are memorial plaques bearing their names.

As a result of this, I have my own theory about the deaths on Kutuzovsky: the theory of the Elite Road. This is the official name for the highways that go from the Kremlin to the West of Moscow, including Rublyov Highway, Kutuzovsky Prospekt and Novy Arbat Street. The traffic police divisions which serve there are also described thus: the Elite Division of the Elite Battalion on the Elite Highway. I don't know whether the personnel also have special titles – 'Elite Major' or 'Elite Colonel' – but they certainly have an air about them of fulfilling a special role for the state. In reality, this is the most important road in the country, and it is there not for the convenience of the public, but so that the country's leaders can have a safe passage from the pine trees of Barvikha (just outside Moscow and chosen by the Bolsheviks in the 1930s), to the centres of power: the White House (seat of the Russian government); Okhotny Ryad (the State Duma); Old Square (the Presidential Administration); and the Kremlin. This is why you won't find any lorries on this road; there are no traffic lights, nor are there police ambushes with speed traps. And that's also why there's a central lane down the middle of the road reserved for the leaders' cars, but no central reservation – the main reason behind the head-on collisions and deaths.

The central lane on Kutuzovsky Prospekt is one of the main symbols and institutions of Russian power in the Moscow 'vanity fair'. This is where you measure your worth; it all depends on your elite number plate and your elite pass. Specially chosen traffic police are there not so much to keep an eye on road safety as to ensure that the hierarchy of the state can travel along their central lane. Ford Focus cars with number plates in the series eKX and xKX (the FSO and the Federal Security Service (FSB)) travel along this lane quietly and without fuss; important limousines glide past with the numbers aMP and aMM (senior policemen) and aMO (the Moscow Mayor's Office); numbers from the 'commercial' series oOO and kKK zip by, carrying bankers with their guards in their Mercedes G-class four-by-fours; occasionally, a Mercedes with blacked-out windows will fly past, with the regional code 95 (for Chechnya). The inspector filters all traffic using the central lane with an eagle eye: he salutes the leadership, waves through those whose rank permits its use and stops any others daring to use the lane to check on their status and see whether they have had the audacity to break the traffic regulations.

The privileged lane illustrates the vertical of power, which has become a horizontal servility. It is the old Russian class society with its table of ranks spelled out in the letters of the elite number plates; it is Russian feudalism in all its glory.[7] It is just like in seventeenth-century Paris, when cavalcades of horsemen with torches charged around the streets accompanying noble carriages, knocking over traders' barrows and pushing those on foot back against the walls – 'Make way for the King!'. Since that time, France has experienced the Enlightenment, revolution, the execution of the monarch, the Napoleonic Code and five republics. The class system has been dismantled and the principle has been established of equality for all before the law; including when it comes to traffic. In Russia, however, the seventeenth century continues, as if there had never been the new times, or the right to life, property and justice; and the way in which you travel around is determined exclusively by your class standing and how close you are to the body of the sovereign.

When the leadership travels along Kutuzovsky it is not just the central lane that is closed off, but all traffic. The Prospekt freezes in a ninety-minute-long court ritual, and the cortège of dozens of cars screams past on the wrong side of the road under the silent gaze of the people sitting in the traffic jam: the patient bosses who are a rank lower; ambulances with their blue lights flashing; and the common people in their cars. Once in the summer I became fed up waiting in the left-hand lane, turned off my engine and got out of my car, stepping into the central lane. In the distance I could see a swarm of coloured flashing lights, and when the cortège drew close I fell to my knees and crossed myself with a sweeping gesture.[8] This earned me a couple of approving beeps on the horn and thumbs-up from some of my fellow sufferers. The reality is that Kutuzovsky Prospekt reveals the whole reality of the Middle Ages in which our oil monarchy lives; its hypocrisy, and its disdain for the law and for the ordinary people. Here horsepower multiplied by power and money allow any excesses; here the right of the powerful to break the law is taken to the extreme, sanctified by flashing lights and elite passes. And all of this is protected by a special police department.

But this permissiveness leaks into the lower orders of society; many of them start to travel at speeds of 100, 120, or 150 kilometres per hour, taking advantage of the width of the lanes, the perfectly smooth asphalt and the almost total absence of any speed control. And the offspring of the wealthy consider it their duty to go tearing along Kutuzovsky at night at speeds of more than 200 kilometres an hour, and bikers go at more than 250. What begins as the imposing procession along the central lane of the boss with the blue light flashing ends with nighttime races along this prestigious Prospekt and horrific traffic accidents.

At some time in the future, they will grass over the central lane along Kutuzovsky Prospekt and construct a central reservation. They will place a number of speed cameras along it, and it will be possible to travel past these shiny windows and impressive façades without fearing for one's life. But that will happen in a different, parallel and more human Russia. Until then, the elite highway, which was built not for the people but for the powerful ones who live in their world, will continue to maim and to kill, turning power and oil into death in this ruthlessly accurate model of the Russian state.

AN ODE TO SHUVALOV'S DOGS

If Igor Ivanovich Shuvalov didn't exist, it would be necessary to invent him. With his name, which makes him sound like a count, and his castle in Austria; with his London apartment on Whitehall in the former home of MI6, and his ancestral estate on the site of the dacha of the chief ideologue of the Soviet regime, Mikhail Suslov; with his million-dollar Rolls-Royce and his pair of Corgis (the same breed of dog as the Queen has!), which he whisks around the world in his private jet to take part in dog shows. He is a walking cargo-cult,[9] a distillation of the post-Soviet transit.

Sometimes it seems as if the Shuvalov project is some kind of PR provocation, a bomb underneath the existing authorities, a modern Russian Marie-Antoinette with her 'Let them eat cake' – a catalyst for the people's wrath. In actual fact, of course, it is not like that at all. There will be no revolution; no heads will roll off the block; and instead of the people's wrath there are humorous posts on the Internet. All the exposure of corruption by the opposition politician, Alexei Navalny, disappears into the quicksand of Russian society, which is both cynical and apathetic, respecting strength and power over the law and morality. Memes and cartoons about Shuvalov's dogs are posted and shared by hundreds of thousands of people on Facebook, while the rest of the country looks on with indifference, ruled by the inescapable saying among the people, 'He does it because he can'.

As the political commentator, Vladimir Gelman, has noted, this is strikingly different from the 'battle against privilege' campaign in the late Soviet period. This was one of the main slogans of *perestroika*. Political commentators called for a return to the Leninist norm of modesty for those in the Communist Party, and the popular rumour did the rounds of the apocryphal tale of Boris Yeltsin travelling to work by trolleybus when he was First Secretary of the Moscow City Committee of the Party. Where has all this gone? Why does society fail to react to information about corruption or about the excesses of state officials? Gelman speaks of weariness and apathy: needs must when the devil drives. 'The unsuccessful experience of the battle against privileges of the time of *perestroika* and the subsequent events in which the Russian public (with rare exceptions) played the role of bystanders, convinced Russians that speaking out against the overbearing leadership was both useless and possibly dangerous.'

On the other hand, there exists a wide social contract under the title, 'everyone steals'. Evidence of corruption and the blatant use and abuse of luxuries by the political and business elites gives people at all levels of society permission to behave in similar fashion. When they look upwards, people feel that they have the moral right to hide their income, take and give bribes and live beyond their means. The example given from on high creates an atmosphere in society that everything is permissible: if the Deputy Prime Minister's dogs can fly around in private jets, why shouldn't the whole leadership of the Volgograd Region fly off to Toscana to celebrate Governor Bozhenov's birthday? If a car with a flashing light can tear along the central lane, why can't an ordinary driver avoid traffic jams by driving on the hard-shoulder?

But besides the traditional cover-up between the various strata of society, there is a deeper reason why this ostentatious display by Shuvalov not only does not discredit, but actually legitimizes the regime. In Russia, power is based not on elections but on strength; on the affirmation of your status; on the symbolic effectiveness of the master of the discourse. Excess is essential to legitimize power: a blatant spanking of the serfs, demonstrative luxury, disdain for the law and moral norms.

In this sense, all of the examples of the demonstration of wealth – Putin's palaces, Patriarch Kirill's thirty-thousand-dollar Breguet watch, Shuvalov's dogs on a business jet, lions in the private zoo of the leader of Chechnya, Ramzan Kadyrov – are the attributes of patriarchal power and important arguments in the hierarchy of the state; and the only people to protest about them are Facebook users and a few other active citizens. The majority of the population accept them silently as inevitable peculiarities of their socially favoured lords and masters. As a powerfully effective symbol, Corgi dogs on a private jet not only do not compromise their owner, they underline his right to power and his standing in the system.

The essence of the modern era of the evolution of society in Russia can be defined as the ruling elite irrevocably separating themselves from 'the people'. They no longer care about creating an image of propriety; on the contrary, they have turned their privileges and personal whims into the norm. All of these lordly mega-projects – from the Winter Olympics and the World Cup to superfast trains and improvements on the streets of Moscow, all taking place at the same time as the dismantling of the social infrastructure and disdain for the needs of the common people which runs through the pronouncements of the higher leadership and deputies – all of this speaks of the final loss of social solidarity and the catastrophic stratification of Russian society as one of the main results of Putin's counter-reforms.

Over the course of the hundred years since the Revolution of 1917, Russia has tried to create a modern society, built on the principles of solidarity, egalitarianism and the social contract (although in many ways these were merely declared aims, while in the USSR the privilege of status ruled supreme). But since the start of the twenty-first century there has been a landslide of the demodernization of power, society, the economy and the mass consciousness. As a result, Russia is rolling back from modern bureaucracy and from the oligarchic state of the times of early capitalism to feudalist, aristocratic rule, to the appearance of the class of the service nobility, as in the time of the godfather of Russian statehood, Ivan the Terrible. And Igor Shuvalov, with his carefully constructed aristocratic ways, sets a political fashion, albeit in a British way – from the royal Corgis to a house on Whitehall.

If we continue this trend down the staircase of history, we should then pass from the age of the service nobility to patrimonial nobility. It was no coincidence that in 2012 the political scientist, Yevgeny Minchenko, declared the second decade of this century as the 'dynastic stage' of the evolution of the system, in which the ruling elite develops the desire to create a hereditary aristocracy, so that they can transfer by inheritance property they have acquired. Only the right of patrimonial nobility could give the elite the guarantees they seek against the next redistribution of property (which will be inevitable when power changes hands again in Russia), and ensure stability and continuity in an era of wars, terrorism and sanctions.

To achieve this, new laws will be needed: hereditary titles and rights; a special judicial status for the new nobility; immunity from justice; guarantees of the inviolability of their private life and their property; classifying information about the aristocracy in registers. It seems that special status will be essential for the animals of the lords and masters, too – just like in the Middle Ages, when a peasant who raised his hand against the master's dog was sentenced to death. And if a hundred years ago the poet Sergei Yesenin could write a touching message to the dog of Vasily Kachalov, a legendary actor of the

71

Theatre of the Arts, then the poets of the new age could compose an ode to Igor Shuvalov's dogs. After all, they are a symbol and a role model for modern Russia.

MISSILE MANIA

Moscow, the end of April, late in the evening. At midnight the police have shut off the Garden Ring Road: there's a rehearsal taking place for the Victory Day Parade on 9 May. There's electricity in the damp April air: a crowd is standing on the roadside; the police cars are stationary, blue lights flashing. From a long way off comes a deep rumbling sound. A few open military vehicles go past; and then, there IT is: the pride and joy of the Russian lands, the symbol of the might of the state and the jewel in the crown of the Strategic Rocket Forces – the twenty-five-metre long Topol-M missile. Bringing up the rear, at a respectful distance, is a column of BTR armoured personnel carriers. The ground shakes, the windows rattle, and the social networks are abuzz: everyone is excitedly snapping away, tweeting, posting and sending photos of the missile on Instagram. The only thing lacking is the battle cry, like that of the last Red Indians, as they carry this war axe.

Watching these primitive rituals in paying homage to the missile, I thought about the nature of Russian sovereignty, about the collective unconsciousness and the sanctification of strength. The missile is immanent and attached to Russia as part of the state's armaments, built into the Russian landscape. It even led to a recent scandal with an advertising poster for Aeroflot in the Brussels metro. The poster carried an aerial shot of the Kremlin; but when you looked closely you could see that on the Kremlin Embankment there was a column of Topol missiles. Alarmed locals tried to work out the hidden message behind the poster; some even took it as a thinly disguised threat from Moscow to the European Union. What had most likely happened, however, was that the designer had been searching for a photograph of the capital at its best. This one seemed the most appropriate, and having military hardware on display was an appropriate symbol of the holiday mood, adding a certain national piquancy. The idea that just one five-hundred-kiloton warhead of this piquancy could wipe out the whole of Brussels never even occurred to the designer.

73

Missiles are a vital part of our mentality: 'But we build missiles', as Yuri Vizbor sang in a humorous song in answer to a foreigner's criticism of the Soviet Union.[10] The missile is the carrier of the Russian myth, from the theorist of interplanetary travel, Konstantin Tsiolkovsky, to the constructor of the first space rocket, Sergei Korolev; from the jet-propelled 'Katyusha' rockets of the Second World War to the submarine-launched intercontinental ballistic missile, Bulava. The missile is the child of the limitless Russian space, and it is also the state's answer to the challenge of this space: a huge phallic symbol of might, in contrast to the horizontal and amorphous flat plain. The missile is the Russian dream; it compensates for the imperfections of life on earth by producing a reckless flight and the wide smile of the first cosmonaut, Yury Gagarin.

At the start of the twenty-first century, when Western countries consider parades of military hardware as an exotic anachronism, we remain one of those ambitious developing countries which still hold them. Columns of heavy technology rolling across Red Square – causing the icons to shake in St Basil's Cathedral, the tea cups to tinkle in the shops in GUM, and the bones to quake of Stalin in the Kremlin Wall and of the holy mummy of Lenin in the Mausoleum – put us on a par with India and Pakistan, with the oil monarchies of the Arab world, and with unbending North Korea, which, full of bluff and blackmail, from time to time shows the world its Taepodong ballistic missile. All these countries are united by a patriarchal picture of the world, which is seen through the prism of fear and strength. Instead of holding parades of inventors and Nobel laureates, of GPs and school teachers (who, according to Bismarck, were the ones who won the Franco-Prussian War), we choose to roll out our huge missile as our final and main argument.

For eighteen years, from 1990 until 2008, Russia lived without demonstrations of military hardware in the capital; tanks appeared on the streets only at the time of the coup in August 1991 and the street battles in October 1993.[11] Vladimir Putin brought the 'heavy parades' back to Moscow alongside other traditional attributes of sovereignty just as the curtain was coming down on his second presidential term at the start of 2008. Just three months after the Victory Parade on Red Square, Russian tanks were flattening South Ossetia during the war with Georgia – the first time for many years that Russia had carried out a military operation outside its borders. Of course, these were different tanks; but such a demonstration of strength is sooner or later put into practice.

Muscovites know about the costs of these 'heavy parades' – and not just through gossip: roads are closed on rehearsal days and there are restrictions on aircraft flying into and out of Domodedovo Airport because the air force is preparing for the parade. There is also the dismantling of the overhead wires for the trolleybus network and other electricity cables, the reinforcement of the ceilings of some metro stations and the checking of all the subways along the route taken by the columns of military hardware. Then, of course, there is the main part of the costs: the resurfacing of the roads. When the parade was revived in 2008, the Moscow Mayor's Office costed the repair work to the almost one million square metres it covered at over a billion roubles (twenty-five million dollars). Today, the total cost for holding the parade, including clearing the clouds from the sky, is around forty to fifty million dollars.

All this leads me to have a theory about who it is that really wants the parade. It is not the military-industrial complex, trying to gain new orders; neither is it the patriotic general public; it is not even the state, in an attempt to scare the West. It is the Moscow road-builders, who have learnt in recent years how to extract billions from the city budget, by resurfacing the same stretches of road three times in a year. It is this sector, which has been given to Vladimir Putin's friends, the oligarchs Gennady Timchenko and the Rotenburg brothers, who are most interested in the destructive procession of military hardware over Moscow's streets. Because, in the first instance, patriotism equals business.

TANK INVASION

The biggest hit of summer 2015 in Russia were tanks! The season opened with the parade on Victory Day, 9 May, and the unveiling of the new Russian tank, the T-14 'Armata' (which, it has to be said, broke down right opposite Lenin's Mausoleum) and the excited discussion of this event in the media and on social networks. The parade passed off; but the love for military hardware did not diminish, and on 12 June, Russia Day, patriotic mothers in Tambov formed their own parade by making up their children's pushchairs as plywood tanks, complete with guns, and dressing their children in soldiers' tops and military side caps. On the same day, a tank-themed Disneyland for older children was opened in Kubinka, near Moscow. The military park, called 'Patriot', cost twenty billion roubles (three hundred million dollars), displays the latest types of weaponry, puts on tank shows and even has a facility for those who wish to sign up for contract service in the army.[12] Twenty thousand people visit 'Patriot' every day.

Woodstock in Reverse

Traditional summer festivals and public holidays are transforming themselves before our very eyes into exhibitions of military hardware. In the last couple of years, the main Russian rock festival, Nashestvie ('Invasion'), has evolved into a military-patriotic show – the main sponsor of which is the Russian Army. It has become Woodstock in reverse: in Russian rock, the culture of protest and pacifism has been replaced by conformity, militarism and a love for weaponry – and all paid for by the state's money. The same has happened with the Grushin bard song festival. At a meeting of the festival's 'military council' it was decided that 'alongside the festival site there should be set up an interactive historical-patriotic and technical exhibition for young people'; in other words, those same tanks are coming to this festival, too.

What next? Holding the Usadba Jazz Festival in the Arkhangelskoye estate outside Moscow to the accompaniment of artillery salvoes? *Afisha* Magazine's hipster picnic supplied by field kitchens? The Tchaikovsky Music Competition with a review of military orchestras? We see tanks on our streets and in our parks; they roll across our TV screens, from 'Tank Biathlon' (not seen anywhere else in the world of entertainment) to documentary films; on state TV channels, films have been shown justifying the Soviet invasions of Hungary in 1956 and Czechoslovakia in 1968. These films showed with pride Russian tanks on the streets of Budapest and Prague.

The degree of military-patriotic hysteria in Russia today is reminiscent of the USSR in the second half of the 1930s: a time of physical fitness parades, mock-ups of tanks and airships, shaven heads and creaking Sam Browne belts. Once again, today the country gladly lines up wearing soldiers' shirts, has its photo taken on a tank and is preparing for war. Russia is bombarded by a continual liturgy of 'the Great Victory'; in the arts, the most important performance of all has become the military-patriotic show; and the war in Ukraine, with its columns of military hardware marching to the border, is simply a continuation of this endless military parade that has hypnotized the nation.

A Child of the Twentieth Century

The tank is one of the principal inventions of the age of steam and metal, a deadly miracle of the period of industrialization, a child of the twentieth century. It was born in the protracted battles in the trenches of the First World War, created almost simultaneously in Britain, France and Russia, and first saw fighting in September 1916 at the Battle of the Somme. Along with mustard gas, the aeroplane and the Maxim machine gun, it was yet another example of the technology of the mass society; a means of killing on an industrial scale. A little under thirty years later, armoured vehicles decided the outcome of the Second World War: two million men and six thousand tanks took part in the Battle of Kursk in the summer of 1943.

World War Two was both the peak and the start of the decline of the might of the main battle tank. The Soviet Union continued to maintain a massive group of tanks in the centre of Europe, with the aim of following up a tactical nuclear strike by defeating NATO forces in a tank battle in the Fulda Gap in the middle of Germany, then pressing on to reach the English Channel within three days. But military planners were already moving on from the idea of the mass tank battles of the industrial era to the post-industrial technology of the 'third wave', as the futurologist Alvin Toffler called it: precision 'smart' weapons, rapid deployment forces, space and information technology, and cyber warfare.

At the same time, in the so-called Third World, low-intensity conflicts started to break out: ethnic and religious wars, in which tanks were superseded by fighters with Kalashnikovs who would simply melt into the landscape and be lost among the local population. The USSR experienced this in Afghanistan, where tanks were useless at exercising control over mountainous terrain. And then Russia had a similar experience in Chechnya, where tanks got stuck in the streets of Grozny and were easily shot up from within buildings. Today, Russian army tanks, with their identifying marks wiped out, cannot bring victory in the Donbass, leaving us to read the reports about Russian conscript soldiers being burnt to death in their armoured vehicles, like the twenty-year-old tankman from Buryatia, Dorzhi Batomunkuev. Tanks have not won a single battle for Russia in the past thirty years, but they still remain an important symbolic resource.

In reality, the tank has become one of the symbols of the new patriotism. One of the pillars of the regime is the Uralvagonzavod Tank Factory in Nizhny Tagil in the Urals. In 2012, the head of the assembly shop, Igor Kholmanskikh, promised to bring his workers to Moscow to sort out protesting intellectuals; and soon after this he became the Presidential Representative in the Urals Federal District. This was the factory where the ill-fated Armata tank was built, the one that broke down on the 9 May parade. Indeed, Putin's Russia has slipped back to the Battle of Prokhorovka, one of the principal engagements on the Kursk Salient in 1943, and has got stuck in the age of geopolitics, mass armies, tank battles, annexation and occupation. Putin sees himself in the role of Stalin, standing over the map of Europe at Yalta or Potsdam in 1945, waving a hand over the territory to be taken over, deciding the fate of the world. And the post-Crimea majority in Russia believe in this archaic illusion, idolizing the Topol and Iskander strategic missiles, creating the cult of the 'little green men' (the special forces soldiers who seized Crimea in 2014), snuggling up to the saving armour of the tanks and the BTRs. Putin has created in Russia a nation at war, which has battened down the hatches and is looking at the world through the sights of a tank.

A Russian Tiananmen

Early on the morning of 19 August 1991, I was woken by the ground shaking. The cups in the sideboard were ringing as they knocked against each other, and the glass in the windows was vibrating. Along the Kiev Highway, not far from our dacha, a column of tanks was heading at full speed for Moscow. Every television channel was showing Tchaikovsky's *Swan Lake*; then they started to show the press conference of the Emergency Committee for the State of Emergency (GKChP), which had seized power in the country. I quickly finished my breakfast and hurried into town.

Tanks were drawn up on Manezh Square, outside the Kremlin. The sun was shining, people stood around gawping, the militiamen looked bored; alongside the old building of Moscow University, the tanks did not look at all frightening. I went up to one, climbed on it and knocked on the hatch. To my surprise, it opened and, blinking against the sunlight, a puny blonde lad of about nineteen climbed out. 'Have you got a fag?' he asked uncertainly. I gave him a packet of cigarettes and one of the leaflets signed by the Russian President, Boris Yeltsin, which called on the people to oppose the coup. Having thought about it, the tankman took the leaflet, climbed back into the tank and closed the hatch behind him.

One of those who helped with the defence of the White House, the building of the Russian Supreme Soviet (or Parliament), and who set up the headquarters of the protest, organized the radio link and prepared a possible escape route for Boris Yeltsin, was Reserve Lieutenant Sergei Shoigu. For this he received the medal, 'Defender of a Free Russia'. How times have changed. Now Minister of Defence Sergei Shoigu commissions research on how to oppose 'colour revolutions'. In his words: 'We do not have the right to repeat the situation of the collapse of 1991' and 'We must not allow the army to stand to the side, as happened in 1991.'[13] Apparently, the best guarantee against 'the orange threat' of revolution is to bring the tanks onto the square; in other words, create a Russian version of Tiananmen Square.

I think about how quickly time flies and the world changes. Since that moment in 1991, the USSR has collapsed, as has Yugoslavia; the USA has elected a black President; in the West they have defeated AIDS; the fourth industrial revolution is under way; Elon Musk is building electric cars and private spacecraft; Google is preparing to spread the Internet to the four corners of the world by satellite; and

Russia ... what of Russia? We are still sitting in the same old tank, playing at war and fighting with imaginary fascists.

Until someone knocks on the armour from the outside.

PURVEYORS OF THREATS

It was in our Basic Military Preparation classes in school that I first heard from our military teacher, a major of the reserve, the phrase, 'the threat period'. It was at this point in our training sessions for nuclear war that we were supposed to grab our gas masks and march to the Civil Defence Headquarters.

It seems that we have reached that point now in Russia. From all sides we hear cries about threats: the Motherland is in danger! We are threatened in turn by all sorts of things: paedophiles, homosexuals, Westerners who adopt Russian children, 'foreign agents', 'the fifth column' of the Russian opposition and the US Sixth Fleet, Western ecologists and Russian separatists, the Kiev junta and the American State Department – even, in recent times, Western food products, against which Russia has introduced sanctions: beware Italian parmesan, Spanish ham, Polish apples and Norwegian salmon!

Every threat has its own lifecycle, its sell-by date. A couple of years ago none of these threats was even on the horizon. As a rule, threats appear out of nowhere (such as 'foreign agents' or Russian separatists). Suddenly there's a concentrated attack in the media and the degree of public hysteria is raised. On a wave of popular anger, a draft bill is introduced into the State Duma, is instantly approved in three readings (sometimes without even the approval of the appropriate committee or a call from the government) and straightaway is signed by the President. After this, the hysteria immediately dies down and everyone quietly forgets about the threat. Who now remembers the 'separatists' whom we were fighting against at the end of 2013: Karelian, Siberian, on the Kurile Islands, North Caucasian, or in the enclave of Kaliningrad? Now, the separatists are held in high esteem – in Crimea, Donetsk and Lugansk – but these are the 'right' separatists in neighbouring Ukraine. From time to time we even forget about 'foreign agents', as a warning closing down a few NGOs. What remains on the battlefield are sick Russian orphans, some of whom have already died because foreigners were not allowed to adopt

81

them; discriminatory, indeed fascist, anti-gay laws; blocked websites and banished media outlets. But no one remembers this now, because Russia has new enemies: Barack Obama, the Ukrainian President, Petro Poroshenko, the German Chancellor, Angela Merkel …

The majority of these threats, when looked at rationally, have been completely dreamt up, from the foreign child adopters to 'the homosexual lobby'. However, it would be naive to suggest that this is simply because of the paranoia of members of the State Duma. The precise mechanism for marking out these threats, amplifying them in the media and drawing up the legal process leads one to suggest that behind this endless flow there is a unified guiding logic. Threats are sought from the outside, but they are formulated within the system. What's more, threats are a key element of the functioning of the Russian state.

The scientific description of the role and place of threats in the state system was given by the sociologist Simon Kordonsky. For him, the very structure of the state, with its role of providing for survival, security and social stability, creates the conditions for apparent threats. Each department comes up with a particular type of threat – natural, military, social and so on – and accordingly this hierarchy of threats requires its own share of resources. The more dangerous the particular threat (be it real or imagined), the greater the flow of state resources dealt out to the various services and departments responsible for dealing with it. In such circumstances, Kordonsky writes, 'services become ever more interested in increasing the number of the threats for which they are responsible, as well as making them appear bigger and more dangerous'.[14]

One method for gaining extra resources from the state is to invent new threats on different levels, from the state level down to the municipal level. One example of such an invention was the creation of the myth about the 'orange threat' after the revolution in Ukraine in 2004. This led to the formation of new organizational structures (such as the infamous Directorate E of the Interior Ministry, responsible for tackling extremism) and a variety of 'patriotic' youth organizations. The state set aside for certain agencies the appropriate resources to fight the 'orange threat', which became a particular type of corporation, interested in continuing the funding of its activity and using any means possible to reactivate the 'orange' myth.

In 2011 the League for a Safe Internet was launched by Konstantin Malofeyev, to combat the threat of 'paedophiles and extremism on the Internet'. This organization was given a budget of tens of millions of dollars. It is still managing to cope with 'its own' threat, while trying to introduce ever more restrictive laws and receiving ever more administrative and financial resources. Sometimes, combatting a threat can bring direct commercial benefits, as happened with the Russian Sea (*Russkoe morye*) group of companies, belonging to the oligarch Gennady Timchenko, which benefited from the embargo on the import of Norwegian salmon. After it was announced that there would be Russian sanctions, the purchase price of salmon doubled, and Russian Sea shares rose by 34 per cent.

Exactly the same thing happened when the Russian Security Council discussed the fantasy threat that Russia might be excluded from the worldwide web (as happened to Sudan in 2007). This was a purely commercial idea, dreamt up in order to sell to the state equipment that would duplicate the infrastructure of the Internet in Russia. The threat of Russia being excluded from the worldwide web remains purely hypothetical; but real funds can be allocated to that idea – including technology costing hundreds of millions of dollars. A very peculiar 'threat market' is growing in modern Russia, and bets on this are constantly growing. As for the growth in the amount of resources that are redistributed, there is 'threat inflation', as new ones are constantly being brought into being. Threats may be genuine or just as easily imagined or carefully designed. The motivation of the players in this market may be purely for their own department, or it may be commercial (frequently these amount to the same thing), but the sale of these threats has massive internal and foreign policy consequences.

The emergence of this market has been dictated by the character of the political elite of Putin's third term. In place of 'Politburo 2.0', which was made up of representatives of the power ministries (*siloviki*), bureaucrats and oligarchs, the leadership is now totally dominated by the *siloviki*. As the political commentator Konstantin Gaaze writes, all the key decisions in the past year have been taken by a closed circle of representatives of the FSB. 'The FSB doesn't concern itself with development, it just reacts to threats as it sees them. The government and the various departments spend years weighing up the pros and cons of any decision, but now the FSB simply "sells" a threat to the President and he immediately takes the decision reached by the Service.' In this way, according to Gaaze, the decision was taken about protecting Russians' personal data (according to which all personal data should be stored on Russian servers); about the embargo on foodstuffs; and also about many questions linked to Ukraine.

The threat-producing machine works on the redistribution of state resources to the advantage of the power corporations and the business structures linked to them. Here you will find means that have been earmarked for the rebuilding of Crimea and the war with Ukraine, the rearmament of the Russian Army and the modernization of the nuclear arsenal. Then there's the expensive reinvention of the bicycle – that is, the production of Russian versions of global technology: GLONASS instead of GPS; a sovereign Internet on local servers; a national payment system, 'Mir', in place of Visa or MasterCard; and a national search engine, 'Sputnik', to take the place of Google. Fascinated by imaginary threats, the Kremlin has diverted funds from the market to the *siloviki*, who follow their own commercial interests exclusively through nonmarket methods. The liberals in the system have been crushed; those that are left carry out rearguard battles in the Central Bank; and market logic no longer works in post-Crimea Russia.

But this is just half the problem. The bitter irony is that the idea is tangible, and these threats, which were dreamt up and sold to the Kremlin, have become reality – only now not as the reasons for Russian policy, but as the results of this policy. The Kremlin is not reacting to threats, but creating them itself. So in the autumn of 2013, for instance, the legend was dreamt up about 'the loss of Ukraine' if it were to sign an Association Agreement with the EU. In many ways this Agreement was a mere formality and did not carry with it any obligations. But because of this, the Kremlin started to tie the hands of the then Ukrainian President, Viktor Yanukovych, which led to mass demonstrations on Kiev's Maidan Square and subsequently the whole spiral of confrontation. As a result, Ukraine went ahead and signed the Agreement; and is now lost to Russia forever. Three months later, in February 2014, the annexation of Crimea was undertaken out of fear of an imaginary 'NATO base in Sevastopol'; and what has happened as a result? Ukraine is rapidly growing closer to the North Atlantic Alliance and NATO is expanding its presence by creating permanent bases in the Baltic States, which are worried by the turn of events. In Russia they started battling with imaginary 'separatists' until they were foaming at the mouth, and as a result created the virus of separatism, coming to us from Crimea and Donbass.

The problem is that the *siloviki*, who have a complete hold on power in post-Crimea Russia, are capable of thinking and acting only in a space full of threats. All they can do is track, describe and neutralize threats. This is their particular way of dealing with the outside world, where they see only challenges, not possibilities. The *siloviki* need threats for bureaucratic domination; for obtaining resources and the redistribution of property. Now, though, the *Chekist* machinery for replicating threats has become a loose cannon and has started to destroy everything around it. It has itself become a threat to Russia's national security. 'The threat period', which our military teacher frightened us with in my childhood, has finally arrived.

CHURCHILL DREAMT IT ALL UP

There's a national sport in Russia – and it's not fishing, or checkers or even hockey. It is exposing global conspiracies. From the false 'Protocols of the Elders of Zion' about the establishment of world domination by the Jews, to the 'Dulles Doctrine' for the moral degradation of Soviet citizens; from the idea that the October Revolution of 1917 was funded by the German General Staff, to the collapse of the USSR in 1991 being planned by the CIA: everywhere we are looking for the false bottom in the suitcase, for secret signs or interests behind the scenes, and we always ask the question, 'Who gains from this?' We are perceptive and vigilant, like the patients in the asylum in Vladimir Vysotsky's song, which said of the Bermuda Triangle: 'Churchill dreamt all this up in 1918'.[15]

Hearing about the terrorist bomb at the finish line of the Boston Marathon on 15 April 2013, our homegrown conspiracy theorists immediately declared it to be a CIA set-up. Bloggers compared photos before and after the explosion and where the policemen were situated and insisted that the wounded could not have been quietly sitting in wheelchairs and that therefore they were simply actors. The television anchor Maxim Shevchenko came right out and said that the scene was part of a secret scenario arranged to cover up the USA's failed policy in Iraq in order to justify sending American troops into the Caucasus.

Conspiracy theories have always abounded everywhere, but they became particularly popular from the time of the French Revolution, which was said to be either the work of the Masons, or the Illuminati, or the Jews. In America itself there are conspiratorial versions of the murder of President Kennedy; or those that say that the Moon landings were staged on Earth. But wherever they appear, conspiracy theories remain the product of immature or sick minds. In Russia, conspiracy has become the dominant worldview. This can probably be explained historically by the long tradition of a lack of freedom, of serfdom and by the psychology of slavery. Not being responsible for their own fate, people became used to blaming everything that happened on a higher power: the peasantry said it was 'all due to the nobles', and the nobles that it was 'the will of the sovereign'.

Today – when horoscopes are published in newspapers alongside the currency exchange rates; when icons are stuck on the dashboard of every other car (and, at the same time, the driver doesn't wear his seat belt); and when religious obscurantism dictates laws and court procedures – conspiracy theories are once again troubling Russians' minds. But what is most frightening of all is that this is becoming state policy.

It all began in 2004, with the terrorist attack in Beslan in Ingushetia, when Chechen fighters seized a school and took the children hostage. Vladimir Putin suddenly announced that this was the machinations of the West, which was trying to snatch Russia's 'juicy morsels'. Then there were the protests on Kiev's Maidan Square, and the carnival of 'colour revolutions', from Bishkek in Kyrgyzstan to Tbilisi in Georgia. This frightened the Kremlin, which saw the spectre of a global conspiracy by the agents of democratization. Next came Tahrir Square in Cairo and the 'Arab Spring' ... Then suddenly there were the protests on Bolotnaya Square in Moscow in the winter of 2011–12, and the paranoia became complete once and for all, producing a locked and hermetically sealed picture of the world. Fantastic scenarios are born in this picture, such as that the West was transferring billions of dollars to Russian NGOs in an attempt to bring about regime change in Russia. This is like Stalin's picture of the world in 1937, when all the facts incontrovertibly pointed to each other and all together added up to a counterrevolutionary conspiracy; but not a single one of them bore any relation to reality. Nevertheless, this short circuit in the brain, this paranoia of the state, sets the political agenda and reflects the moral atmosphere of a closed and cynical society, where the individual is not free to make his own decisions: 'the boss' is behind everything, and everything is done simply for money.

The conspiracy theory is poor and flawed; it does not understand all the complexity, multitude and subjectivity of the contemporary world, where behind all major events there stand not secret forces but many different players, each with their own interests. And these interests are far from always being material ones; people are prepared to sacrifice their personal well-being – and even their lives – for the sake of ideas, taking part in an act of terror or going out onto the streets to protest. Nor is the conspiracy theory prepared to accept that we live in a 'Risk Society' (as the German sociologist, Ulrich

Beck, wrote); that history is unpredictable and perverse, more likely to obey the law of incompetence and chance than an evil will. As Margaret Thatcher's press secretary, Bernard Ingham, said: 'Many journalists have fallen for the conspiracy theory of government. I do assure you that they would produce more accurate work if they adhered to the cock-up theory.' It seems that we find ourselves right in the middle of that cock-up now.[16]

A RACKETEER WITH ROCKETS

Reasons seem to come thick and fast these days for relations between Russia and the West to pass the point of no return. The international investigation team looking into the shooting down of the Malaysian airliner MH17 over Ukraine in July 2014 confirmed that the aircraft was shot down by a 'BUK' missile, brought from Russia and fired from territory controlled by pro-Russian separatists. Immediately in the wake of this report, Western countries held Russia and its Syrian ally, Bashir Assad, responsible for the barbaric bombing of a hospital in the Syrian city of Aleppo; the French Foreign Ministry described it as 'a war crime'.

It probably makes sense to point out at this juncture the West's foresight in ensuring that the Western legal process moves slowly but reliably. And to remember the bombing in 1988 by Libyan special forces of the Pan Am airliner over the Scottish town of Lockerbie: it took eleven years before Colonel Qaddafi gave up the suspects and fifteen years before compensation was paid to the families of those who died in this terrorist attack ... But even this is not a fair comparison: the analogy with a small country such as Libya doesn't work, and these latest revelations evoke a sense of déjà vu. Over the past three years there were many such points of no return, and on every occasion Russia and the West crossed yet another 'red line' and continued downwards on the slippery slope with mutual accusations and verbal exchanges, as if they were connected by an invisible chain. There will be no Nuremberg Trials, nor Hague Tribunals, nor, indeed, any other tribunal. What is much more likely is that Russia can expect trials *in absentia* lasting many years, and convictions, and demands for payment of multimillion-dollar compensation – all of which, of course, Russia will refuse to acknowledge. This will start a new round of sanctions, rows over the seizure of Russian assets abroad and litigation drawn out over years, if not decades. A better parallel to draw than Lockerbie is the tragedy of the Korean airliner shot down by a Soviet fighter jet over Sakhalin on 1 September

1983. To this day, there has never been a full explanation of what happened, no one has been held responsible, and you can no longer find on the map of the world the country that shot down the aircraft.

In other words, it is highly unlikely that there will be catastrophic consequences for Russia as a result of this deterioration in relations. It may even have the opposite effect: the West's latest accusations play into the Kremlin's long-term strategy of creating an image of Russia as an unpredictable and dangerous player, one that breaks all the global rules and therefore should be feared. Clearly, neither the shooting down of MH17 nor the bombing of civilian targets in Syria were actions planned in advance by Russia; but they come out of that high-risk environment created by Moscow in the post-Soviet space and in the Middle East, and are inevitable consequences of the hybrid war that Russia is waging around the world. Yet another act of this war was the decree signed by Vladimir Putin suspending the work of the intergovernmental agreement with the USA on the use of plutonium. Russia raises the stakes in the geopolitical game, showing everyone that it is willing to hold the West to nuclear blackmail (like the television presenter Dmitry Kiselyov – one of the Kremlin's main propagandists – talking about reducing American cities to 'radioactive ash') and to dismantle all the agreements reached about nuclear weapons.

The Kremlin's hybrid war is a policy of weakness and cunning in the information age. Having insufficient military, economic and diplomatic resources to achieve victory in Ukraine or Syria, Russia carries out precise operations so as to destabilize the situation in these two countries and provoke a confrontation with the West that it shies away from at the last moment. It conducts a powerful campaign of disinformation and propaganda with the aim of distorting the picture of what is going on and blurring the position of the West, which itself appears unclear and indecisive. The aim of hybrid warfare is the projection of unpredictability, chaos and fear; the creation of an unstable environment in which it is much easier to bluff when you hold weak cards in your hands.

In the twenty-first century, Russia's principal export has become not oil and gas, but fear: the price of the former will fall over time; the price of the latter will rise. In the risk society that the leading contemporary philosophers and sociologists write about, from Ulrich Beck to Anthony Giddens, the winners are those who can create and capitalize on fear, turning it into a political and economic resource. In this, Russia is a leading player and provider. The manufacture of fear is part of the very essence of Russian history, both in Russia's relations

90

with the West and in the day-to-day relationship of the individual and the state. The system of international relations in the twenty-first century dates from 11 September 2001 (in Russia, slightly earlier – from September 1999, with the mysterious bombings of apartment blocks in Buynaksk, Moscow and Volgodonsk, in which many saw the hand of the FSB). The structure of this system fits the scenarios laid out by Thomas Hobbes, who predicted anarchy in interstate relations and a 'war of all against all'; but not that of Immanuel Kant, who sought 'eternal peace' in Europe. Putin's Russia is one of the producers and beneficiaries of this Hobbesian world, in which its main resource – fear – and its main services – security measures – are in great demand. This is the classic strategy of the racketeer, who symbolically creates a threat, and then suggests 'protection' at a decidedly non-symbolic price.

The key word here is 'weakness'. Having lost the Cold War and the postwar world, and having squandered its oil profits and the remaining shreds of its reputation, Russia is incapable of constructively solving the world's problems. Instead, it prefers to make them worse. It doesn't welcome and settle refugees from the Third World on its own territory; instead, it sends wave after wave of them into Western Europe across its land borders with Finland and Norway, using them as an instrument of hybrid warfare in order to deepen the migration crisis in Europe and provoke anti-immigrant sentiment there. It doesn't solve humanitarian and political problems in Syria, but meddles in an already existing conflict with selfish geopolitical aims, thus taking it to an even higher level. It doesn't assist the objective international investigation of the shooting down of MH17, but tries to knock it off course, constantly putting forward versions that contradict each other. And Russia didn't cooperate with the World Anti-Doping Agency (WADA) and international sporting federations in order to eliminate the epidemic of doping in modern sport, but tried to discredit and destroy WADA with information overload and attacks by hackers.

And it has to be said that for now it is all working out well for Russia. The combined efforts of the Ministry of Defence, the Foreign Ministry, the Russia Today (RT) television channel and the individual assault squads of 'people's diplomacy' – from football fanatics in European stadiums and so-called 'Orthodox bikers' touring Europe to hackers and Internet trolls flooding Western networks – are ensuring that the export of fear and uncertainty is growing at maximum volume with minimum cost. The Russian threat seems to loom over the West on every corner: in the movement of Assad's forces and the provocations of the Donetsk separatists; in any cyberattack, be it breaking into the servers of the headquarters of the Democratic Party in the USA, to attacks on Yahoo's servers (which, the Internet company confirmed, were linked to Russian government agencies); in the unidentified submarines in the Baltic Sea; in the waves of migrants in European cities; and in the financing of Donald Trump and Marine le Pen. It no longer matters to what extent Moscow is linked to each of these episodes, or whether it was a carefully planned special operation or simply the actions of individual patriotic citizens. Russia has created a shimmering space of uncertainty in which its role is demonized and, most likely, exaggerated; but that's exactly what Putin is trying to do.

The amount spent on the production of fear is minimal: according to the RBK news agency, Russia's operation in Syria came in at under one billion dollars: chickenfeed by Russian standards, the cost of just a few hours of the Sochi Olympics. As President Putin said cynically about Syria: 'We can train our army there for quite a long time without having any real effect on state finances.'[17] Add in the cost of the Russia Today information agency, the work with the various Russian diasporas in the West and with politicians like Gerhard Schroeder and Silvio Berlusconi, and aid to right-wing populist and separatist parties in the West, and you still get a comparatively small sum; certainly, one that cannot be compared to the ruinous investments in the infrastructure of fear during the Cold War.

On the other hand, compared to thirty years ago the West today simply does not have either the necessary organization or the will to resist. Relaxed by a long period of peace, and demoralized by the postmodern, 'post-heroic' era, the West is passive, disunited and too dependent on consumerism: Russia exploits this weakness. Minimal funds were dug up to deal with the archetypal Russian threat, which had been dozing in the back of the West's consciousness since Gorbachev's time; but this threat has raised itself once more to its full height, like an emaciated bear coming out of hibernation in the spring. It is no coincidence that whenever their team plays away, Russian football fans – in the front row of Putin's hybrid war – take with them huge banners with a roaring bear, or that the group of hackers who broke into the WADA server call themselves Fancy Bears. On their logo they have a bear wearing the Anonymous mask. Thirty years on, the symbolic economy of the Cold War has returned to its starting position: Russians blame Obama for everything, and Americans look for the Russian threat under the bed.

However, the West is not rushing to buy life insurance or security services from the 'Russia' defence factory. The racketeer's strategy works when he manages to tie the client into his 'protection', his defence; but the West is not exactly falling over itself to enter into talks about 'a new security system', and it does not see Putin as a new Stalin of the 1945-type, with whom you have to sit down around the map of the world and divide it up into spheres of influence. That is why it is more accurate to compare Russia less with a racketeer than with a small-time thug. As they say, Russia may have got up off its knees, but it is still only squatting. Since he doesn't have real strength, the thug holds the neighbourhood in fear and manipulates the law-abiding parts of society by issuing small threats. All he has in his arsenal is a collection of petty ritual gestures (such as beating up a weakling, nicking a mobile phone, cheeking the police, flashing a knife, baring his chest), all designed to show those around him that he's prepared to break the law and violate convention. But the thug immediately shrinks in the face of any outside force or organized opposition. For that to happen, though, such opposition must be evident, and in the current system of international relations, with Obama on the way out and the EU weakened by Brexit, that strength simply isn't there.

What next? At first glance, it seems that the aim of this hybrid war has been achieved: the world has started to listen to Russia and started to fear it; but this is on a par with the fear that the world has for Iran or North Korea, which have been global scarecrows for decades. Russia has not so much returned to the club of the leading world powers, which it was a part of before 2014, as turned into a worldwide horror story. And in this it should be compared not with Libya or North Korea, but with the Soviet Union at the start of the 1980s. In the very same way, that country squandered the resources and the respect it had, lost all its allies and, not having the strength to solve global problems, carried out a destructive foreign policy, from the arms race to the war in Afghanistan. Pathetic in its global pretensions and its dreams of past greatness, inflated on the outside, but empty within, the Soviet Union turned into a warhead stuffed full of rubbish, a shadow of what it once was. It seemed to be eternal and unshakeable – until it collapsed overnight. 'This was forever, until it ended', as the sociologist Alexei Yurchak wrote in his book on the collapse of the USSR. But projects such as this always end unexpectedly, ridiculously and unstoppably.[18]

THE TORCH PROCESSION

In the build-up to the Sochi Winter Olympics, the Olympic Flame continued its march around Russia's wide expanses, accompanied by hundreds of security personnel, police, guard dogs and patriotic bikers (who nowadays carry out the role of the emperor's mounted guard). Life along the route of the VIP cortège came to a standstill: whole towns froze; roads were closed; trains came to a halt. From being a celebration on the move, the Olympic Torch Relay became a mobile police operation. The centre of Moscow shut down for three days; in St Petersburg, thousands of soldiers cleaned Palace Square and cordoned off the city's main thoroughfare, Nevsky Prospekt.

The mind boggles at the scale of this gigantic performance. Ever since the first Torch Relay took place – the idea of Josef Goebbels before the Berlin Olympics of 1936 – this one became the longest, the biggest and the most technologically accomplished relay ever. It lasted 123 days, covered 65,000 kilometres, involved 14,000 torch bearers and used every form of transport possible: from atomic ice-breakers and spacecraft to dog-sledges and teams of reindeer. When it travelled by railway, the Flame was transported by a Russian Railways staff train, made up of eleven carriages, including two restaurant cars, and accompanied by five hundred people. The Olympic Flame went to the North Pole, into outer space and on the International Space Station (ISS). There followed a trip to the bottom of Lake Baikal; it was taken down a coalmine and to the summit of Mount Elbrus. The Olympic Torch Relay even became a religious ceremony: in the railway carriage and on the ice-breaker, the Flame travelled in a special sacred case; and when he sent the Torch on its way from Vladivostok to Khabarovsk, the Head of Russian Railways, Vladimir Yakunin (who also happens to be a patron of the Orthodox Church, and who has experience of transporting the Blessed Easter Flame from Jerusalem to Moscow), made the sign of the cross over the Flame.

Like an animal in the forest, Russia was marking out its territory. With precise points, here we had Kaliningrad (Russia's outpost inside the European Union); Sakhalin (a message to the Japanese: don't even think about the Kurile Islands); the North Pole (relevant for the dispute over the territorial ownership of the Lomonosov underwater ridge, where the polar explorer, Artur Chilingarov, hoisted the titanium flag of Russia in 2007). Most important of all, though, was the parade of Russian sovereignty in the North Caucasus, where the last two weeks of the Torch Relay took place before it reached its final destination in Sochi. The true meaning of the holding of the Olympics in this troubled region was that it conclusively confirmed Russian sovereignty over the North Caucasus – the final victory of the two-hundred-year Caucasian war.

And it was no coincidence that the Olympic Torch Relay took place against the background of a discussion of the sovereignty of the Russian Federation. In the State Duma a draft law was being considered that would make the propagation of separatism a criminal offence: 'The spreading in any form of views, ideas, or calls for action that would question the territorial integrity of the Russian Federation.' It was proposed that the punishment should be severe: for the thoughtcrime against sovereignty, a twenty-year prison term was suggested – much longer than for murder! However, in Russia crimes against the state were always punished more harshly than crimes against individuals. The Deputy Prime Minister, Dmitry Rogozin, even proposed renaming the Russian Far East 'Our Own East' in order to prevent it from moving even further away.

Oh, this childish belief in the power of the word – that if you forbid people from speaking about a problem, it will disappear all by itself! The taboo about having any conversations about the territorial make-up of Russia brings on a generic trauma in our political elite. There is a phantom pain after the collapse of the USSR – 'the greatest geopolitical catastrophe of the twentieth century', as Vladimir Putin called it – and a panic attack about the threat of further disintegration.

Where does this fear come from? Why has 'sovereignty' suddenly become such a painful place for the regime? There are two problems here, neither of which is caused by external (and, indeed, imaginary) threats to sovereignty, but by Russia's own internal psychological hang-ups. The first is the deepening post-Soviet identity crisis of trying to understand what Russia is: a country for the Russians or a multinational empire? And where do its borders lie? In the Baltic States? In the North Caucasus? In Crimea? In Eastern Ukraine? In Northern Kazakhstan? It is not the separatists who want to dismember Russia, but the Russians themselves who cannot understand where the borders are; this is where the paranoia and hypersensitivity springs from whenever the issue is raised of sovereignty or of Russia's borders.

The other problem is much more serious: it is a crisis of belief in Russia's future. Here, once again, it is not a question of Russia's territorial integrity or of imaginary threats to sovereignty, but the fact that the raw, authoritarian model is worn out and it is impossible to conduct any long-term planning in our country. Today's Russia has been robbed of any model for the future, any long-term perspective, or any economic or social model other than the export of raw materials and the plundering of the state budget. The elite compensates for fear of the future with ever more paranoid ideas of sovereignty. Instead of coming up with genuine ideas for strengthening the state, such as a strategy of development for the depressed regions and the single-industry towns, or investment in education, healthcare and culture, in human capital and the future of the country, all they propose is rhetoric, prison terms for thoughtcrime and fantastic ideas about renaming the Far East. Once upon a time we had a country that tried to patch up holes using mere words; but this country collapsed in 1991.

This is why religious rituals of sovereignty and the Olympic Torch Relay are so important for the state, and the Olympic Games as a model for the future and the medal count as a prototype for war: it is the containment of fear, an exorcism of the eternal Russian emptiness. This is where the seriousness of the state comes from and the extreme security measures, turning what should have been a jolly carnival procession into a special operation by the security forces.

But it didn't turn out as it should have done. The faulty torches went out (the Olympic Flame was extinguished on more than fifty occasions) and the ungrateful public laughed and whistled. It became essential to have a member of the Federal Guard Service standing by with a Zippo lighter to relight the Olympic Flame, which is exactly what happened when the rally reached Red Square, right opposite Lenin's Mausoleum. But where can we find enough guards who, with their Zippos, can reignite the dying belief in Russia's future?

OLYMPIC SCHIZOPHRENIA

Everyone is asking whether the 2014 Sochi Winter Olympics can be compared to Berlin in 1936. I decided to ride on the wave that this historical analogy has created and look again at the legendary film, *Olympia*, directed by Leni Riefenstahl. I saw masses of happy faces, a parade of muscular bodies and a whole host of ingenious camera angles and original editing techniques. Up in the stands, Hitler smiled in a rather embarrassed way, Goebbels and Goering appeared at his side, and the crowd threw up their arms in the Nazi salute. The spectators got excited, jumped out of their seats, supporting equally enthusiastically their own athletes and those from other countries; they were very friendly towards the American fans in their white hats. Flags were waved bearing laurel wreaths, the Olympic Flame burned brightly in the Temple of Light designed by Albert Speer and the sky overhead was full of aeroplanes.

The sensation never left me that everything taking place had a dual meaning. In just three years, these people would begin crushing each other with tanks. In nine years, the Americans would bomb Dresden and Hiroshima. In ten years, the Nuremberg Trials would be held. We would learn about Dachau and Auschwitz; about Khatyn and Babiy Yar.[19] Can we today watch Riefenstahl and not be burdened by this knowledge? Can we take the Olympics out of their historical context? How can we watch Ludwig Stubbendorf ride to victory in the equestrian event, knowing that he will be killed on the Eastern Front in 1941; or see the record shot-put of the great Hans Welke, who was to become a policeman and be captured and executed by partisans near Khatyn in 1943? And if we cast our net wider, how can we read the works of the philosopher, Martin Heidegger, and the 'court lawyer of the Third Reich', the political theorist Carl Schmitt? How can we listen to the works of genius that are the recordings of the conductors Wilhelm Furtwängler and Herbert von Karajan with the Berlin Philharmonic Orchestra, knowing that they both served the Nazi regime, and that Karajan somehow managed to join the Nazi Party twice?

For seventy years now we have been trying to separate the wheat from the chaff, to separate politics from culture. Leni Riefenstahl was cleared by a postwar court, but still came up against a secret ban which prevented her from working in her chosen profession, and she went into photography instead. Nevertheless, at the 1948 Lausanne Film Festival, she was awarded an Olympic certificate; and in 1956 a Hollywood panel named *Olympia* one of the ten best films of all time. In 2001, the President of the International Olympic Committee, Juan Antonio Samaranch, presented the ninety-nine-year-old Riefenstahl with a gold medal of the 1936 Berlin Olympic Games.

Sochi 2014 is not Berlin 1936. It is not worth comparing one of the most terrifying totalitarian regimes in history with the populist authoritarianism of modern Russia. A better comparison would probably be with Mexico in 1968 and Seoul in 1988. Mexico and South Korea in those years were each ruled by one-party dictatorships, just as, incidentally, Japan was in the decades after the Second World War, if we think back to the Tokyo Olympics in 1964 and the Winter Olympics in Sapporo in 1972. Even a comparison with the capital of what Reagan described as 'the Evil Empire', Moscow 1980, is a limp one; Beijing 2008 would be closer.

Nevertheless, in the Russian discussion the Sochi Olympics inevitably brings up moral dilemmas similar to 1936: we are used to thinking on a grand scale. The question stares one in the face: should someone who is in opposition to the regime wish for a successful Games and victory for the Russian team, if each triumph raises Putin's rating? Can you join in a celebration if it is supported by billions of stolen dollars and the destruction of a region's ecology, and every Russian medal is simply an indulgence to redeem evil?

But if we put extreme views to one side, a normal citizen, even one who is critical of the state (and, after all, isn't that one of the usual human criteria for normality?) cannot actually not support his country and cannot actively wish for it to fail. A significant section of the reading and thinking public has developed Olympic schizophrenia: they are torn between typical Russian *Schadenfreude* about the incompetence of the managers, the thieving ways of the contractors and the crisis in many sports (such as in figure skating and biathlon), and pride in our sportsmen, the volunteers and the unusually amicable policemen as well as the inspirational opening ceremony. This is not about President Putin, or the Sports Minister Vitaly Mutko, or the authorities; this is about Russia as a country testing itself before the whole world over the course of two weeks.

Schizophrenia is a peculiarly Russian characteristic. Power is separated from the country by the crenelated Kremlin Wall. And for centuries the educated class was not only alien to its own people but even became used to being ashamed of Russia, while at the same time surprisingly remaining Russian patriots. As the poet Alexander Pushkin said: 'Of course, I despise my Fatherland with my whole being; but it annoys me when a foreigner shares this sentiment with me.'[20] Shame and pride, love and hatred, give rise to the typical Russian split personality. Russian patriotism has been schizophrenic from the time of the Russian philosopher of the first half of the nineteenth century, Pyotr Chaadaev. He was the author of the critical 'Philosophical Letters', who dared to love Russia warts and all, and for his ideas was declared mad by the authorities.

The problem, clearly, lies in the binary nature of Russian thinking, noted by the late twentieth-century philologist and semiotician, Yury Lotman. In one of his later works, *Culture and Explosion*, Lotman talks about the typical black and white Russian view of the world: 'He who is not with us is against us'; it's us and them; Russia versus the outside world. A war rages between these two positions – for the Olympics, for social networks, history, faith, memory. In this battle, the state tries to claim all the significant national symbols: the Great Patriotic War and the Victory in 1945, spaceflights and sporting achievements. Any alternative point of view is dismissed as traitorous: either you accept these events with all the glory of the state or you are condemned as a slanderer: there can be no spots on the Sun. It is impossible to honour the Victory in the Second World War, but at the same time cast doubts on the role of Stalin; it is impossible to revel in the Olympics, yet at the same time to speak about theft, the destruction of homes, the forced resettlement of local residents and the destruction of homeless dogs in Sochi ahead of the Olympics. War is war.

Here we should remember Lotman's warning that binary structures are doomed to lead to a catastrophic resolution of conflicts, to self-destruction and to a total explosion. We will collapse as a country if we do not put a stop to this spiral of hatred and polarization; it is a civil war in the making. We need to look for a way out in an acceptance of a multilayered reality. As Lotman wrote, European culture is resistant because it is ternary. It rests on the idea of overcoming binary structures, of allowing for a third position that accepts both of the others. It's like in the joke about the wise rabbi, who says to the two men who are arguing: 'You are right; and you are right, too.' And when a third man asks, 'How can that be, rabbi?', he replies: 'And you are right as well.'

The Olympics is a gigantic carnival where Russia appears in all its greatness and its provinciality, where fifty or sixty billion dollars are turned into a giant hecatomb, like the Great Pyramid of Giza, rebuilt in the spirit of the eternal Russian desire to prove something to the world. It is a combination of the work of world-class producers of mass spectacles and Asiatic *Gastarbeiter* who have no rights; wonderful architecture but poor finishing; selfless volunteers and indifferent bureaucrats; a mix of global ambitions and parochial bluff. In this schizophrenia, no doubt, there is also the essence of the Russian soul, which is capricious and paradoxical; just like holding the Winter Olympics in the subtropics.

THE THUGS' GAME

They're celebrating yet another victory in Russia. On the eve of the first match in the European Football Championship 2016, a couple of dozen Russian fans chased away a much larger group of English fans in the Old Port in Marseilles. The next day, immediately after the match, they started a pogrom in the stands where the English fans were, beating everyone they could get their hands on, including families and elderly people. The results were upsetting. At least thirty-five people were injured, and one fifty-year-old English fan was hit over the head with a crowbar and died. By way of punishment UEFA threatened the Russian team with expulsion from the tournament and fined the Russian Football Union 150,000 Euros, taking into account also the racist behaviour of the Russian fans during the match. The Russian fans were the first item in world news; but wasn't that exactly what they wanted?

Perhaps this disgraceful episode did not deserve such attention: 'The thugs' game',[21] as the movement of football thugs has become known, long ago turned into a safari park of violence and a close relative of world war; fans of all countries fight and cause trouble. This can even lead to carnage, such as the tragedy at the Heysel Stadium in Brussels, when thirty-nine people died. That led to all English clubs being excluded from UEFA competitions for five years. Indeed, Marseilles remembers only too well the English fans at the World Cup in 1998, when they started a fight against Tunisian fans, which smashed up half the city. But here's the difference: whereas in England society and politicians alike condemn such outrageous behaviour by the fans, in Russia these football hooligans are presented almost like national heroes. The correspondent of the newspaper *Sovietsky Sport*, Dmitry Yegorov, carried out a live transmission of the carnage on Twitter, commentating on it as if it were a football match, lauding the organization and physical fitness of the Russians. Social networks were full of praise for the Russian fans 'slapping' the English softies and standing up for Russia like the three hundred

101

Spartans; one sports journalist even put out on Twitter that he was ashamed of the Russian fans who didn't take part in the beatings.

Even more interesting was that the Russian thugs were supported by high-ranking officials, from the representative of the Investigative Committee of Russia, Vladimir Markin, to the Duma deputy and member of the Executive Committee of the Russian Football Union, Igor Lebedev. And here one has to acknowledge a very unpleasant thing: the fans in Marseilles were representing perfectly the official policy and mass consciousness of post-Crimean Russia.

They carried out the same hybrid war that is so popular in our propaganda, when well-prepared fighters trained in hand-to-hand combat are sent into Crimea or the Donbass under the guise of 'soldiers on leave'; when violence is carried out selectively and purposefully; and when attacks take place in unexpected places. Rumours abounded on the Internet about how, on many of the video clips, these Russian fans looked so muscular, organized and sober that they could almost have been *spetsnaz* soldiers from military intelligence; but let's leave that theory to conspiracy lovers. What certainly appears to be the case is that in Marseilles an organized group of fighters, the 'Ultras' (as the organized fans who go to fight are known), gathered from various 'firms' of fans and schooled in street battles, attacked the 'casuals' – ordinary English fans. Some of these English fans had their families with them. What's more, they were tanked up on beer and had come there not to fight but to cheer for their team and enjoy themselves. One of the Russian fans came straight out in an interview and admitted that our fans had gone there to fight: 'It doesn't matter which towns our fans are from or which team they support. All that matters is that we're from Russia and we're going to fight the English fans. They reckon that they're the biggest football hooligans. We're here to show that the English fans are just girlies.'

So even if the Russian attack wasn't a well-planned military operation, there is fertile ground for rumours to start. For Russia this was not the first 'hybrid' interference in social movements in Europe; others include organizing protests and spreading propaganda, influencing the media, subtly stirring up anti-immigrant sentiments, cooperating with right-wing radicals and neofascist movements and supporting odious populists and separatism in European regions. Just as when the Comintern[22] existed the USSR carried out subversive activities in the countries of the West, so Russia is getting into the cracks and splits within European society, trying to weaken the West from the inside, and explaining this as a total 'information war'; and the nervous Europeans see these Russian fans exactly in that light.

Second, football fans really are one of the Russian state's fighting groups. The state is irresistibly drawn to these dressed-up actors who like to put on a display of strength: Cossacks, bikers and football fans. Representatives of these tough male brotherhoods drink tea in the offices of high-ranking officials. They are held up as examples of patriotism and are given government grants for the development of civil society; and when necessary they are sent to support the 'Russian Marches' with the nationalists or to attack opposition rallies. In all this, the football hooligans are as far away from the traditions of football as the so-called 'Orthodox bikers' are from rebellion and the freedom of the 'easy riders'; and the pot-bellied Cossacks with their stuck-on forelocks are from the honour and glory of the Russian Cossack tradition; these are all carnival fakes of the Putin era. In the conditions of total simulation of civil society in modern Russia, these protest countercultures become the representatives of pathetic officialdom, official patriotism and the fat cats who receive government grants.

Finally, the Russian fanatics (at least, those who are caught on camera) are readymade products of official propaganda, displaying on their tee-shirts and their bodies all the caricature-like kitsch of the era of the annexation of Crimea and 'Russia rising up off its knees': tee-shirts with 'the little green men' (the *spetsnaz* troops with no distinguishing markings on their uniforms who seized Crimea in 2014), and slogans such as 'We don't abandon our own'; Russian hats bearing the red star; banners with the roaring bear and Slavic warriors. And as the apotheosis of all this patriotic trash, there is a huge Russian tricolour covering half the stand bearing the words, 'VSEM PI..DEC' – 'F.UCK YOU ALL': for them, it seems, this is the national idea of this new Russia.

However, these excesses began long before Crimea: the Russian fans saved the most vile displays of great-state chauvinism and racism for their trips abroad. In the Czech Republic, Russian hockey fans unfurled banners with pictures of tanks and promises to repeat the Soviet invasion of 1968; and in the centre of Warsaw in 2012, football fans put on a procession in honour of Russia Day, almost provoking a massive fight with the Polish 'ultras'. In the stands at football and hockey matches, Russian resentment rises up to its full height, pumped up with beer and propaganda; the Soviet empire taking its symbolic revenge: yes, we lost a great state and still haven't learnt to play football, but we can still break chairs and 'slap' the Europeans around; 'kick the hell out of the bastards', as Vladimir Putin said one day, using the language of the fanatics. Ultimately, wasn't it he who in one of his interviews shared the folk wisdom gleaned from his difficult childhood in the backstreets of Leningrad: 'get the first punch in'? That's exactly how the thugs behaved in Marseilles, and in this sense they are worthy representatives of the state: football hooliganism in hybrid Russia is a matter of vital importance for the state.

The term, 'the thugs' game' exactly sums up what is going on: despite the 'grown-up' budgets of the clubs and the national team, despite buying world-class star players (the typical strategy of superficial modernization), Russia remains an average country in the world rankings, both in terms of its national championship and the performances of its national team. Just before the start of Euro 2016, our country was twenty-ninth in FIFA's top fifty world teams. But our fan movement has very quickly and in a very organized way adapted the British model. The books of the English historian of football hooliganism, Dougie Brimson, achieved cult status among Russian football fans. Russia may not have become a football superpower, but it has excelled in the hybrid world of 'the thugs' game', bursting onto the international stage with a deep-rooted culture of violence that is accepted by society.

But Russia is up to that same hybrid 'thugs' game' in Ukraine – not carrying on an open war but delegating the task to well-prepared groups of fighters – and in Syria, interfering in an overseas war in order to demonstrate its strength, and in Europe, betting on populism, separatism and the break-up of European society. 'The thugs' game' is a substitution for the honest game, for real work, for the painstaking development of institutions with simple acts of strength and demonstrations of hooliganism. Our whole society has been playing 'the thugs' game' for years; the hooligans in Marseilles were simply the away team.

THE SOVEREIGN FROM THE BACK
STREETS OF ST PETERSBURG

In order to understand the evolution of contemporary Russia, its politics and its society, books about Germany in the 1930s are becoming ever more useful. Even so, the collection put out by the *Territoriya budushchego* (Future Territory) publishing house, *The State: Law and Politics*, by the political theorist Carl Schmitt (who was known as 'the Hobbes of the twentieth century' and 'the court lawyer of the Third Reich') is amazingly relevant.

Schmitt's works were written at the start of the 1930s, when the Weimar Republic was deep in a constitutional crisis and on the threshold of fascism. As a lawyer, Schmitt proposed subjugating the law to specific political tasks, opposing the abstract legality of the state governed by the rule of law, with the 'substantial legitimacy' that comes from having the people united. In the book's central chapter, 'The Guarantee of the Constitution', Schmitt called for the replacement of the multiparty system by just such a 'substantial order', where the state acts with a unified will. And for this, he argued, it was essential to have a presidential dictatorship to protect the constitution.

A member of the Nazi Party from 1933 and an active supporter of the Hitler regime, Carl Schmitt died in 1985, aged ninety-six. Even after his death he remains one of the most contradictory figures in modern political theory. On the one hand, his ideas lie at the heart of the right-wing theory of National Socialism. On the other, he exerted a huge influence over all political thought in the twentieth century, from Walter Benjamin and Jürgen Habermas to Giorgio Agamben and Slavoj Žižek,[23] and even on the modern constitutional structure of the Federal Republic of Germany. Schmitt's harsh criticism of the interwar liberal world order and of the idealism in the spirit of Woodrow Wilson found resonance at the start of the twenty-first century, when the wonderful liberal world that had risen out of the remains of the Berlin Wall began to fall apart.

American neo-cons and the European 'new right' enthusiastically quote Schmitt today; but nowhere has Schmitt's renaissance been as turbulent and politically significant as in Putin's Russia. Oleg Kildyushov, who has translated and researched Schmitt, calls him 'the theoretician of the Russian 2000s'. Political scientists close to the Kremlin are particularly excited by his theory of 'the state of emergency'. This argues that a politician becomes a sovereign only from that moment when he steps outside the law and declares a 'state of emergency', at the same time creating a new norm and receiving a genuine and tangible legitimacy. According to Schmitt, sovereignty means the ability to go outside the boundaries of legalism and abstract law and declare a state of emergency.

This is exactly how Putin's Russia is behaving today, acting according to the logic of the 'state of emergency', tearing up the rule book and expanding the boundaries of its sovereignty. Some were frightened and others euphoric over the annexation of Crimea; but now that we can assess what happened in a sober way, it should be acknowledged that nothing significantly new took place. This was not a 'Putin 2.0', nor was it any sort of decisive new direction, capriciousness or madness, which Angela Merkel hinted at when she said that Putin had 'lost touch with reality'. The President continued to act exactly in the logic of Schmitt's sovereign, taking a political decision (the word 'decision' is key in Schmitt's thinking) in violation of existing judicial norms. Furthermore, says Schmitt, the sovereign can rely on a host of 'organic factors': 'the will of the people', tradition, culture, the past, political expediency, emergency conditions – but not on the law, nor on universal human values. Just remember the unexpected 'asymmetric answer' by Putin to the terrorist action in Beslan in Ingushetia in 2004, when Chechen terrorists seized a school with one thousand children. In response, Putin cancelled the elections of governors all over Russia. One might well ask, what on earth did the governors have to do with this? But in the paradigm of Schmitt's sovereign, the most important thing is the act of violating the existing judicial norms so as to declare a state of emergency.

Just about all of the authorities' decisions over the past ten years fit into this logic, from altering the constitutional moratorium on two presidential terms right up to the 'Bolotnaya Affair' (the repression of people who took part in the protest meetings on Bolotnaya Square in Moscow in 2012), and the prison sentence for Pussy Riot (two years in jail for singing a punk prayer in the Cathedral of Christ the Saviour in Moscow): these were all 'state of emergency' actions, a violation of accepted conventions and norms for the sake of a symbolic assertion of sovereignty. For a while, this logic worked

106

solely within the country, causing merely a few standard reprimands from the West about the authoritarian drift of the Russian state. The case with Ukraine, however, saw internal policy spill over onto the outside, shocking the world. But the Crimean gambit showed exactly the same sovereign logic of the 'state of emergency' by citing 'the will of the people', only this time it meant violating not the Russian Constitution but international law, undermining not the social consensus within the country but the international order. Looking back at Putin's actions over the previous ten years one could see that the annexation of Crimea (or a similar piece of foreign policy adventurism) was inevitable.

At the same time, it is interesting to see how Carl Schmitt's theory fits into typical Russian sociocultural practice. The objective logic of Schmitt's sovereign, which causes Putin constantly to alter the game's scenario (from where we get his trademark 'unpredictability') and to tear up the template in order to show his superiority over his opponents, apparently coincides with his subjective beginnings, with his 'lads" (*patsany*) view of his status, which he brought from the backstreets of Leningrad in the 1960s, preserving the language and the romanticism of the St Petersburg criminal underworld (they would be known today as 'city ghettos'). This concept is well understood by the vast majority of the male population of Russia, who are concerned less with what they can make of their lives and more with the ceaseless promotion of their own status. In Russia you have to be a 'real lad' (*patsan*): to know how to put down (humiliate even) your enemy; to stand on your own dignity; to show no sign of weakness; and to answer for your own words. According to this logic, it's important to be able to break the law; indeed, it's this arrogance and preparedness to break the law that marks out a real 'lad' from a 'nerd' ('ordinary man').

For Putin, who came from the sleazy world of the St Petersburg backstreets and who loves to show off that he knows the foul language of the criminal fraternity (remember his famous phrase, 'we'll wipe out the terrorists in the shit house'[24]) these status games are second nature. This typical Russian disdain for norms and rules so that you can assert your own status can be seen at every level of society: it might be displayed by cutting out your business partner; by overtaking a car that's cut you up and thus punishing the other driver; or by stealing land from an annoying neighbour. In this way the logic of the backstreet bandit becomes the logic of Schmitt's sovereign and the 'code' of the criminal underworld which formulates contemporary Russian politics.

107

PUTINISM AND QUESTIONS
OF LINGUISTICS

A new enemy has appeared on the scene for the Russian authorities: the English language. A scandal erupted in the State Duma over a speech made by deputy Dmitry Gudkov in the US Senate in March 2013, which was critical of Russia. When he returned to Russia, the Duma Ethics Commission recommended that he be removed from the Duma on the grounds that his speech 'was written and delivered in English'. Furthermore, Gudkov was charged with preparing his text in good English; in the opinion of the deputies this could be a sign of high treason.

Around the same time, the Chairman of the Cultural Commission of the Russian Federation Public Chamber, Pavel Pozhigaylo, who served in the Strategic Rocket Forces and also in the Main Intelligence Directorate (GRU) of the Russian Armed Forces, gave an interview to the Voice of Russia radio station, where he said with military directness: 'We have a small population and a serious demographic situation. So I am absolutely certain that for a period of time we shouldn't teach foreign languages at all, so that people don't leave the country. The Russian language is all they need. Russian literature is all they need.'[25]

In Soviet times having bad English was a good sign for people in authority. Die-hard Soviet international affairs specialists Valentin Zorin, Yevgeny Primakov and Georgy Arbatov knew the language perfectly, but in international meetings they would speak with a heavy Russian accent in which you could hear the arrogance of a superpower: if you need to know what I'm saying, you'll get it. And if we dig down even deeper, into the Stalinist era, then, according to a number of witnesses, foreigners in Moscow in the late 1930s were afraid to be heard speaking their own language on the street because they could immediately be arrested as spies.

In the 1990s and at the start of the twenty-first century there appeared among Russian politicians and in the business community bright young people with degrees from Harvard and who spoke wonderful English. They mixed on a par with their partners in the G8 and the World Trade Organization (WTO); but they are not the ones today who set the tone in Putin's Russia with its *Chekist* vigilance and its paranoid searches for 'foreign agents' and 'the hand of the US State Department'. The patriotic revelations of Pozhigaylo and the Duma's démarche about Gudkov are typical of the political discourse in modern Russia, in which anti-Western pathos, cultural isolationism and aggressive provinciality have become the norm.

Russia has fallen way behind when it comes to foreign languages and overseas contacts. According to research carried out by the organization EF, English First, on the knowledge of English in forty-four countries where English is not the official language, Russia came thirty-second, behind the other BRIC countries, China, India and Brazil. According to data from sociologists from the Public Opinion Foundation, only 17 per cent of Russians know any foreign language; and a mere 20 per cent have ever been abroad (and that includes the countries of the former Soviet Union and largely Russian-speaking resorts in Turkey and Egypt). Statistics from the Federal Migration Service show that only 15 per cent of Russians hold a foreign travel passport, and only about half of those use it regularly.

It is almost impossible to hear a foreign language in the cinema or on television: all films and foreign programmes are dubbed. The dubbing industry is flourishing. The best actors and pop stars are brought in for this, and their names appear on the billboards in larger letters than the names of the director and the cast. Films in the original language with subtitles are shown only in selected cinemas in Moscow, or at closed screenings. It is a fact that hiring and watching films with subtitles is one of the cheapest and most effective ways of studying foreign languages, as the experience of North European countries and the Netherlands shows, where virtually the whole population has a good knowledge of English, especially the younger generation.

The same language war is taking place on the streets of Russia. The law on advertising forbids the use of foreign words in advertisements without a translation unless the foreign advertising slogan is a registered trademark. The Federal Anti-Monopoly Service wants to ban shops from using even the inoffensive word 'Sale', saying they should use the Russian words *skidki* ('discounts') or *rasprodazha* ('sale'). Legal cases have already been brought in some parts of Russia against companies that have used foreign words in their advertising.

The supporters of language sovereignty often point to France as a country where cultural protectionism flourishes, where films are also dubbed (just like in Germany), and where there are quotas for the hiring of foreign films. They are even more enthusiastic in taking the USA as an example, where the population is perhaps even more ignorant than ours when it comes to travelling abroad and speaking foreign languages. But America and France can allow themselves this luxury. America is by rights the only global superpower, a major exporter of culture and the language standard bearer for the modern world. And France can do this because it is a cultural superpower, the ruler of a worldwide Francophone empire and the most popular country in the world for tourists.

Russia remains a country on the periphery of capitalism, squeezed into an inhospitable corner of Eurasia, and with a culture and a language that, throughout history, have been largely imported. There was a brief period in the twentieth century when we exported culture, when the world saw the dawning of the Russian avant-garde; and then we exported our social model and our image of modernization, educating in our universities and our academies hundreds and thousands of representatives from countries of 'the Third World'. Today Russia has lost its empire, its territory, its reputation and its global attractiveness. It seems determined, too, to lose its population, for whom the Russian language is its native language; and even those native speakers have disastrously lost their literacy. In such conditions, to introduce linguistic isolationism just to satisfy national pride is suicidal for Russian culture. It will become simply a provincial sideshow, a subject of interest only for professional ethnographers and Slavists. The only way to preserve Russian culture is to broadcast it to the world. And for that you need English.

We shouldn't be comparing ourselves to America; we should learn from our neighbours, such as Finland. Of course, the scale and the ambition there is not on a par with Russia's, but the problems are similar. Like Russia, this is another country on the periphery, with a borrowed Western culture and a language that is out on a limb. The Finns acknowledged pretty quickly the lack of perspective in linguistic nationalism. Moreover, while the second language of the state is Swedish (even though no more than 5 per cent of the population speak it, it is compulsory to study it), in practice the third language is English. You hear it on the radio and on television; up to half of all university courses are taught in English (by Finnish lecturers to Finnish students); you can go up to just about anyone on the street – and this is not even counting policemen or state officials – and speak to them in English, and if they can't answer you they will be embarrassed. What's more, Finnish culture is in no way marginalized; on the contrary, it is becoming ever more competitive in the world. They export unique items, from design and electronics to consulting and educational services.

Of course, our political elite is hardly likely to learn any lessons from little Finland. In their dreams they put themselves on a par either with the Roman Empire or with the USA; but behind these global illusions they are sinking ever deeper into the bog of cultural and linguistic isolationism.

WAR OF THE AVATARS

Russia is a unique country, always managing to find its own particular way of doing things. While the whole world (or the Western part at least) was declaring its solidarity with the victims of the terrorist act in Paris on 13 November 2015, when in one evening hundreds of people were shot in restaurants and in the Bataclan Concert Hall, yet another massive scandal exploded on social media in Russia. Tens of thousands of Russian Facebook users coloured their avatars in the red, white and blue of the French tricolour as a sign of mourning for those who had died in the Paris attacks; and then other, patriotic, users started to reproach them for the fact that they hadn't mourned the 200 Russians who had perished when their aircraft exploded over Sinai on 31 October 2015, two weeks earlier. A 'holy war' erupted, a sacred Internet-war, about the right way to mourn, about what colours you should use for your avatar and where you should lay your flowers. Thousands of friendships, subscriptions and reputations fell victim to this war. In answer to the French flag, a Russian emblem was put forward: the silhouette of an aeroplane against a background of the Russian tricolour, stylized under the pacifist sign. Tens of thousands of users adopted this as their avatar. Some tried to act as peacemakers, colouring their profile photo horizontally in the Russian colours and vertically in the French.

In the nervous reactions of the Russian domestic networks to the terrorist attacks, substituting sympathy and solidarity for internal squabbles and blame, we could see the agonies of the Russian mass consciousness. The first diagnosis was one of resentment, a sense of being deeply wounded, a readiness to mourn for any reason, to search everywhere for Russophobia and a worldwide conspiracy against Russia. Indicative in this sense was the unanimous insult felt by Russian politicians and media at the cartoons published in the French weekly *Charlie Hebdo*, and which in their own peculiar way they immediately linked to the Sinai terrorist act (parts of the Russian aircraft fell on the Islamic fighters and it was deemed to

112

be a 'continuation of the bombing'). On the day the cartoons were published, according to the magazine's own analysis of hits on its website, there were more viewings from Russia by a long way than from any other country – 42.5 per cent, two and a half times greater than from France itself. It looks as if *Charlie Hebdo* is much more popular in Russia (where hardly anyone can read French) than in France. So Russian 'worldly sensitivity' (*vsemirnaya otzyvchivost*), exalted by Fyodor Dostoyevsky, quickly turns into international touchiness. It could be in Kiev, in Paris, or on the Internet; and a lack of attention is taken as an insult: they didn't notice us! They didn't appreciate us! They didn't take account of us! This is true *Lust am Leidenschaft*, passion for suffering, as the Germans say who are familiar with this feeling; they lived through such a period of resentment during the Weimar Republic, which led, as we well know, to fascism. The American Slavist, Daniel Rancour-Laferriere, described this characteristic of Russian culture as 'moral masochism and the cult of suffering'; a desire to be humiliated and insulted.

The second diagnosis one could make about the discussion on avatars is that this is hypocrisy. Those who had painted their avatars in the French colours were accused of being insensitive to people suffering in the Third World. A Facebook user from Krasnoyarsk, Dan Nazarov, published a horrible photograph of a terrorist act in Kenya, where, on 2 April 2015, Islamic terrorists blew up a university building in the city of Harris and shot 147 Christian students. He posed the rhetorical questions: 'Did you hear about this in the media? Did people lay flowers outside the Embassy? Why are we so selective in our sympathy? One group are people; who are the others?' (This received 13,000 likes and 20,000 re-postings.) The author's reproach is, of course, justified – only not in our country. Russia is one of those places where such indifference to suffering in the Third World has become a virtue of the state; where federal television channels scare viewers with fables about refugees flooding Europe, where the terrorist acts in Paris were accompanied by malicious commentaries in the spirit of 'they got what they deserved, messing around with their ideas of tolerance and openness'; but we're not going to show any compassion for the Third World.

And we have a third problem here: the deepening split in the Russian mass consciousness. For many countries, days of celebration and days of sorrow become causes for national solidarity; but for us they have exactly the opposite effect. Victory Day on 9 May and the Day of National Unity on 4 November; the terrorist actions at 'Nord-Ost' (when terrorists seized a theatre in Moscow in 2003) and Beslan (the seizure of a school in Ingushetia in 2004); the terrorist acts in the *Charlie Hebdo* editorial offices and on the streets of Paris: these all become causes for social division. In fact, Russia has witnessed these divisions for the past hundred years, since the time of the 1917 Revolution and the unfinished Civil War of 1918–21; and perhaps even from the time of Peter the Great's reforms at the start of the eighteenth century. Our mass consciousness is deeply and painfully politicized, and precisely in the way that Carl Schmitt understood politics: as a search for enemies. If anyone is expressing sympathy with MH17, *Charlie Hebdo*, Paris or the West in general, our propaganda castigates it as 'a fifth column'. The very act of laying flowers, if it hasn't been sanctioned by the state – for example, outside the Embassy of the Netherlands – is considered suspicious and potentially an enemy action.

This is why the Russian Internet bursts into a holy war at the slightest provocation; no kind act can pass without some reproach: you grieved over the victims of the Paris attacks, but for some reason you didn't grieve over the Russians who perished in the Sinai, which means you're a Russophobe; you expressed sympathy for the victims of MH17, but not for the miners in the Donbass, which means you're a traitor; you help stray dogs, but you don't help children, which means you hate people; you plant trees, but you don't think about people, which means you're an eco-fascist – and so on. Our public space has become a territory of hatred and mutual accusations; our society has been atomized and struck by social anomie, deprived of any moral guidance or authority, incapable of showing solidarity or uniting in protest. Such a shattered society is very convenient for authoritarian powers, and is the ideal object for manipulation by the media and propaganda.

All this shows that this disunited social sphere can be divided into two groups: the first is convinced that the whole world is against Russia; and the second, that Russia is a part of the world. These two groups are the party of post-imperial resentment and the party of globalization. The former blames the outside world for all the country's ills, from terrorist acts in the North Caucasus to the loss of Ukraine, from the fall in the oil price to Russia's social problems: 'Obama, hands off our pensions!' as the signs read at the official celebration of the Day of National Unity. It is worth recalling what Yevgeny Fyodorov, the deputy from the ruling party 'United Russia', suggested: that the protests by the long-distance lorry drivers against the outrageously high road tariffs were directed by the USA to bring about the collapse of the state in Russia.

In the second group are people who consider that Russia is a part of the global community, and who react to tragedies in the world. I looked at how the avatars and cover of my Facebook profile had changed over the last few years: *'Je suis Paris'* after the terrorist acts in Paris; a photo of Boris Nemtsov, after the murder of the opposition politician; *'Je suis Charlie'*; a black ribbon in memory of the victims of MH17; the Ukrainian flag (after the annexation of Crimea); the Boston Marathon (the terrorist act in April 2013); the crew of the submarine Kursk (on the anniversary of the tragedy in 2000); the Norwegian flag (for the terrorist act by Breivik in July 2011) ... The memorial ribbon waves as a ribbon of grief, and each time my personal sorrow moves out to the wider political context; an act of sympathy becomes an act of citizenly solidarity and identity.

It is no less interesting to analyse the link between the 'avatars of sympathy' (with the victims of the terrorist acts in Paris, with *Charlie Hebdo*, with MH17) and the 'avatars of protest' against the ruling regime (usually a white ribbon, which has become a symbol of the opposition in Russia). Clearly, there is a strong link between those who went to the protests on Bolotnaya Square in 2011–12 and on Moskvoretsky Bridge in 2015, where Boris Nemtsov was killed, and those who changed their avatars and laid flowers at the Netherlands and French Embassies after the MH17 and the *Charlie Hebdo* tragedies. It is basically the same 14 per cent of the population who, according to the opinion polls, do not agree with the current political regime. It is here in this opposition segment that new ways of remembrance are born: wearing the white ribbon, laying flowers on the spot where Nemtsov was shot and repainting their avatars. As opposed to the official, state forms of collective remembrance – such as the official cult of Victory Day on 9 May, or the formal celebrations like 'Day of the City' – this practice is deeply private; it comes from below, out of civil society.

At this point we should remember other forms of commemoration: 'The Last Address', in which plaques are attached to homes from which victims were taken during the Stalinist repressions; and the annual action of 'Returning their names', the reading aloud of the names of those who were shot, which is held at the Memorial to the Victims of Stalinist Repressions on Lubyanka Square in Moscow.[26] The state looks on these actions with suspicion; but they are the points where civil self-awareness crystallizes, where memory becomes an act of resistance to the machine of terror, be it Communist, Islamic or the terror of the police state. In Putin's Russia, the civil memory becomes a challenge to power; and for those protesting, sympathy and grief become a common cause, *res publica*. Private emotion develops into social commotion, and as a result becomes political – which in no way detracts from the sincerity of the original personal concern.

Therefore, by painting our avatars in the colours of the French flag, many of us are grieving not only for the 130 people who died in Paris, but also for the 224 passengers who were killed in the sky over Sinai, and about whom, disgracefully, President Putin said nothing for two weeks; for the victims of Beslan and 'Nord-Ost'; for Kenya and Beirut; and at the same time for us ourselves, who against our will were drawn into the Middle East conflict and the global war against terrorism. Paraphrasing John Donne: 'Think not for whom your avatar grieves, it grieves for thee.'

PART III: THE WAR FOR THE BODY

PUNITIVE HYGIENE

The battle for a healthy lifestyle has reached new heights. The Interior Ministry has introduced a draft containing corrections to the Code on Administrative Infringements of the Law, according to which, as well as testing drivers, the police will be able to test pedestrians to see if they are sober and in general carry out a medical examination on anyone they want to. (Especially if that 'anyone' had turned up at an opposition rally.) It seems that cleaning the social space is becoming the principal task of the authorities, and the instrument they are using is punitive hygiene.

The crusade for cleanliness began fifteen years ago after the 'Orange Revolution' in Ukraine, when the authorities spoke about the 'orange infection', and the main strongman in the country became the Chief Sanitary Inspector, Gennady Onishchenko, who banned the import of Moldovan wines, then of Georgian mineral water, then of American chicken legs, depending on the demands of the day. In the course of these ten years the country did not actually get any cleaner; but hygiene and the cult of the clean body grew to become a mass political campaign with military sports camps of the pro-Kremlin youth movement, *Nashi* ('Our people'); with Putin meeting patriotic young athletes; and with the President visiting the 'Pankration' 'no rules' fights, with their classic male torsos on display. Not surprisingly, the heroes of the day, looking out at us from the advertising hoardings, were the Russian fighters Nikolai Valuyev and Fyodor Yemelyanenko.

At the same time, the nationalists became interested in health and social hygiene: their main topic became eugenics and demography, and they held marches with the slogan, 'Being Russian means being sober'. Back in 2005, Dmitry Rogozin (now a deputy prime minister) put a call in an election video for his party 'Rodina' ('Motherland') 'to clean Moscow of rubbish' (meaning get rid of people from the Caucasus, who are known as 'blacks'). This has now become a reality, with raids carried out by skinheads in army boots, to clear the

119

streets of the city of 'scum' (as they call Asian immigrants) and the homeless; and 'sanitary' raids by dog hunters to destroy stray dogs.

Finally, the Russian Orthodox Church joined in the battle for hygiene, preaching sermons about celibacy outside marriage, promoting the family and the procreation of children. In response to the Western feast of St Valentine's Day, they brought in the Orthodox feast of Peter and Veronica, sacred patrons of the family. And advertisements assure us that the best protection against AIDS is not a condom but abstinence and marital fidelity.

In Vladimir Putin's third term, the crusade for cleanliness was formalized in a series of laws against alcohol, tobacco, swearing, 'homosexual propaganda', 'foreign agents' and other 'evils'. Laws were passed placing age limits on television programmes and censoring the Internet, thus beginning a battle for digital hygiene. It would be naive to suggest that this was all the work of the State Duma: in reality, all these laws helped to formulate the protective sanitary line of the Kremlin. At the same time, the state's priorities in the area of reproductive policy were clearly spelt out. One of Putin's first decrees on the day of his inauguration for his third term in office in May 2012 was 'On measures for the fulfilment of the demographic policy of the Russian Federation', in which the government was ordered to 'raise the summary coefficient of the birth rate to 1.753 by the year 2018'. And in Putin's instruction to the Federal Assembly in December 2012, demographic policy played a key role and it was announced that, 'in Russia the norm should become three children in a family'.

The French philosopher, Michel Foucault, described such intensive attention on the part of the government to issues of hygiene, nutrition the birth rate and sexuality as 'biopolitics'. The state regards the population simply as a collection of bodies; it is biological capital, which it can regulate and multiply, and from which it can make a profit. Biopolitics is a higher form of sovereignty: the state appropriates the bodies of its citizens and then interferes in areas that, up until then, had been considered private matters, such as sex, choosing what to eat and drink, food, domestic life, smoking, the spoken language and social network interaction. This unceremonious interference by the state in private life, under the banner of 'the battle for a healthy way of life' is nothing less than repressive hygiene.

Biopolitics flourishes in totalitarian and fascist states. In the Third Reich, the idea of 'racial hygiene' included: sorting out the 'genetic rubbish', such as homosexuals, the mentally ill, the disabled and 'lesser races' (like the Jews, gypsies and Slavs); the fight against smoking; the cult of children and youth; and supporting the healthy Aryan family. All of this was supplemented by the simultaneous cult of the body as epitomized by Leni Riefenstahl, mass rallies and the Olympic Games. Stalin's USSR carried out similar biopolitics: abortion and homosexuality were criminalized; having large families was made a virtue of state policy and awards were handed out for having many children; and World War Two veterans who had lost arms and legs – of which there were many – were carted off to special facilities, where they simply disappeared from view. Instead of racial hygiene and 'the Aryan family', there was class hygiene and 'the Komsomol wedding'.

In today's Russia, biopolitics is the continuation of the traditional approach to resources. The state takes and disposes of resources, labelling them 'strategic' (in other words, not for private use). Just as with oil and gas, the population has become a strategic resource, and the state's biopolitics means the strategic enlargement of the population, in order to fill out Russia's empty spaces and to increase its weight on the world stage. It is only the size of the population and not the quality of life that is the strategic argument for a resource-minded state.

Under the logic of biopolitics it is easy to understand (though in no way approve of) the 'Dima Yakovlev Law', which forbids US citizens from adopting Russian orphans, in practice making these children into hostages of the state. This is not just about the orphans' right to happiness and a family, this is about the state's right to deal with its population as it wishes. Orphans, including disabled orphans, suddenly become a strategic resource, mere biological material, which can be used as an 'asymmetric answer' to America. From the point of view of humanity, this law is pure cannibalism; but in terms of biopolitics it is a rational resource approach: in exactly the same way as we occasionally turn off the gas tap to Ukraine to make that country more compliant, and in the 1970s we used to turn on and off the Jewish emigration tap as a great power trade-off with America. We no longer have the Jews at our disposal; all we have left are the orphans.

Biopolitics also explains another law that has caused commotion in society: the law banning so-called 'gay propaganda'. It's not because of the retrograde homophobia of a large part of the Russian population; it's because the state sees homosexuality as an infringement of its reproductive policy. Any sexual activity that does not bring about an increase in the population is considered 'unclean' and should be banned by law. According to this same logic, therefore,

121

condoms are also unclean, and so conservatives are trying to restrict their sale. Should we now expect Old Testament laws forbidding masturbation?

The state's new Orthodox hygiene policy is designed to turn the population into an obedient mass, which is loyal to the idea of the family and dutifully produces children, and which has turned its back on polygamy, contraception, homosexuality and other attractions of the devil. The most important thing here is not the quality of life; it's the number of children you have.

The paradox and the cynicism of the situation is that modern Russian biopolitics bears no relation to biology (since it is based on wholly false assertions, such as that homosexuality is not 'normal'), nor does it improve the health of the nation, as it is accompanied by a radical cutting back of state financing of the health system and the destruction once and for all of free Soviet healthcare. Biopolitics is above all a matter of politics and ideology, the privatization of the human resource, the disciplining of the collective body of the nation. It is the drawing up of the state's sanitary contours, the task of which, as in times past, is to discipline and punish.

THE KING'S BODY

On 5 March 2015, the anniversary of the death of Stalin, Russia's President disappeared. There was nothing unusual in this. Vladimir Putin had gone missing on other occasions, and the television audience were fed what they call 'preserves' – recordings of earlier business meetings and speeches. But on this occasion, in the particularly evil atmosphere surrounding the recent murder of Boris Nemtsov, when there was a seething mess of versions concerning who was responsible for this crime, the void in the Kremlin was especially keenly felt. The omnipresent journalists found out about Putin's disappearance and the broadcasting of old recordings on TV and sounded the alarm.

Ten tension-filled days passed. Commentators talked of 'Cheyne–Stokes respiration', the pathological breathing pattern that often accompanies a stroke, which Soviet newspapers had written about shortly before Stalin died, and which has come to be a political term in Russia. By coincidence, it was at the same time of year, in March 1985, that Konstantin Chernenko died, the last General Secretary of the Communist Party, during the period of stagnation,[1] and his demise was also somewhat inopportune. After the subdued growling of the Kremlin's 'bulldog fight under the rug', and after the fantastical suggestions that Putin had been taken away by aliens and the absurd rumours about helicopters over the Kremlin, a medical explanation began to emerge. There was a feeling that Putin's absence was something pathological, as if the whole nation was writing the story of his illness: there was talk of 'flu and stroke, of back injury and pancreatic cancer; but there was even more talk of rejuvenating medicine: of plastic surgery, or scheduled Botox injections. There were even rumours about a trip to Switzerland, to Canton Ticino, where the gymnast and Duma deputy Alina Kabaeva, whom people called Putin's common-law wife, had given birth to a son or a daughter. The life and death of Putin, his appearance, his reproductive capabilities, his facial muscles, his spine – all of this became the heart of political discussion; the sole topic of conversation.

123

Such close attention to the body of the sovereign is an ancient and venerable tradition, born in the late Middle Ages and at the start of the modern era. The well-known German American historian of the medieval period, Ernst Kantorowicz, devoted a book to this subject, *The King's Two Bodies*. According to Kantorowicz, in the twelfth and thirteenth centuries the Christian concept of the dual nature of God (Father and Son) and man (soul and body) was mixed with ancient legal tradition and produced the idea of the two bodies of the king: the physical body, which is perishable and exists in time; and the 'political body', which is sacred and lasts for eternity. This political body is the nation; but it is wholly linked to the physical, anatomical body of the king. The king is no longer in charge of his own body: the nation decides its fate. Kantorowicz cites as an example the English Revolution, when in January 1649 Parliament judged and executed Charles I. This was treated at the time not as a popular uprising against the monarch, but as a legal action of the political body of the king (what was known as 'the King in Parliament') against his physical body.

I recall how this idea amazed me when I was in Versailles – in reality, a vast theatre – where the spectacle of the king's body in all its guises was played before the nation as represented by the court. Inside the palace the king was effectively deprived of any privacy; everything physiological was as public as it could be: in one place the king slept; in another he appeared as an ordinary man in his night-shirt; in a third he sat on the pot and washed, also in the presence of members of the court. The queen's birthing room had places reserved for observation. There were chambers for the king's lovers; his virility, his productivity, his male health: all was a carefully guarded ritual, a guarantee of the political health of the nation. As Michel Foucault wrote: 'In a society such as that of the seventeenth century, the body of the king was not a mere metaphor but something political: his bodily presence was necessary for the life of the monarchy.'[2] And it is no coincidence that, just as in England, the French Revolution announced, via Robespierre's mouth: 'Louis must die so that the Republic may live.' On 21 January 1793, the king was executed, as were, after him, Marie-Antoinette and her sister Elizabeth – the political body of the nation got rid of the physical body of the monarch. A similar act was carried out in Russia in the basement of the Ipatiev House in Yekaterinburg on the night of 16–17 July 1918. But by an irony of fate, having got rid of the body of one sovereign, the nation immediately installed another, which to this day lies unburied in the Mausoleum.

In implementing Putin's de-modernization programme, Russia has been knocked back into the same political theology of 'the king's body'. Medicine first broke into politics with the arrival of Boris Yeltsin: his great size created the effect of a bodily presence. After the decrepit old men of the Kremlin and then the lively Gorbachev, Yeltsin stumbled onto the political scene like a lumbering Siberian bear. His habits, including rumours about his drinking and his love affairs, became the stuff of legends; and his illness and the operation he underwent in his second term (when his Press Secretary, Sergei Yastrzhembsky, explained his absences by saying that the President was 'working on documents') became a metaphor for the weakening of the political organism.[3] This was the background to Vladimir Putin's arrival in the Kremlin: young, sporty, with no bad habits and with the halo of a Soviet James Bond.

With Putin's coming to power the appearance of the body of the leader who emerged from the entourage becomes a subject of carefully thought-out image-making, an object of close attention for society: ambiguous photos are published of a semi-naked man in dark glasses; there's a blatant demonstration of his torso, a public show of machismo (with his judo, hunting, swimming and horse-riding). At the same time rumours are put out about just how masculine the sovereign is, about his divorcing his wife and his love affair with Alina Kabaeva. This doesn't seem to fit into the background of an Orthodox renaissance and the propagation of family values, but in the logic of the sovereign, 'what's not allowed to an ox, is allowed to Jupiter'. Putin is able to go outside the traditional moral framework in order to demonstrate his extraordinary right to be the alpha male. (It appears likely that the supposed 'leak' of this description of Putin as an 'alpha male' by Wikileaks may have been organized by Russia in order to create just such an image of the Russian President.) The propaganda machine has created the image of a middle-aged man who says little, doesn't drink or smoke, who uses the language of the criminal underworld and is a lover of patriotic pop music such as his favourite group, 'Lyube': he appeared as the dream guy for the downtrodden Russian woman, who sighed, 'I want a man like Putin'. The President became the ideal bridegroom for Russian women (as is well known, there's a shortage of men in Russia); he stepped into the sexual pantheon of the post-Soviet consciousness.

Putin's body became a glamour object. He is a child of the era of exciting spy stories, the cult of the young body and plastic surgery, when the young-looking, tanned President suddenly sits himself down at a white grand piano and with feeling plays 'What the Motherland begins with' and 'Blueberry Hill', as happened at a charity concert in St Petersburg in 2010. The first decade of the century, when the country was swimming in oil riches, gave birth to a glossy presidency, based on political pretence and plastic manipulations, on high ratings and Botox. The main thing is to call a halt in time, before he starts to look like his friend Silvio Berlusconi, who, with his dyed hair and desperate attempts to look young, has already turned into a political clown. The body of the sovereign expanded to cover the whole nation. It entered every home; it stares out at us from tee-shirts and the covers of school exercise books; it led the Deputy Head of the Presidential Administration, Vyacheslav Volodin, to the natural conclusion that 'Putin exists, therefore Russia exists; there is no Russia today if there is no Putin'.[4]

Then suddenly there were rumours about the President being ill or possibly even dead; in place of political theology we had political thanatology.[5] The body of the nation was shaken to the core; the political system immediately trembled. And even the return to public view of a younger-looking and wrinkle-free Putin was not taken as being back to normal for the political body: observers commented that the Tsar had been replaced, that this was not the same Putin; he smiles in a rather strange way, rather like the little girl whose mother has tied her plait too tightly. The traumatic experience of the President's ten-day absence and the rumours about his illness presented Russia with a bald medical fact: Putin's body had become the body of the nation; it had taken the place of politics. Instead of executive power, we now had Putin's spine; instead of a work schedule, we had his pancreas; instead of parliamentary debates, we had an analysis of the President's gait. And so the rumours about his illness instantaneously led to political chaos: in Russia there are no institutions apart from the body of the sovereign, and any hope of political change is inextricably linked to this body. We are all hostages to its fortune. This is exactly how it was in March 1953, when all the inhabitants of the USSR were hostages to Stalin's body, and again in March 1985 when the whole country became a hostage to the decrepit body of Konstantin Chernenko (and before him to the terminally ill General Secretary Yury Andropov, who had been linked up to an artificial kidney apparatus) – and the country fell apart before our very eyes.

In order to break out from this model from the Middle Ages and to tear up our dependence on the body of the king, we have to do what they did in Europe in the early modern period: replace this body with institutions, to divide the person of the ruler from the function of government, so that Russia can finally become a civil nation and the President an ordinary person made of skin and bone, with illnesses and weaknesses and not a receptacle for abstract ideas and sacred thoughts. Only then will we be able to rid ourselves of the periodic necessity to listen out with holy fear for the Cheyne–Stokes respiration.

THE CONDOM AS A
SIGN OF PROTEST

This object was always taboo in Russian culture. When I was a young man it cost two kopecks in the chemist's, sold in envelopes made of rough, official paper, under the code name, 'Product No. 2', and made in the Bakovka Factory for Rubber Products ('Product No. 1', of course, was the gas mask). As teenagers, we were too embarrassed to say this word, as if it was a swear word; the sacred word 'condom' caused Soviet schoolchildren to catch their breath and speed up their pulse rate; occasionally, we would run to the chemist's to look at this semi-forbidden fruit tucked away in the corner of the shop window.

We saw a similar flash of discomfort cross the President's face during his press conference in December 2011 when he was answering a question about the 'white ribbons' worn by the opposition movement on their clothes. Faltering, Putin said: 'To be honest, I think it's rather inappropriate, but nevertheless I'll say it: I thought it was publicity for the campaign against AIDS; I thought that they were contraceptives.' Because of old Soviet habits he, too, couldn't bring himself to say the taboo word 'condom', using instead the neutral euphemism, 'contraceptive'.

The sanctimonious nature of Soviet culture, in which 'there was no sex' (in the famous words of a Soviet woman who was taking part in a tele-bridge between Leningrad and Boston in 1986), is now returning along with other types of Soviet absurdity. The Duma proposed banning advertisements for condoms outside specialized publications. In fact, even without any changes being made, condom adverts have effectively already disappeared from the media and migrated to the Internet. And considering the growth of the campaign in support of having children and promoting the family, almost to the point of introducing high duties for divorce and a suggestion to bring back the Soviet tax on singles and childless families, we cannot exclude the possibility that sooner or later condoms will go the same way as cigarettes: they'll disappear from open sale at petrol stations and by the checkout in supermarkets and they'll be hidden away in closed drawers at the chemist's, where they'll be available only with special permission. And why not then bring in an age limit for their sale, like for women below forty; or restrict the number of condoms one person can have? If in the new state–church ideology contraception is declared to be a sin, HIV to be God's punishment and the best way to prevent pregnancy and infection to be self-restraint and marital fidelity, then condoms should be seen as a Western perversion, contradictory to the national traditions of healthy sex; a latex 'fifth column', threatening Russia's demographic security.

Condoms were always considered to be foreign agents in Russia, little French things passed around the aristocracy in the gallant time of Ekaterina, in the period of Voltaire, the Marquis de Sade and Casanova, which, as everyone knows ended with the French Revolution. Two hundred years later in the Russia of the 1990s, they once again became the symbol of liberalization and moral emancipation. Western charities brought them into Russia as humanitarian aid and gave them out to all who wanted them, along with syringes; sex education programmes were introduced in schools and on television; and on Myasnitskaya Street in Moscow a specialized condom boutique opened, offering not the mass-produced condoms you would find in the supermarket, but an individual selection of items. At the same time, a lot of amusing advertisements appeared in the media (such as 'Come properly to the end of the evening'), which didn't just sell the product but educated people in their use and quietly got across the idea that you can talk about sex and joke about it, and that sex is fashionable, prestigious and happy.

The condom became as much a part of everyday life as the aspirin or the toothbrush. At the same time, the patriarchal, sanctimonious foundations of post-Soviet society also began to change. According to an All-Russian opinion poll carried out by the Levada Centre in 2012, only 23 per cent of Russians considered premarital sex to be immoral, compared to 29 per cent in 2007 and 42 per cent in 1992. More than half of those asked (55 per cent) considered it acceptable for someone to have more than one partner, while 77 per cent of young people approved of cohabitation, against 30 per cent of the older generation.

Russians' sexual habits are rather relaxed. According to the annual Global Sex Survey carried out by the research department of the Durex Corporation, Russians have more sexual partners than almost any other country, losing out only to the Austrians. On average, our men will have twenty-eight partners in the course of their lives, while Austrian men will have twenty-nine. Russian women on average have seventeen partners. And 42 per cent of those questioned say that they are totally satisfied with their sex lives, which is higher than in Europe or the USA. Finally, and most importantly, thanks to widespread sexual education and modern methods of contraception, for the last twenty-five years the number of abortions carried out in Russia has been consistently falling (although we still remain the world champions): the annual rate has fallen from six million per year in the 1960s, to four million in 1990, and down to under a million in 2013.

Today's conservative attack on sexual freedom in Russia goes against these trends. Advertisements for condoms are being banned, sex education lessons in schools are being replaced by the 'God's Law' programme, and social adverts on billboards in the cities aggressively call on people to turn away from the idea of safe sex. The results of this puritanical propaganda could turn out to be completely the opposite of what is intended. They won't be able to destroy the sexual freedom that people are now used to, but restricting the availability of condoms will lead to widespread unprotected liaisons, as a result of which the number of abortions and sexually transmitted diseases will rise; this will lead to a drop in the reproductive capability of the population, which the conservatives are so zealously fighting for. And this is to say nothing about the proposed bans on advertising and the sale of condoms, which will make people's lives worse, restrict their choice of sexual practices and scenarios and limit people's freedom in one of the last areas where the citizen is relatively free from the unsleeping eye of the Tsar – in bed.

It turns out that in that press conference in December 2011, Vladimir Putin was right: in an era of total biopolitical prohibitions, the condom does indeed become a symbol of the opposition and the citizen's self-awareness. Free citizens choose safe sex; and also they decide themselves whether they have children, without any instructions from above.

THE PROTOCOLS OF THE
ELDERS OF SODOM[6]

I've made an important discovery: the 'worldwide homosexual lobby' really does exist. And beavering away behind the scenes, it really does rule the world. One warm autumn evening I stood on the corner of Castro Street in San Francisco, right in the heart of the most famous gay quarter in America, not far from the well-known glass-walled 'Twin Peaks' gay bar. A mixed crowd was going past, which included the city's most varied types – gays, transvestites, freaks, queers, old hippies, tramps – and I was surrounded by a large group of curious tourists. There was music playing, police sirens wailing, lights of clubs flashing, rainbow flags hanging from balconies; and the sensation grew that this never-ending carnival of human variety, this display of eccentricity, was the heart and soul of this place, an essential part of the identity of this great City by the Bay.

I went off to have supper in the Chinese Quarter, where the Great Eastern restaurant serves (as they assure you) the best dim-sum on the whole US West Coast, and where Barack Obama once ordered takeaway dumplings. San Francisco's Chinatown is the most famous in America, as well as the oldest. Chinese migrants started arriving in the middle of the nineteenth century in their tens of thousands, men who came to work on construction of the Pacific and transcontinental railroads. The history of Chinatown is full of tales of xenophobia (such as the Chinese Exclusion Act of 1882), fires and ethnic crime; but today the Chinese make up 20 per cent of the population of San Francisco and are one of the more successful communities. The Chinese Quarter has become one of the symbols of the city.

Silicon Valley didn't spring up just by chance among the rolling hills and serene gardens of Palo Alto and San Jose. At its heart lay the freedom-loving spirit of California, 'the promised land', which attracted the adventurers in their covered wagons. Here was to be found the entrepreneurial excitement of the frontier, which resonated to the sound of the wheels of stagecoaches and the crack of the Winchester rifle; but there was also an unimaginable mix of races and cultures: Hispanics, Anglo-Saxons, Scandinavians, Chinese, Japanese, Russian Old Believers,[7] all seeking happiness in this golden, oil-rich and now digital El Dorado. California meant not only gold fever, but also an unprecedented freedom: the hubbub of the saloons, the can-can cabaret, the dubious entertainments in the alleyways of the port of San Francisco. In the rebellious 1960s, the hippy revolution developed in the warm Californian climate – as Scott McKenzie sang in the unofficial hymn of the counterculture of the 1960s: 'If you're going to San Francisco, be sure to wear some flowers in your hair.' It was there that the first gay revolution took place, linked with the name of Harvey Milk;[8] and there, too, in San Francisco, where the AIDS epidemic broke out in 1981.

Without all of this, Silicon Valley would never have come into being (and also, incidentally, without the huge government investments that the USA made into new technology after the shock caused by Russia's Sputnik programme between 1957 and 1961, and without the Stanford Industrial Park). Its location is on the reckless west coast of the USA and not on the stiff and starchy east coast, even though it would appear that the country's best intellectual resources used to be in the east, from Yale and Harvard to the Massachusetts Institute of Technology (MIT). This is not because hippies, Chinese and gays are especially gifted, nor that unique creative enlightenment comes thanks to the influence of LSD. The point is that in post-industrial society an atmosphere that is multinational and tolerant and allows for sexual freedom encourages the flowering of entre-preneurism, innovation and creativity. A person who is prepared to accept another with all their differences is also prepared to accept new business ideas or finance a risky start-up. And give ten thousand dollars credit for someone to construct a computer in a garage – from where the Apple empire grew.

After all, it is all about complexity management. Post-industrial societies have a high density of horizontal connections, and demon-strate a wide variety of identities, and religious, ethnic and sexual practices, each of which relies not on domination but on equality. The ability to understand and accept this complexity (also through the rituals of political correctness and tolerance, which they love to laugh at in Russia) is the key to managing and modelling complexity. In today's world, all the major centres of creating value and meaning – New York, London, Berlin, Paris, Barcelona – are marked out by their multiculturalism (another favourite target for Russian critics of the West), broadmindedness, and acceptance of variety in ethnicity, race, religion and sexual orientation. And it is no coincidence that a number of the greatest global cities today have had an openly gay mayor: Bertrand Delanoë in Paris, Klaus Wowereit in Berlin, Ole von Beust in Hamburg, Glen Murray in Winnipeg ... [9]

Moreover, the author of the fashionable concept of 'the creative class', Richard Florida, suggested creating a 'Gay Index' as a way of measuring tolerance. The level of openness to sexual minorities is an indicator of how low the barriers are for the development of human capital. According to Florida's research, centres of the innovation economy are exceedingly popular places for the gay community to live. And the Russian political scientist, Andrei Shcherbak, carried out similar research in fifty-five countries between 1996 and 2008, in the course of which he studied the influence of tolerance on economic and technological modernization, measuring it in relation to gender equality, sexual minorities and xenophobia. In putting together his modernization index, Shcherbak took into account the role of hi-tech goods produced for export, the percentage of GDP spent on research and development, the number of academic articles on science and technology, the number of patent applications, the size of seed capital investment as a percentage of GDP and the level of foreign investment as a percentage of GDP. With all of this, his results correlated with the index of acceptance of gender equality, sexual minorities and foreigners. Statistics over an extended period of time show that it is the level of acceptance that helps society to develop, and not the other way round.

In a sense, the 'worldwide homosexual conspiracy' that Russian politicians love to talk about actually does exist. The point is, it's not some sort of collusion between gay politicians in order to seize power across the globe and ravish the last bastions of morality like Russia, but the encouragement of reflexivity and greater flexibility in society in managing complexity, allowing for people to take up key posts notwithstanding their sex, race or sexual orientation. And the reaction to homosexuality as probably the strongest social irritant is the litmus test for society's ability to accept differences.

As always, Russia is following its own difficult path (or, to be more precise, it's going down the path which the West trod half a century ago). The growth of the homophobic mood in society and the authorities and the declaration of the country's sexual sovereignty coincided with the time when all conversations about modernization and innovation were being wound up; all the slogans to do with this now seem to have been merely a fad of Dmitry Medvedev's interim presidency from 2008 to 2012. At the same time, an anti-immigration mood has been growing in society, as witnessed by the pogroms against people from Central Asia that occurred in the Moscow suburb of Biryulyovo in 2013; 'tolerance' became virtually a swear word.

All this reflects society's nervousness when faced with the complexity of the post-industrial world and the uncontrolled flows of people and information; there is an inability to accept this complexity and transform it into social and market technologies, or to use it to the benefit of state governance. Fear produces such chimeras as 'a paedophile conspiracy', 'the gay lobby', the 'orphan killers'. Most probably, it would be appropriate for the guardians of the nation's morality to forge yet another set of 'Protocols of the Elders of Zion' – this time it would be 'The Protocols of the Elders of Sodom'.

But what we have to understand is that along with the growth in paranoia, we are losing our competitiveness. Closed systems are no longer capable of tackling complex problems. They will be affected even more strongly by global flows, but they will no longer be in a position to control them, thus condemning themselves to becoming peripheral. In our interdependent world, questions of sex, gender, race and tolerance are no longer matters of ethics or identity, but to do with the economy and the survival of the country in global competition.

Therefore, I would switch from an ideological approach to a pragmatic one. For a start, by special decree alongside the Skolkovo Innovation Centre a gay quarter could be set up, like Castro in San Francisco. Maybe something non-traditional would grow out of it – or, at least, something innovative.

TEST FOR HOMOPHOBIA

Sometimes it seems that those who were drawing up Russia's laws in 2013, banning the promotion of homosexuality, achieved completely the opposite effect to the one they actually wanted. You hear speeches about homosexuality now on every corner, in the Duma and on television. They use the term to insult opponents and to frighten parents. An acquaintance of mine told me that she called the doctor out to examine her sick child. The doctor, a woman of about fifty years old, prescribed antipyretic suppositories, having explained that they don't use rectal suppositories now for boys over three years. When asked why, she answered emphatically: 'Homosexuality!'. It seems that at long last Russia has found its national idea; and this idea is homophobia.

Homophobia has become the platform on which the state's repressive laws and the Stone Age instincts of the mob have been brought together. According to a sociological survey by the Russian Public Opinion Research Centre (VTsIOM), the law banning the promotion of homosexuality is supported by 88 per cent of Russians. Being openly antisemitic or racist in Russia is already considered not quite proper, at least in politics; but being a homophobe is normal, worthy and even patriotic. The bastards who beat a gay man to death in Volgograd on Victory Day, 9 May 2013, said that they did it for patriotic reasons. The official rhetoric has opened up a carnival of hatred in Russia; it's hunting season on homosexuals. Each year there are now dozens of attacks recorded on gays, many of them ending in death, and the number of unrecorded crimes are too many to count. And even tortures carried out by the police – at least, the ones that become known, such as the rape of people who were detained, one using a champagne bottle in Kazan and another a crowbar in Sochi – follow the same homophobic logic: the state degrades people, using the kind of sexual violence that is common in the criminal world.

Politics in Russia has been brought down to the level of vulgar physiology; what the Italian philosopher, Giorgio Agamben, calls 'the naked life'. The biological becomes political, whether we are talking about the hunt for paedophiles or the ban on foreigners adopting orphans; about the censorship of homosexuality or the concept of family policy, as put forward by Duma deputy Elena Mizulina, according to which 'normal' should mean a patriarchal family with four children, living together with their grandparents. The state intrudes upon the sphere of what should be intimate and private, using repressive measures to impose from above a patriarchal and authoritarian 'norm', which it then calls 'a national tradition'. Aggressive homophobia rises up from the depths of the patriarchal consciousness to meet it. In this way homophobic fascism is born.

This is exactly what it is: fascism. These 'spiritual bindings', which President Putin loves to talk about, tie together the lictor's bundle, the fasces, from which the word 'fascism' comes. Fascism always appeals to biology, to the primacy of birth, blood and soil; it is no coincidence that the head of the SS, Heinrich Himmler, considered homosexuality 'the syndrome of a dying people'. Homophobia becomes the focal point for national self-awareness. It relies on masculine stereotypes, which are written about in folklore, jokes and swearing, and on rituals of initiation and stigmatization in school, the army and prison. What's more, homophobic fascism is simple and convenient for the state, because it is not aimed at a particular group on national or race lines (at least the Caucasian people can fight back) but against a defenceless minority with no voice in society. Virtually no one will stand up for homosexuals in Russia, unlike human rights activists in the West. In Russia, sexual minorities are the ideal target for hatred, just like the Jews were in the Third Reich.

Homophobia is an anti-Western and anti-globalist idea: it seeks out internal enemies from amongst its own, be they paedophiles, gays or 'foreign agents'. The insult 'liberast', a corruption of the words 'liberal' and 'pederast', shows that in Russia homosexuality is associated solely with the liberal West, which is mired in tolerance, same-sex marriages and debauchery; conservative and Orthodox activists insist in all seriousness that in the West paedophilia and incest are actively encouraged. Such hysteria demonstrates an embittered, alienated and provincial consciousness, one that is unable to adapt to the post-industrial and post-patriarchal world, in which producing children is no longer considered to be man's principal task. It is a consciousness that finds itself lost before a multicoloured contemporaneity, just like our principal homophobe, Duma deputy Vitaly Milonov, who was shocked when the highly genial Stephen Fry dropped in on him. Homophobia is a characteristic of weak people who are uncertain of their own orientation, and who are afraid of losing what they are sure of when they first come up against reality. The weaker the country and its identity, the more fiercely homophobic it is.

This is exactly why Russia desperately needs an injection of tolerance in order to defend and publicize the rights of sexual minorities. One often hears that 'sexual orientation is a private matter, let them carry out their sexual preferences at home, among their friends, and not bring it out in public'. But a call for 'closet homosexuality' is false at its very root. In the same way, you could say that Jewishness is a private matter: they should just sit at home, not go to their synagogues or wear their kippahs on the streets, because this annoys normal citizens and is opposed to Russian national traditions and foundations. After the Holocaust, Jewishness is no longer a private matter for Jews, but a subject of public policy. Analogous to this, the Russian state was the one that made sexual orientation a public matter, taking away homosexuals' human rights, from the right to create a family to the right of self-expression, and thus the answer to this discrimination should be public and political.

As Michel Foucault taught, a person's sexuality remains one of the last bastions of freedom and also one of the main targets for repression; and the battle takes place on the territory of the sovereignty of the individual. Russia is in desperate need of collective therapy: people coming out; gay parades; a battle for full citizens' rights for homosexuals, from same-sex marriages to the right to adopt children. Support for sexual minorities is not easy: people may sympathize with them, but they won't speak out openly for fear of being marked out as one of them. But it is important to understand that this is where fascism makes itself most apparent, supported by the whole weight of the legislative, law enforcement and propaganda machine. And that's why each of us must go through a test for homophobia in our own souls: these days examining our own feelings about citizenship and humanity is as important as it once was in terms of antisemitism.

THE 'MISS PRISON' CONTEST

Another notable chapter has been written in the annals of Russian judicial practice. The Supreme Court of the Republic of Mordovia refused to grant Nadezhda Tolokonnikova early release from prison. Nadezhda is a member of the feminist protest rock group Pussy Riot, and was sentenced to two years' detention for singing a punk prayer in the Cathedral of Christ the Saviour in Moscow. She was refused early release for a curious reason: the court deemed her unworthy of such clemency because she had refused to take part in the 'Miss Charming' beauty contest that was held in correctional colony No. 14 in Mordovia, and therefore they could not say that her behaviour in the colony had been exemplary.

Nadezhda refused to take part in the beauty contest not as a protest against the rules of the camp, but because she was taking a principled civil position. As an activist in a feminist group, she cannot by conviction take part in a sexist ritual dreamt up by a patriarchal society; it would be like asking a vegan to join in a barbeque. In her deposition to the court, Nadezhda said that her aesthetic values would not allow her to participate in such a competition. This is the very same reason given by another dissident, the writer Andrei Sinyavsky, half a century ago when he had a 'stylistic disagreement' with the Soviet state.[10]

Feminists the world over should applaud the Mordovian court for uncovering the truth: it actually acknowledged that women were obliged to take part in the beauty contest, and that a refusal to do so would bring disciplinary sanctions. According to this logic, the whole world is one big women's prison colony, in the middle of which there stands a catwalk on which the entrapped women are required to show off their charms so as not to be penalized. In a patriarchal and sexist society, a woman is imprisoned in her own body from the very beginning, in a cage of social norms and male expectations. She is controlled far more than a man is by the discipline of her body, the dictates of physiology and the battle with

138

age. Throughout her whole life, a woman has to walk a particular line; and beauty contests simply take to extremes the stereotypes of gender slavery.

Criticism of beauty contests has been growing around the world as being one of the more odious institutions of the patriarchal society, a symbol of exploitation, standardization and commodification of the female body; and it's not just feminists or left-wingers who protest about this. Even organizers of beauty contests themselves have been trying to adapt to the new mood, doing away with the line-up in bikinis, as the Miss World competition has done. Another approach has been for the women taking part to answer questions to show how bright they are. The supposed value of these tests was shown up by the Mrs Russia competition in 2012. In conversation with a correspondent from Russian television, Inna Zhirkova, wife of the footballer Yury Zhirkov, failed to answer the simplest of questions: 'Does the Earth go round the Sun, or the Sun go round the Earth?'; 'Who composed the Ogiński polonaise?'; and 'Who is Agniya Barto?' (a well-known Russian children's poet). She also admitted that she had never done a day's work in her whole life. Following the public outcry following this test, Mrs Zhirkova refused to accept her crown.

Of course, most people in Russia aren't bothered about the ethics of beauty contests. This is a country that adopts laws regulating people's private lives and enforcing heterosexual 'normality'. It's a country where, for a significant part of the female population, the indicator of a successful life is a good marriage. In such a country, beauty contests are a way for a girl to climb the social ladder; they are considered the norm, and an example of how a girl should behave. A Russian girl's dress code is clearly laid out on the catwalk: long, flowing hair, a nice dress, high heels and expensive make-up are still considered the measure of femininity; and if a man has a wife who's a model, he's thought to be a success.

In October 2013, Russia hosted the Miss Universe contest. This was run by Donald Trump, who is renowned for his weakness for tastelessness and kitsch, and it was held at that bastion of Russian glamour, the Crocus-City exhibition centre. The organizers and sponsors were unaware that the real Miss Russia hadn't been able to appear in the spotlights of their competition, wearing a tight dress and with her mascara running down her cheeks. She was working as a seamstress in a prison colony in Mordovia. Nadezhda Tolokonnikova won her crown not in a prison beauty contest or on the catwalk, but in a cage in the Khamovinchesky Court,[11] where she was sentenced to two years in a labour camp; she accepted her sentence simply and with dignity. But the jury of a beauty contest wouldn't be able to understand that.

BREAKING 'THE SILENCE
OF THE LAMBS'

In the summer of 2016, Russian society experienced a totally unexpected show of collective psychotherapy; and society is still trying to come to terms with what happened. Following the English language flash mob #MeToo, there appeared in Russian social media a flash mob called #yaNyeBoyusSkazat, ('I'm not afraid to speak out'). This became the largest 'coming out' in Russian history. Thousands of women shared their memories of the violence that they had suffered at the hands of men – rape, beatings, harassment, stalking and humiliation. Most of these stories were being heard for the first time, because these women were scared of sharing their experiences even with those closest to them, afraid of being judged, stigmatized or labelled as a victim; but thanks to the strength and solidarity of social media, for the first time in their lives they were able to speak about their trauma.

This prompted an explosion of comment: there was a strong and widespread reaction against this unasked for, unexpected and frightening truth. Thousands of social media users, men and women, greeted these revelations with ridicule, calling it 'public striptease', suspecting that it was all PR or some kind of provocation, making fun of the 'erotic fantasies' of these women, or hypocritically fearing for their mental health. Two visions of hell met in this flash mob: the women's hell of pain, fear and a lack of understanding, and the hell of male chauvinism evident in these comments. But these are two sides of the same coin; two rooms in one hell; two articles of our main social agreement: on the one hand, violence as the norm in our life and the main bond of society, and, on the other, 'the silence of the lambs', as the unspoken recognition of the right to violence.

No, this was not a 'war of the sexes', nor was it a display of feminist propaganda. Society wasn't split into men and women, nor divided between the violators and the victims. The division was between those who see violence as the normal way of sorting out relations in society, and those who oppose it and are prepared openly to speak about this. This flash mob, started by women, about women and for women, had taken the lid off the microphysics of power in Russian society: there is a source code of violence at the heart of the Russian matrix.

Violence starts in the family with a tradition blessed by the Church of the practice of corporal punishment ('the sensible and measured use by loving parents of physical punishment in the upbringing of their child', as the Patriarchal Commission on Matters of the Family, Motherhood and Childhood puts it). This then continues in kindergarten, school, youth camp and hospital – in other words, all the disciplining institutions of society – as one of the principal methods of socialization. The main institution for educating by violence is the army, where *dedovshchina* (hazing), the humiliation of junior soldiers by their elders, is a key element for teaching soldiers, even more important than military training.[12] It instils in the new conscript the sense of the hierarchy in the barrack block and of the unquestioned pecking order, and it's no surprise that no one tries seriously to do anything to stop it. It's worth pointing out here that men are also the objects of violence, but their stories are even more deeply buried than those of the women. It is much more difficult for the so-called stronger sex to acknowledge publicly their personal traumas and humiliations, so as not to be known as a victim.

But the most widespread evil, which seems everyday and banal, is sexual violence. The flash mob uncovered the universal and routine nature of this phenomenon. According to psychologist Ludmila Petranovskaya, in Russia 'at least one in two women has had the experience in her life of either being raped or suffering attempted rape (it was interrupted or something stopped it), and just about all of them, with very rare exceptions, have been subjected to some kind of sexual abuse (harassment, groping or sexual threats)'. What's more, if in public there is some semblance of normality in relations between men and women, behind closed doors at home these rules do not apply and a genuine war begins: 40 per cent of all serious crimes are carried out within the family. Between 12,000 and 14,000 women die in Russia every year as a result of domestic violence – that's one murder every forty minutes. And those are just the official statistics: how many deaths are covered up by the police as 'serious heart problems'? How many beatings go unrecorded or simply not mentioned to anyone?

Like *dedovshchina* in the army, these violent practices are neither an exception nor excessive nor 'non-statutory relations'; they are actually part of the 'statute', the ruling patriarchal norm, which determines that the strongest lays down the law and sets the hierarchy of people and status. For a man it is important to be the conqueror, the subjugator, to take what is yours by force – this is how you raise your self-esteem and earn the respect of others. The ability to demonstrate your strength is part of the behaviour of 'the normal bloke' (*muzhik*): in your speech (the ability to use threats and insults); in all-male company, especially in the way you behave on the road (this is where the cult of the big car comes from, driving like a bully, and punishing anyone who upsets you); and, of course, in relations with women. In its concentrated form, the logic of force is expressed in a prison subculture, which in contemporary Russia has moved from being on the margins to being dominant. It becomes vitally important to bend the person to your will, to humiliate sexually the object of your power relations in order to establish the social order.

But that same code of the rule of the strongest, that unspoken agreement based on violence and silence, operates in politics, too. Recognizing the 'natural' right of man over woman, we must also recognize the right of the state over our bodies: the right of the authorities to falsify the results of elections; the right of the police to beat and torture suspects; the right of the courts to hand down unjust sentences; the right of Russia to annex Crimea from a defenceless Ukraine and without any justification to bomb Syrian towns simply to satisfy the geopolitical ambitions of our leader. It is exactly the same mechanism of power and the re-establishment of the hierarchy: when you recognize the right of a man to take a woman by force, you should also be ready to accept that the police can do with you as they wish with a champagne bottle or the shaft of a spade; this is two sides of the same biopower.

Russian power is extremely archaic and physiological: it is based not on the mechanisms of a rational system, nor even on the faceless machines of Weberian bureaucracy, but on direct physical contact, on dealing with people's bodies by force. In order to prove the right to power in Russia, acts of excessive violence are essential, such as the demonstrative murder of farmers by the crooks who were terrorizing them in the village of Kushchevskaya in the Krasnodar Region in 2010; the torture of suspects in the Dalny police station in Kazan, which became public in 2012; the murder of the opposition politician, Boris Nemtsov, in Moscow in 2015; burning down the houses of suspected terrorists in Chechnya; the demonstrative destruction of sanctioned foodstuffs ... It is no coincidence that at the head of the state stands an 'alpha male', who has legitimized the cult of strength, starting with physiological half-naked photo sessions, right through

143

to the use of force against opposition and against neighbouring countries; a leader whose lexicon and arguments ('the weak get beaten', 'get in the first punch') come straight out of criminal rituals of demonstrating brute force. This is why, behind the patriarchal gender models revealed so clearly by the flash mob, there is the whole archaic matrix of Russian power, carried out by 'blokes'.

And if male violence is not a private matter, but, rather, the universal law of the state, then the protest against it is also not a private matter, but a political one. This is about the 'de-automatization' of violence, about acknowledging that force is not a legitimate instrument, about breaking out of the vicious circle of violence and silence. This circle can be opened up in the first place by speaking out: by publicly announcing her pain, by speaking about her trauma, a woman can find her voice and the right to her memories. And along with it, political subjectivity.

And once again we are talking here not only about women, about their pain and fear and humiliation. The problem is that we are totally unable to speak about trauma – for example, about the legacy of Stalin's repressions. We are unable to work through traumas in our recent history – the war in Afghanistan in the 1980s, the Chernobyl disaster in 1986, the painful transition of the 1990s ... The hysterical reaction to the women's flash mob can be compared to the inability in contemporary Russia to cope with the documentary stories (not to mention the Nobel Prize awarded for them) of the Belarusian writer Svetlana Alexievich. People in Russia are unable to speak in public about the problem of cancer, or AIDS, or disability; and after the passing of homophobic laws the subject of homosexuality has become an even more taboo and repressed subject. Such forbidden topics are typical of an undeveloped mass consciousness – just as the state governs us with the help of archaic rituals of physical violence, so the mass consciousness reacts as primitive magic would have done: if you don't talk about a problem, it simply disappears and apparently resolves itself.

But nothing will change by itself. By speaking out about their trauma, women are making the first step towards overcoming the conspiracy of silence. Russia is a country trying to catch up with modernization and, as usual, it is about forty or fifty years behind the discussions of emancipation that Western society went through in the 1970s and 1980s, when they worked out the rituals of political correctness and guarantees of the defence against sexism and harassment, which we are so used to laughing at. Russia is going to have to go through the same 'sentimental education', shedding the myths about the submissive 'Russian woman' and daring 'real bloke', 'the hussar', and the practice of gender violence, which have built up over centuries. Today this may seem unimaginable; but the ice has started to crack. In the small space of social networks and the media, the first step towards freedom has been taken – not just to liberate women from fear and the dictatorship of men, but to free us all from the practice of social and state violence that has hung over Russian history like an age-old curse. We must return the right to memory and the right to speak out: two things that distinguish the free man from the slave. As so often happens, these courageous women with their personal stories have shown themselves to be in the forefront of a social movement, and it is already too late to hide or forget their uncomfortable truth.

THE POLITICS OF THE
FEMALE BODY

Unexpectedly for many, political life in Russia has moved into the area of the female anatomy – not in a metaphorical sense, but in the most direct way. The liveliest discussions taking place now are not about Ukraine or Syria and not even about the next Duma elections, but about the womb and the clitoris; about female genital mutilation in the North Caucasus; about the new children's ombudsman, who is actively fighting against abortion; about the age of consent; and about the schoolgirls who were seduced in School No. 57 in Moscow.

Everything began with a declaration by the Chairman of the Muslim Coordination Centre of the North Caucasus, Ismail Berdiev, who explained the barbaric practice of female genital mutilation in the remote villages of Dagestan as a desire to 'calm women down': 'Women do not lose the ability to give birth. But there will be less debauchery.' In the discussions that followed, Orthodox fundamentalists supported the Islamic cleric. At their head was Archpriest Vsevolod Chaplin, who declared his sympathy for the mufti on the matter of 'this feminist howling'.

Discussions about the details of the female anatomy became stronger with the appointment of the new children's ombudsman Anna Kuznetsova. Journalists quickly uncovered a declaration by Kuznetsova – the wife of a priest and mother of six children – in which she supported the pseudo-science of 'telegony', which maintains that the cells of the womb have 'an information-wave memory', and when a woman has a number of partners this leads to 'confused information', which affects 'the moral basis of the future child'. The ombudsman's posts on social media show her to be a conservative Orthodox believer: she is against abortion, surrogate motherhood, vaccinations for children and even ultrasound examination, which she describes as 'a paid-for mutation' that will ruin the health of the patient in ten to fifteen years. 'It's no wonder that the Old Believers hide their children away in Siberian villages', she writes on her page in the *VKontakte* social network.

146

As well as this, Anna Kuznetsova's charity foundation, *Pokrov* (named after the Protective veil of the Virgin) speaks to women who have decided to have an abortion and tries to persuade them not to do it; in other words, the foundation tries to get doctors to go against their professional ethics, and even the law, by telling them they should come up with reasons why they should refuse the patient what she is guaranteed by state medical help, thus frightening and manipulating women. The sociologist, Ella Paneyakh, who has studied the activities of the foundation, describes its behaviour as 'reproductive violence'.

Now we come at last to the scandal of Moscow School No. 57, where a history teacher (and, more than likely, not just he alone) over the course of many years had been sleeping with his schoolgirls. So as to avoid publicity and scandal, this fact had been covered up by the girls, their parents, the school administration and even the media, which had started to investigate on a number of occasions, but had dropped the case soon afterwards. The matter came to light only thanks to a post on Facebook from a girl who was a former pupil of the school, the journalist Ekaterina Krongauz, which led to an absolute avalanche of similar stories about this and other schools. It is worth pointing out that this wave happened against the background of another, which had already gripped Russian and Ukrainian social networks. This was the flash-mob #yaNyeBoyusSkazat, ('I'm not afraid to speak out'; see above, 'Breaking "The Silence of the Lambs"'), in which thousands of women for the first time in their lives spoke out about their experience of sexual violence, humiliation and harassment. The revelations by these women – from battered wives to schoolgirls who had been seduced by their teacher – was a real eye-opener for the Russian mass consciousness; not because people learnt anything new, but because the taboo on speaking out about such matters had been shattered.

The way in which public speech has drifted towards sexuality, physiology and even anatomy shows how the battle for the body in society's perception has turned around. It is here, and not in the imaginary struggle against NATO, nor on the Russo-Ukrainian border, that we find the frontline in the battle for 'the Russian World'; it is the line where the citizen faces up to the state. The attack unravels by the conservative, Orthodox forces, behind which stands the authoritarian figure of Putin's spiritual adviser, Bishop Tikhon, whom some are now calling a modern-day Rasputin because of the level of his influence on the affairs of state. They say that it was he who lobbied for the appointment of Kuznetsova as the children's ombudsman.

More importantly, though, is that it is not just a case of a few notable individuals, but rather that towards the end of Putin's third term there was the formation of a new consensus with a particular view of the world; a new profile of power in which the pragmatic, Westernizing technocrats, such as the former Minister of Education Dmitry Livanov, were being replaced with the 'correct' sort of fighters on the ideological front, whose ideas are rooted in Orthodoxy. In this profile we find the new Human Rights' Commissioner, Tatyana Moskalkova, who suggested after the action by Pussy Riot in the Cathedral that a new law be brought onto the statute book on 'attacking morality'; and Anna Kuznetsova with her 'telegony'; and the new Head of the Presidential Administration, Anton Vayno, with his fascinating 'nooscope' apparatus, for 'studying mankind's collective consciousness' and 'the registration of the unseen'.

These are all products of the past decade, fruits of the crisis in scientific knowledge and the new cultural condition of society, where on our TV screens 'Word of the Preacher' competes for ratings with 'Battle of the Psychics'; where priests bless spacecraft and astrologers discuss pregnancy with gynaecologists. A post-secular world is developing in Russia with the anti-modernist agenda of a new Middle Ages. Apparently, this is what sets the ideological tone after the 2018 presidential elections, to ensure the loyalty of the elite and social stability in a time of economic crisis and the transit of power. Here we have a parallel with the collapse of various empires, be it the Roman or the Byzantine, when all sorts of sects and Gnostic teachings sprang up; or the Russian Empire on the eve of the First World War, the time of the 'wise man' Grigory Rasputin, the favourite of the Empress; or the Third Reich, with its occult organization, the Ahnenerbe, and its searches for Shambhala in the Antarctic. As all great empires have declined, people have sought solace in mysticism.

Coming to meet this anti-modernist wave is a growing civil wave of a totally different hue, characterized best of all by the 'I'm not afraid to speak out' flash mob and the revelations of the girls of School No. 57 – a spontaneous modernizing network, linked by both freedom of expression and the removal of taboos. Thanks to social networks, people are breaking the ages-old vow of silence and coming out with their personal stories, which tear away the authority of the principal patriarchal institutes: the family and the school, and the orders of closed groups (be they a clan of relatives or an elite educational institution). They are throwing down a challenge to power, which is much stronger than the state Leviathan. This is the power of tradition, written into the very grammar of the language, in the fear to violate spoken etiquette, in the judgement of the collective ('everyone does it like this'; 'there was no need to be provocative'; 'don't wash your dirty linen in public'; 'the most important thing is to preserve the school (or the family)'). All these figures of speech preserve the patriarchal contract even more strongly than the OMON riot police and the Church – and it is against them that these first flash mobs are rebelling. Their language is that of the body: the body is speaking about its independence, its maturity, pain and fear; about the right to choose and the right to speak out.

There is a political logic in this. Where you have an authoritarian regime that has completely cleared the political field, the body becomes the frontline in the battle between the individual and the state. The body is the final frontier, which the state still cannot take over completely in the way that it can take political and civil freedoms. The anatomical protest becomes the answer to the state's biopolitics; and in this sense the symbol, slogan and brand of this new era of political protest has become the name 'Pussy Riot' – literally the uprising of the female being.

It's no surprise, therefore, that political discussions in Russia revolve around 'female' themes. Historically, it is the female body that has been much more repressed, marked out and objectivized than the male body, and today it is the female body (even more precisely, its reproductive organs as the receptacle for the traditional idea of the role of woman as a machine for bearing children) that has become the arena for the battle between the biopolitics of power and the biopolitical protest of the individual. It is here that the gender gesture becomes a civil and a political statement. In essence, it is a battle for sovereignty and for what we understand by this word: the sovereignty of a patriarchal state symbolized by the ritual carrying of a phallic symbol – the Topol-M intercontinental ballistic missile along the streets of Moscow during military parades – or the sovereignty of the individual, which is born out of Goethe's *Ewig-Weibliche* – the eternal female depths.

A FOUR-BY-FOUR AS A
TEACHING AID

A new bizarre moral dispute is taking place in Russia: this time, everyone's arguing over whether a driver, Vladimir Belsky, from the town of Priozersk in the Leningrad Region, was right to chase down in his four-by-four a group of boys who had fired plastic balls at his car. He knocked down one of them, ten-year-old Vanya Shchegolyov, then made him kneel while he waited for the police to arrive, before handing him over to them. Didn't he go a little over the top in teaching the boy a lesson (it turned out that the lad had concussion from falling on the road and later lost consciousness)? Wouldn't it have been better to punish the parents for allowing their child to play on the road? What about the school?

Everything in this story reads like some kind of grotesque fantasy; yet it is all so familiar. Children playing on the dirty spring road after school. A nasty driver in a four-wheel drive, who knocks over a child and then forces him to kneel for half an hour, crying, until the police arrive. The police, who interrogate the boy and then take him back to his parents – but don't say a word about the fact that he's been knocked down. But most surprising of all were all the comments on social media supporting – no, not the boy! – but the driver, for giving the lad a good lesson that you should never damage someone else's property and that you have to answer for your actions.

Russians' pathological fetishism for their cars is well known. People put their own personality into their vehicles, as well as their own privacy (hence the desire for darkened windows, even though the Russian climate isn't exactly spoilt by too much sunshine). They invest them with their own rights, notably that you can't violate my individuality. The car – especially if it's a black four-by-four – is an extension of the Russian's own body; it is sacred and unpredictable, and anyone encroaching on this body must be swiftly and demonstratively punished. This leads to hysterical reaction to any wear and tear or chipped paintwork, which in turn leads to aggressive behaviour while sorting out any incident on the road, and to traffic jams stretching back kilometres because two drivers have stopped in the middle of the road to argue over a tiny scratch.

Russians accept violence against their person far more readily: crushes on public transport or in queues; the inability to maintain a distance during a conversation and respect the other's personal space; drunken brawls and beatings at the hands of the police; assault and battery in the home – all of this is the norm in a society where all social transactions are defined by brute force. But people won't tolerate anything that harms their car or even the space around it. Recently, when I was parking on a Moscow street, I came close to the car behind me, and was subjected to an aggressive shout from the driver who was sitting in the car: 'And how am I supposed to get out?' This despite the fact that behind him was an empty space of nearly a metre; but he took anyone coming close to his vehicle as a threat.

What we have here is a transfer of the principle of *habeas corpus* from the individual to the vehicle. The car becomes the carrier of the citizen's body not only as a marker of identity and the uncrossable line where they mustn't be touched, but as an instrument of aggression, giving greater possibilities or else compensating for the shortcomings and complexes of its owner. When you buy these extra kilogrammes of metal and horse-power (and it's crucial that you have a foreign four-wheel drive; it's possible that the incident in Priozersk could have happened with a small Russian-made car, but it is far less likely), the owner receives extra rights along with the car, including the right to be aggressive. In Russian traffic there is a strict hierarchy of vehicles, based on their cost, the size of the engine, the size of the car, the colour, the number plates and, of course, the flashing light on the roof – the special blue light given to representatives of the organs of power. In such a hierarchy, a small boy who dares to raise his hand against the black four-by-four of a local businessman deserves a suitable punishment; and according to this logic, the driver is behaving correctly – going after him over the grass, knocking down the young hooligan, making him kneel and calling the police. Everything, in fact, like in a real gangster film.

The deliberate chasing after the child; the concussion; the horror and the humiliation that he experienced; being made to kneel in the slush for half an hour; the terror of being interrogated by the police – in a word, the trauma of all this, which could affect him for the rest of his life, all comes from the vicious lessons of the street, repeating the eternal models of power and violence in the Russian space. I remember when I was about nine years old, in the blissful 1970s, I

151

was playing near our house in Moscow. I'd just made a snowman and was throwing snowballs at it. Accidentally, one of them hit a passing car. Out jumped a guy and came straight at me and hit me in the face. He broke my nose and cut my lip. Then he swore at me and drove off. Somewhere in the far-off and decaying United States he could have been given twenty years for that; but in Russia that's called acting like a man. I put some fresh snow on my nose, stopped the bleeding, and went home blubbing. In such cases, nothing changes in Russia. The law that was recently passed in the Duma decriminalizing domestic violence in Russia, which has already been criticized by the European Union, is a tribute to the archaic patriarchal traditions of male domination and an upbringing which humiliates and destroys women, children and anyone who is weak.

But there is another side to the story in Priozersk. The children were firing plastic balls from a toy rifle, imitating the computer game 'Grand Theft Auto' (GTA), which is based on street battles. The problem here is that in the education of Russian children the cult of the weapon and the glorification of war have not been thought through and no one doubts the need for it. The multiplicity of toy guns and computer shooting games; children's beds that look like tanks; morning exercises in kindergarten, where the children wear military hats and tops with pretend medals on them; and the main thing, when the toy guns are replaced by real ones, taking children through their teenage years – in school, at firing ranges, in lessons of military training and security issues; and then on to the conscription process and into the army. The necessity for the whole male population to be able to use a gun is a controversial topic that deserves wider discussion; but at least they could instil into the minds of a young man or a girl from their school lessons on military training and the initial training unit that what they have in their hands is a deadly weapon. For young children, holding a rifle in their hands means no more than holding a rattle or a magic wand, for which they have been taught no responsibility whatsoever.

Here we must question the whole system of symbolic violence, through which any person is socialized, but especially a small boy from whom society demands that he 'becomes a man'. Shooting ranges and the biathlon have become the paramilitary fun of an era of mass armies; and paintball, an outlet for modern workers slaving away in offices. But these popular amusements actually legitimize weapons and the point of these weapons, which is to penetrate, to harm and to kill. It is no coincidence that many educational systems, such as the Waldorf System, carefully protect children from any kind of weapons, from the very concept of taking in your hands something that could – even in a pretend way – cause pain or death to any living creature. When someone plays with a rifle, they develop the idea of the rights of the strong man. And when they grow up, they can easily get behind the wheel of a black four-by-four and start to crush everything around them, from the grass to small cars.

None of this, of course, justifies the actions of the driver from Priozersk, nor does it lessen the sympathy for the child, whatever he was playing. It is simply that in this incident on the dirty Russian roadside there was a short circuit, something that brought together the circle of violence, which includes children's games with weapons, our military-patriotic education, beatings in the family and the aggression of drivers. The subject of 'shooting games' like GTA has come off the computer screen onto the street. And just the same sort of scenes from another shooting-game, 'World of Tanks', has burst out onto the streets of towns in Ukraine, with Russian tanks in the Donbass. Because symbolic and pretend violence sooner or later turns real and deadly.

A RUSSIAN POTLATCH

In the summer of 2015, in the twenty-fifth year of Russia's independence and the second year of the embargo on foodstuffs (a ban on bringing into the country products from countries carrying out economic sanctions against Russia), our country strengthened its sovereignty by the demonstrative destruction of sanctioned products. Thousands of tons of European cheese, fruits and meat products were cast into the fires of mobile crematoria or crushed by bulldozers. The very pinnacle of this struggle for sovereignty was the destruction by a bulldozer of the carcasses of three frozen Hungarian geese in Tatarstan. The film-clip of this immediately went viral.

This media spectacle was an instant success. No one could be indifferent to the spectacle of burning cheese and crushed fruits. It really touched a nerve; it appealed to the genetic memory of a nation that throughout history has frequently gone hungry. From a political point of view, this action achieved the maximum effect. We saw the energetic young customs officer reporting on what he was doing; we heard television commentators obediently blaming the destruction of the products on a Western virus that would be a threat to the health of the nation. Meanwhile, Russian Facebook was indignant about the amoral destruction of food and began to gather signatures for a petition to say that it should be given to needy citizens – this at the same time as these same citizens were gathering up the squashed peaches in order to turn them into home-made vodka or *samogon*.

In fact, this has nothing to do with food safety in Russia, nor the effectiveness of the embargo, nor EU farmers. 'The forbidden fruit' still found its way to the shelves, and most likely will continue to do so through a third country, taxed by an even higher corruption fee. Salmon and oysters will still appear for sale from that great seafaring power, Belarus. The European Union did not suffer either: in the year of the Russian embargo, exports of foodstuffs from the EU rose by 5 per cent, thanks to increased sales to China and the USA. The bonfires of the product inquisition will soon die away, the customs

154

and supervisory officials will also cool off and find new ways to extract corrupt dues, and the media will obediently turn to attacking new enemies. Why was this whole circus necessary?

This is just symbolic politics, or, to put it more simply, trolling. Trolling of the West; trolling of the Russian opposition, which protested, as they knew they would; and a way of frightening retailers, who in the course of the year had already found a multitude of loopholes to get round the sanctions. The state has been carrying out widespread trolling for a number of years already: the Kremlin bots from the 'Troll Factory' in Olgino in St Petersburg are simply a caricature of state policy. With the absence of any political will and strategic thinking, and with a shrinking resource base, trolling represents the thoughts and the main method of state policy; the real Olgino is situated in the Kremlin and in the home of the State Duma on Okhotny Ryad. There is nothing behind this but a desire to muddle public discussion, to provoke the opponent (or the opposition) and to throw disruptive ideas into the political field.

There is a fundamental weakness at the root of the Kremlin's trolling: because the state is unable to cope with the challenges of the outside world, or even with its own society, it puts all its efforts into propaganda and the creation of information 'bombs'. It creates a constant flow of information in the media, trying to have a finger in every pie, just like the troll who joins an online forum in order to break up a serious discussion. Russia is unable to oppose the West in a military sense, so instead it rolls out its Topol-M intercontinental missile in parades, flies its ageing Tu-95 strategic bombers and encourages conversations about 'radioactive ash' – like TV presenter Dmitry Kiselyov, who was threatening the nuclear annihilation of the United States. Its unsubtle nuclear trolling makes it look like North Korea. It carries out similar trolling in Europe, secretly financing the most odious and marginal allies, from right-wing radicals to separatists, in an attempt to sow discord among Western societies and politics.

Not wishing to give orphans or disabled children a decent life in Russia, the state bans foreigners from adopting them, condemning many of these children to death, shocking the West and openly trolling the opposition and human rights activists. And lastly, unable to change the situation on the food market, to halt inflation and supply products to take the place of those no longer being imported, the state orders the destruction of sanctioned foodstuffs, creating the maximum media effect, which is aimed at the West, business and their own population. This changes absolutely nothing. The state looks like some kind of primitive native, performing a ritual dance wearing war paint, crying out, rolling its eyes and beating itself, under the astonished gaze of European tourists. It is no coincidence that the German magazine, *Der Spiegel*, placed Russia's action of destroying food on a par with the behaviour of Somali extremists, who burnt foreign products, or the radicals of Islamic State, who destroyed American humanitarian aid parcels dropped in by parachute.

From an anthropological point of view, burning food does indeed have much in common with the traditions of primitive tribes, notably with the Potlatch of the North American Indians. This was a traditional tribal festival, in the course of which, as a demonstration of the ambitions and power of the leader, property was handed out or destroyed without any plan, which sometimes caused irreparable damage to the whole tribe. In order to demonstrate the greatness of the leader and his disdain for wealth, they gave away, threw into the sea or burnt skins, blankets, furs, boats and wigwams, kitchen implements and food reserves. For some time after the Potlatch, the tribe appeared to be on the brink of ruination, which was why such a festival was remembered for years, legends grew about it and were handed down to the children.

The Kremlin is following exactly the same logic of the Potlatch. The first sacrifice was of sick children. Next was the Russian rouble and the prospects of economic growth. Finally, sanctioned foodstuffs were cast into the sacred hecatomb. All this, apparently, has been done to demonstrate the greatness and sovereignty of Russia, its special path, fortitude and disdain for material values.

The French writer and philosopher, Georges Bataille, has called the Potlatch a political and economic expenditure, which is the opposite of the economy of consumption and accumulation. It is a particular religious action that crosses borders and prohibitions, an ecstatic spectacle of death, like the corrida. We are reminded about our own frailties and about the moment when man finally casts off his material shell. In contemporary Russia, the demonstrative destruction of food products is a move from the conspicuous consumption of the oil era to the demonstrative destruction of the post-Crimea era. Being unable to change the world, Russia is trying to frighten it: it is calling up the spirits of the past, digging out the tomahawks and painting its face with mud. It is burning cheese, crushing the carcases of geese and waving its missile at the world.

All we need to do now is wait for the anthropologists.

A REQUIEM FOR ROQUEFORT

Among the losses of recent years – the free press, fair elections, an independent court – what has hurt especially has been the disappearance of good cheese. As Oscar Wilde said, 'Give me the luxuries and I can dispense with the necessities'; and right now, most of all, we have a shortage of luxuries. Going into the supermarket, I plan my route so that I don't inadvertently walk past the shelves holding Russian-made cheese, because the bright packaging with the pseudo-European names brings on mild signs of nausea: 'Maasdamer', 'Gruntaler', 'Berglander'. And underneath this colourful packaging are concealed tasteless blocks, which are a mix of soap, plastic and the Russian national product – palm oil. If you wanted to point out one place to illustrate the fantastic failure of the policy of import substitution, then look no further than the cheese shelves.

This is reminiscent of the writer Vladimir Sorokin, a visionary genius, who foresaw it in his anti-utopian novel, *Day of the Oprichnik*. In a totalitarian future in Russia, all foreign supermarkets have been closed down and in their place stand Russian kiosks, in which there are just two types of each item: 'Russia' brand cheap *papirosi* cigarettes and 'Motherland' (*Rodina*) cigarettes; *Rzhanaya* (rye) vodka and *Pshenichnaya* (wheat) vodka; white bread and dark bread; apple jam and plum jam – 'Because our God-bearing people should choose from two things, not from three or thirty-three.' The only product of which there is but one type is cheese – Russian, and the *oprichnik*, the officer of the security services, struggles in vain to come to terms with the deep and meaningful thought: 'Why is it that all the goods are in pairs, like the beasts on Noah's Ark, but there's only one kind of cheese, Russian?'[13]

There is a logic to the Russian state's war on cheese, which is understandable and culturally determined. For the state, cheese is a marker of the dangerous *Other*, a symbol of the decaying West. It is the rot and the mould of that fluid urban class, which, having travelled around Europe, has come to think too highly of itself and demanded not only cheese but also honest elections; and these people went out onto the streets in December 2011, on Chistoprudny Boulevard and Bolotnaya Square, protesting about the falsified elections for the Duma. There is a direct route from 'Maasdam' cheese to 'Maidan', as the Ukrainian Revolution was called, and evil must be destroyed at its root – at the customs border of the Russian Federation.

If we analyse this, quality European cheese belongs in the territory of the sensible middle class, because it falls into the category of democratic, affordable refinement. Cheese is not one of those luxuries that can be shown off, like Louboutin shoes and lobsters, Breguet watches and Bugatti cars. Russian sales in this particular consumer market have not fallen off in the time of sanctions. Parking his Porsche Cayenne outside the shabby entrance to his crumbling Soviet-era block of flats and buying *foie gras* and XO cognac to enjoy in his tiny eight-square-metre kitchen, the Russian man can feel that he is taking part in the cargo-cult of the consumer, that he is in communion with civilization: but he has not become a part of it. But a piece of French brie, a bottle of Italian chianti and a warm baguette in a paper bag from a local bakery drew him close to Western values and were acts of social modernization.

Removing cheese from this formula broke the model of consumption, and, in exactly the same way actually, it showed that there was no demand for it in Putin's model of the redistribution of raw materials and the whole ephemeral post-Soviet 'middle class'. Striking against cheese was equivalent to carrying out a strike against the quasi-Western idea of normality and bourgeois values, and a return to the strict Russian archetype: for the Russian it is *kolbasa*, salami-type sausage, that is symbolically valuable, while cheese is simply urban capriciousness, because you don't follow a shot of vodka with a piece of cheese. So in this sense cheese underlines the narrow dividing line between Russian tradition and our superficial Westernization.

Here we have to state the obvious, sad though it is. Despite multiple attempts to establish a culture of cheese production in Russia's vast expanses and poor soils, from Peter the Great through to Stalin's Head of Food Production, Anastas Mikoyan, and today's heroic Russian dairy farmers, cheese remains a product that is alien to the Russian soul. Its lifecycle is too long for Russian history and everyday life in the country. Like wine and olive oil, cheese is the product of a stable culture. Roquefort has been made since the eleventh century; Gruyère and Cheshire cheese since the twelfth; Parmesan, Gorgonzola, Taleggio and Pecorino since the fourteenth. But it's less a question of the length of the tradition than it is the time it takes for the cheese to mature: thirty-six months for Parmesan; five to six years for mature Gouda. For cheese to able to spend such a long time maturing, you need political and social stability, guarantees of the rights of ownership, credit and a steady demand. Cheese is an investment in a reliable future.

In Russia they made *tvorog* (a kind of cottage cheese), which can be made quickly and which also goes off very quickly. You put the milk out in the evening, drain it the next morning, and eat it the following evening, by which time it's already beginning to go sour. The Russian peasant had no certainty about the future: tomorrow there could be war, a military call-up, a *corvée*[14] or Bolshevik demands for extra produce. The peasant didn't manage his own life or his own property; he didn't have time to make cheese, he just wanted to stay alive. Russian production of both material goods and foodstuffs has always been the victim of the climate and the country's history, which dictate quick production and use; and also the victim of weak institutions under which there is no right to ownership, nor the possibility for long-term planning and storage. There is just a single Leviathan state, which can never be satisfied and which will gobble up any surplus – and cheese comes about as the result of a surplus of milk.

As a result, the question of cheese (also, incidentally, of wine) is a question of roots, about a person being tied to a place; it's about identity, locality and regionalism. It's about a village that has stood for the past two thousand years, where there are houses that are three hundred years old. It's about family traditions, generations of peasants, about handwritten housekeeping books, alfalfa, which is at its best on the western side of the hill. Charles de Gaulle asked the rhetorical question: 'How can anyone govern a nation that has 246 different kinds of cheese?'[15] In fact, the General was mistaken; there are at least 400 different cheeses in France. And it is precisely that variety of tastes, regions, cultures and traditions that has made France the most popular country in the world for visitors, attracting up to a hundred million people every year. In Russia, the tradition of producing cheese arose only in the non-Russian regions on the periphery of the empire, in the Caucasus, the Baltic States and Finland; in other words, in those areas where there was no serfdom and where the sense of kinship, soil and roots was strongest. In the central spaces of the empire, where there was serfdom, cheese never caught on; it never became a tradition or a favoured taste, but remained a sort of foreign amusement, the forbidden aroma of the West, of satiety – of freedom.

The present war against cheese in Russia is following in the footsteps of this long cultural tradition, and it is no coincidence that alert citizens continue to use the 'hot line' to report shops where they find 'the forbidden fruit', and the television stations continue to show the destruction of cheese in mobile crematoria, and the health authorities continue to tell people how bad Western cheese is for the Russian stomach. Wiping out cheese is eternal Russia's answer to the mouldy West and to curious citizens: 'Your predecessors didn't have a rich lifestyle, why the hell should you start now?' And at one and the same time, these are symbolic gestures of Russia's political independence, a step into the future, where there won't be 246 types of cheese, as de Gaulle had to cope with, but just one, Russian, like in Sorokin's *Day of the Oprichnik*. True, it will be made of palm oil, but that's like just about everything in our sovereign state.

THE LAND OF
ABANDONED CHILDREN

Loveless, a film by Andrei Zvyagintsev about a boy who runs away from home after a row between his parents and disappears into the forest, hit the Russian screens on 1 June 2017, which happens to be the Day for the Defence of Children. Even though this was, no doubt, a complete coincidence, the timing is deeply symbolic.

Children have indeed become one of the painful subjects of our time, from the fake propaganda about the 'crucified boy' in Slavyansk (a well-known lie put out by Russian media supposedly to illustrate the cruelty of Ukrainians in the Donbass), to the hysteria in the Duma about the 'groups of death' in social media, which allegedly were trying to provoke schoolchildren into committing suicide. From 'the children's crusade' of those school kids who unexpectedly took part in the protest rally in support of the opposition politician, Alexei Navalny, on 26 March 2017, to 'the Arbat Hamlet' – a boy who was reading Shakespeare aloud on the Arbat pedestrianized street in Moscow and was arrested for begging. With this film, Zvyagintsev hits right at the sore point where politics, propaganda and collective trauma all meet.

Just about all of Zvyagintsev's films revolve around the subject of abandoned children. In *The Return* (2003), a prodigal father visits his two abandoned sons, and their lack of understanding ends in tragedy. In *The Banishment* (2007), the abortion of an unwanted foetus starts a chain of deaths. In *Elena* (2011), one of the central conflicts is between a father and his daughter (but there is also in the final scene the shot of a small baby writhing on a huge bed, as a symbol of thoughtless reproduction). In *Leviathan* (2014), the son of the main hero is taken off for adoption. Unborn, unwanted, abandoned children, children who are taken from their parents – this forms a key image for the director, and a symbol of the decaying cosmos and the moral catastrophe which he shows in every one of his films.

In *Loveless* (2017), a child is once again placed at the heart of the story; or, to be more precise, the child's disappearance. The film has an overwhelming emptiness, a lacuna, which begins to grow like a funnel, drawing into it all the main characters, those close to them, their homes, the areas where they live, and the forest park. The aesthetics of absence, marked by traces of the boy who has disappeared – his jacket, notices about his disappearance, the cries of those searching for him in the empty forest – all heighten the suspense, turning a family drama into a psychological thriller. The tormented search for the child reminds us more than once of Andrei Tarkovsky's *Stalker*. Zvyagintsev always uses the same cameraman, Mikhail Krichman, whose lens gives even the simplest details a merciless sharpness and metaphysical depths; Krichman's gripping shots and dim palette turn a Moscow suburb into the kingdom of the dead, relieved only by the fleeting beauty that is brought by the first snow, which just for a second turns the scene into a Bruegelesque winter landscape.

In line with the laws of thermodynamics, entropy grows in this space. There is no god here (although there are bearded office workers in the company of an Orthodox businessman), just as there is no state – a policeman immediately warns the parents that the police won't go searching for the boy. Here, families are dead and the school is hopeless: the schoolteacher helplessly drags a cloth across the blackboard leaving chalk smears, while outside the window the snow gradually starts to fall. There are not even guilty people here: everyone has simply been born and lives in a loveless space, which they diligently reproduce as the only method available to them for survival and communication.

The apotheosis of this emptiness comes in an abandoned building somewhere in the forest, the boy's last refuge. The leaking roof, the puddles on the floor, the fragments of human civilization – all this reminds us of The Zone and The Room in *Stalker*, which was for Tarkovsky a metaphor for the deserted soul. Even the brilliant final scene in the mortuary (which, for its intensity and lack of resolution should go into a handbook for directors) is constructed around absence. We do not see the actual fact, the events, the dead body: all we see is the reflection in faces and the reactions of the characters. But the most frightening emptiness opens up in the film's epilogue, in the eyes of the main female character, walking on a treadmill while wearing a fashionable Bosco tracksuit with the word 'RUSSIA' written in English. The camera seems to fall into that totally vacant stare.

The simplest thing of all would be to see this as a caricature of Mother Russia, having lost her child and walking on the spot on a treadmill on the balcony of an elite home, while her new husband mindlessly watches news from the Donbass on the television, as presented by Russian TV's chief propagandist Kiselyov. But Zvyagintsev doesn't use such obvious metaphors. He does not convict, he makes a statement; he doesn't lay blame, he presents a diagnosis. He's made a film about a broken family and it's come out as being about Russia, and the Donbass and Kiselyov; the final scene is not a political pamphlet, as in *Leviathan*, but the *Zeitgeist*, a frozen picture on the TV screen. Ultimately, is Alexander Pushkin's *Boris Godunov* a tragedy about a murdered boy, or is it about Russian power? It is a similar question with *Loveless*: it reveals a moral flaw, an abandoned boy, at the very core of our existence, but the war in the Donbass is simply one of the partial consequences of this comprehensive moral disaster.

It is crucially important that the time of the action is clearly shown in the film. It begins in December 2012, the eve of the passing of the Dima Yakovlev Law, otherwise known as 'the scoundrels' law', which doomed dozens of sick Russian orphans who were waiting to be adopted by foreigners to a miserable life, worsening illness and, in some cases, death. It is exactly from this moment, when the ruling class was bound by the blood of the children, that the definitive moral decline of the state set in, accompanied as it was by the overwhelming indifference of the population. The film ends in 2015, 'the year of normalization', when the shock of Crimea and the shooting down of MH17 had passed, when Russia had grown used to the sanctions regime and understood that this new relationship between the state and society was serious and in for the long run. Zvyagintsev makes films about the family, but the action takes place in conditions of an unprecedented moral decline. And the basic problem here is not Putin and Kiselyov; it's not in the Kremlin and the Donbass; and it's not even corruption and theft: these are all merely symptoms of the disease. The director addresses the disease itself – it is society, mired in lies, cynicism and a lack of trust, having lost all hope for the future and for change; and Putin and Kiselyov simply cast this lie in the form of politics and the mass media, thus exporting it to the whole world.

It is certainly not a coincidence that in 2016 in the Russian public space the conversation turned to ethics: here we had the flash mob, 'I'm not afraid to speak out' (see above, 'Breaking "The Silence of the Lambs"'), in which women spoke about the sexual harassment they have had to put with; about domestic violence and torture in Russian prisons; and about historic memory and the responsibility of Stalin's executioners. The reflective part of society has begun to be aware of the moral dead-end in which we all find ourselves, and the conspiracy of silence that has surrounded the problems of violence, humiliation and trauma. These are exactly the questions that Zvyagintsev has been raising for many years, including the problem of not speaking out and the break in communication. In conditions where there is no state with a social policy, no church that is socially responsible or close to the people, no culture of public dialogue on questions of the family, childhood, or relations between the sexes, Zvyagintsev's films present us with the very fundamental moral questions about which we prefer to remain silent – or leave them at the mercy of cynical populists like deputies Vitaly Milonov and Elena Mizulina, official defenders of 'traditional values'. Andrei Zvyagintsev is now the main person in Russia raising the question of values – real values, not those dreamt up by propaganda – but the state will never acknowledge him in this role, preferring to limit the distribution of his films and defaming him in the press, as happened with his previous film, *Leviathan*, which they accused of being Russophobic.

One of the fleeting images in *Loveless* is signal tape. Right at the start of the film, the boy finds some in the forest. He ties it to a stick and throws it at a tree. The years pass, new children are born, but the tape remains there. It is as if Zvyagintsev has wrapped our society in this tape, marking the perimeter of the contours of the humanitarian catastrophe and the moral quagmire into which we have plunged. Like Pushkin's 'bloody boy' in *Boris Godunov*, his lost child speaks about the fundamental crime lying at the base of our silent well-being, about the things we are trying unsuccessfully to forget. This is why this film is so ruthless, so discomforting – and such essential viewing.

THE AMPUTATION OF CONSCIENCE

The season of tolerance and humanity opened in Russia: as its representative at the finals of the 2017 Eurovision Song Contest in Kiev, Russia chose Yulia Samoilova, a singer in a wheelchair. Shortly before the competition, it had seemed as if Russia would boycott it, given that it was taking place in the capital of a country with which Russia is de facto at war. But suddenly, in a single magical moment, everything changed: with one generous gesture Russia was returning to the bosom of this international festival, rising above the military conflict, and announcing that it was adhering to global standards of tolerance and equal opportunities.

And everything would have been wonderful in this Hollywood-like story, demonstrating that music and the will to live can triumph over hatred and division – except that the shadow of the Kremlin propaganda machine could be seen sticking out from underneath this great humanitarian subject. The problem was that in July 2015 Yulia had performed in Crimea after it was annexed by Russia, and had travelled there without the permission of the Ukrainian authorities. Thus, Ukraine was presented with a cynical choice by Russia: either allow a singer who had broken the law in Ukraine to take part in the competition, thus violating its own principles and norms; or refuse her entry, thus opening itself up to a guaranteed artillery barrage of Russian propaganda and the judgement of the international community. The Ukrainian musician and actor, Anton Mukharsky, even proposed greeting Samoilova at the airport in Kiev accompanied by hundreds of Ukrainian Army soldiers who are now permanently disabled as a result of the battles in the Donbass.

In the end, the Ukrainian Security Service did ban Samoilova from entering Ukraine for three years, and Russia was not represented at Eurovision 2017; but, at the same time, it made Ukraine look like a miserable host that had politicized the song contest. This was a masterful propaganda stroke from Moscow's point of view, which had been prepared to send its singer deep into the rear of the enemy as a diversionary tactic in its hybrid war against Ukraine and the West.

However, the main problem with nominating Yulia Samoilova to take part in Eurovision 2017 was that Russia did not have the moral right to send someone in a wheelchair from a country that does not provide its disabled people with equal rights for treatment, mobility or work opportunities. There are huge problems with medication for the disabled and with the provision of ramps in housing blocks. As a result, the vast majority of disabled people are confined to their apartments. It is impossible to live on the miserly disability benefits provided, or to look after a disabled child, even in the poorest Russian regions. As has always been the case, Russia has a shortage of quality protheses, wheelchairs and spare parts for them; furthermore, virtually none of these items is produced in Russia itself. Yulia, who suffers from spinal amyotrophy (an inherited disorder, exacerbated following a polio vaccination as a child), is hoping to go to Finland for an operation, and is collecting money for this via crowdfunding. As they joked bitterly on Twitter: 'It's only in Russia that a disabled person could go to Eurovision, but can't go to the shop next door.'

Our Paralympic sport is also just such a Potemkin Village, if not more so: first and foremost, it is a shop window for national pride, and only after that is it a humanitarian project. When there is no infrastructure, nor any tradition of people with restricted abilities taking part in sport (it would be a great rarity in Russia for a blind runner or skier to take part in a mass marathon accompanied by a specially trained sportsman), all that exists is a state system for choosing people with disabilities to take part in top-level sports. They identify gifted people with restricted abilities – for example, former sportspeople who have been in a car accident – and suggest to them a professional career that would be the envy of any disabled Russian person: everything is paid for by the state, they travel abroad and, if they are victorious, there are generous prizes. Paralympic sportspeople are a part of the elite Russian sporting machine, and huge financial and administrative resources are thrown at their success; but it's no coincidence (judging by the unprecedented sanctions imposed by the International Paralympic Committee) that they were drawn into the massive doping programme. And, as dependent people, they couldn't refuse. Then, when they were caught out, the moralizing machinery of state propaganda went into overdrive, blaring out about the 'unheard-of cynicism' of the international sporting organizations, which had decided 'to take revenge on Russia' and 'make an example of disabled sportsmen'.

Samoilova's situation is similar to the Paralympic one in that the state draws vulnerable groups into its special propaganda operation, hiding behind their weakness like a living shield. In its clearest and most distilled way, this policy was evident in the passing of the Dima Yakovlev Law in December 2012: the state took as hostage orphaned children with disabilities, the most vulnerable group, completely lacking in rights, who were critically dependent on foreign adopters (as is well known, it is very rare for sick children to be taken into Russian families), and used them as a bargaining chip so as to 'punish' the West for the 'Magnitsky List'.[16] In reality, what we are talking about here is the state's right over the body of the individual, where even their disability is taken away from them and becomes a state resource. This is a specific type of biopolitics: the nationalization and politicization of disability, the creation of a medical exclusion space, which allows for no external criticism ('they are insulting the weakest!') and can be used to cover any special operations by the state, from the doping programme to the hybrid war against Ukraine and the West.

Yulia Samoilova is far from being the first contestant with particular features to take part in the Eurovision Song Contest. We had the Polish singer, Monika Kuszyńska, who is partially paralysed following a car crash; there was the blind Georgian woman, Diana Gurtskaya; a pregnant woman; the bearded Conchita Wurst; and the Russian grandmothers' chorus: this competition long ago turned into a parade of variety and tolerance. It's time we stopped paying attention to who is performing in front of us: a man or a woman; bearded or not; straight or gay; a cute-looking actress or a youthful old man; someone with one leg or two; standing up or sitting in a wheelchair. The only thing that matters is that he or she should perform best of all. But our lens is so configured that we pay special attention to, stigmatize and politicize these particularities, while Eurovision is a special kind of magnifying glass and a false mirror, a safari park of archaic and wounded national pride. Here the show is ruled by complicated coalitions and mutual back-scratching. Old historical scores and childish grudges are settled; national pride preens itself and defeat is taken very badly. No one could have guessed that, out of the forty-three countries, two would find themselves at war. It would have been far more honest for Russia to have boycotted the Eurovision final in Kiev from the start, bearing in mind the events in Crimea and the Donbass. But Moscow unexpectedly made the knight's move (or, more exactly, the wheelchair move) and short-sightedly considers that it has had a propaganda victory; while in reality it is a moral defeat.

The Samoilova problem exists on two levels: the human and the political. From a human point of view, one could only wish that she had been able to take part in the competition, something she had dreamed about for years. It's possible that the honorarium and the publicity she would have received may have helped her to pay for her operation in Finland, which would have allowed her to be able, in the future, to breathe, sing and perform normally. Perhaps her performance would have given support to all those who struggle with their traumas and their ills, so that they didn't have to hide them, and so they could overcome their pain, isolation and anonymity. But on the political level, one is stunned by the cynicism of the producers of the show in nominating Samoilova to take part: they solve their own propaganda tasks by using the most vulnerable and dependent bodies. In reality, they have already had their consciences amputated, just as, for the rest of us, the ability to be surprised by anything has long ago atrophied.

THE FIASCO OF
'OPERATION SOCHI'

Taking back the Olympic medals won at Sochi from Russian sportsmen and women as a result of the doping scandal, and the subsequent unprecedented ban on the national team from taking part in the PyeongChang Winter Olympics in February 2018, became the greatest failure of Russian foreign policy in recent years. Victory in Sochi had been one of the main international achievements, a personal triumph for Vladimir Putin, who stood, emperor-like, on the podium of the Fisht Olympic Stadium and reviewed the parade of the victors. It was a symbolic prize, which remained in place even after Russia tore up the modern world order in 2014 and turned into a revanchist state.

And now there are no medals, nor victory in the medal table, where Russia had come out on top. There is a certain logic to all of this. The medals from Sochi were the final legacy of that old, pre-Crimea, Russia, which proudly showed the world its history and the masterpieces of the Russian avant-garde in the impressive opening ceremony; which triumphed in the snowy arenas and not in the back streets of hybrid wars; and which was a part of the global world. Now everything has been put in its place: the medals have been taken away and the last link with the previous era has been severed. It turns out that the 2014 Olympic Games were just a sham, a cover for doping, a special operation by the Federal Security Service, the FSB, all part of the hybrid war with the West.

The most banal and useless answer would be to blame the West for everything – which is exactly what the state propaganda did. They produced from up their sleeves a whole set of absurd excuses about an anti-Russian conspiracy: 'Everyone's involved in doping, it's just that the Russians are the only ones they catch'; 'They've done this to us because of Crimea' (or even because we were victorious in the War in 1945, as was recently put forward in the Duma); 'Sport can't achieve the highest results without doping'; 'Norwegians all take asthma medicine', and so on. They can try all they like to take comfort in myths about an anti-Russian conspiracy in the International Olympic Committee (IOC) or the World Anti-Doping Agency (WADA) and curse the whistle-blower, Russian doping guru and defector, Grigory Rodchenkov, who revealed all the details of the doping system. But none of this changes the principal, inconvenient question: were the facts that became known from Rodchenkov's diaries, from Richard McLaren's report about Russian doping, from the documentary films of the German ARD television channel, and from Bryan Fogel's film *Icarus*, which won the Oscar for best documentary film, all actually true? By way of an answer, there was just an eloquent silence and conciliatory statements from our normally combative official spokespersons, which de facto served as an acknowledgement of the facts as presented. What's more, the evidence was apparently so convincing that the Kremlin preferred to accept the IOC's comparatively soft verdict so as not to threaten the Football World Cup, which took place in Russia in 2018.

The fact is that doping in Russia is a deeply systemic phenomenon, the logical result of the resource machine in Soviet and Russian sport, where plans and norms on the number of medals are handed down from above, and medals and results are expected to be produced from below. Every trainer in each of the sports schools answers with their head and their salary for the smooth production of leading athletes; every federation in each sport answers for the preparation of Olympic champions; and the Olympic Committee is responsible for victory in the medal table. The very pinnacle of this pyramid comes when, right outside the Kremlin, Olympic champions and prize winners are handed the keys to Mercedes and Audi cars, as well as being given flats and gifts worth millions of dollars from regional governors and oligarchs. In this administrative and bureaucratic machine, honed only so as to demonstrate the superiority of Russian sport, the bodies of these athletes are turned into a mere biological resource, and doping becomes an essential method for the solution of the state's strategic tasks. This machine has been working for decades, from children's sport to the Olympic level, in a process of Darwinian selection culling hundreds of thousands of people who didn't pass selection, meaning that someone who has gone through many years of ruthless training to reach the level of 'Master of Sport', but who didn't then make it into the Olympic reserve, will, as a rule, be thrown by the wayside, their health ruined, and be left with a deep disgust for sport.

And this machine would have carried on working with regularly interspersed individual doping scandals. But then the Sochi Winter

Olympics came along as the main image-making campaign of the decade for Vladimir Putin and became his pet project. After the poor showing of the Russian team at the previous Winter Olympics in Vancouver in 2010, only victory on home territory would be good enough. So now the FSB became involved in the sporting-medical machine, turning the Olympics into a special operation straight out of a cheap spy novel: a doping cocktail nicknamed 'Dyushes'[17] masked by alcohol; the collection and preservation of the urine of athletes over the course of many months; drilling a hole in the wall of the anti-doping laboratory, hidden behind a cupboard; disguising FSB operatives as plumbers; opening up and switching urine samples; and carrying out other favourite spy tricks. As became clear, everything was done in a very clumsy way – it was a typical Russian cock-up (Rodchenkov's diaries reveal only worries and cursing over the mixed-up test-tubes and samples – you couldn't make it up!) It appears that even the FSB hasn't managed to avoid the overall drop in professionalism and responsibility in government service which has come about as a result of the general corruption and fall in standards in the selection process.

As a result of this poorly organized and well-publicized special operation, the scandal over Russian doping became a serious political defeat, and the negative media reporting around it was on a par with the shooting-down of MH17 (although not, of course, comparable in terms of human tragedy). And this draws the boundaries of the hybrid war and special operations which in Putin's time have taken the place in Russia of diplomacy, sport, mass media, administrative procedures and rules. In other words, the problem is much wider than doping. It is in the whole political system, where power has been usurped by the *Chekists*, who have plunged the state and society into a condition of permanent threat and hybrid warfare. And this is not only internally, but in foreign affairs, too, where all the normal bureaucratic procedures have been replaced by special operations. Procedures for reaching agreement, consulting experts and taking informed decisions; all the usual mechanisms of accountability, openness and audit. The *siloviki* have turned all these complex processes of public policy into a bad spy movie.

In reality, everything surrounding the Sochi Olympics became a special operation, from the lobbying for Sochi during the selection process in the IOC, to the construction of the facilities, thanks to which whole territories were put under a state of emergency, limiting constitutional rights for citizens, such as the right to property and freedom of movement. Another special operation was the long-planned annexation of Crimea, with its multilayered cover-ups and lies. The war in Ukraine is a special operation, too, with the separate episode of shooting down MH17. The war in Syria has been carried out in many ways according to the laws of a special operation, with disinformation about the scale and the aims of the military presence and the covering-up of Russian casualties. A huge special operation involved Russia's meddling in elections and internal political discussions in Western countries, through an ever-expanding system of state propaganda, fake news and trolling on social media, the culmination of which was the Russian interference in the 2016 US presidential elections. And finally, it was the poisoning of the Russian former spy Sergei Skripal and his daughter in Salisbury, UK, in March 2018.

There are three problems with the special operations that have taken the place of Russia's policies. First of all, they're ineffective. The Sochi doping thriller not only saw Russia lose its Olympic medals and the right of the national team to compete in PyeongChang, but it also ruined the country's position in world sport for many years ahead. The annexation of Crimea left Russia not only with a toxic asset on its hands and one for which it is paying with sanctions, but it cannot even get any use out of it: as well as the well-known problems with banks and the provision of electricity (see above, 'A Sovereignty Full of Holes', for the scandal about the turbines built by Siemens, which were taken to Crimea illegally, in contravention of sanctions), there is also the collapse of the tourist industry there and the criminalization of every level of authority on the peninsula. In the same way, the war in Eastern Ukraine has seen the final separation from Russia of a vital part of its former empire, exactly as the late Zbigniew Brzezinski predicted, and the irreversible drift of Ukraine into the bosom of Western institutions (precisely what the Kremlin tried to prevent). What's more, Russia has been left with yet another toxic asset – the pirate republics of Donetsk and Lugansk, which are totally dependent on injections of Russian cash, military equipment and personnel, and on the economy of violence.

Finally, all the Russian special operations to support forces that are against the system in Western countries – from right-wing populist and proto-fascist parties, like the National Front in France and Germany's *Alternative für Deutschland* ('Alternative for Germany'), to the former hope of the Kremlin, the populist Donald Trump – have collapsed. The established parties proved to be more stable than the Kremlin thought, and Trump became a headache for the whole world, including Russia. So the Kremlin has ended up with a huge number of toxic assets on its hands: compromised Olympic medals; Crimea and the Donbass, not recognized by international law; Assad's cannibalistic regime in Syria; radicals, separatists and quasi-fascists in Europe; accusations of staging a chemical weapons attack in Salisbury; and now even the unpredictable, poisonous Trump. These are all the fruits of special operations and hybrid wars in which Russia, as they say, has shot itself in the foot.

Here we have the second problem of the policy of special operations: they are highly toxic. Even in places where Russian interference went unnoticed and was merely symbolic, its policies and representatives are marked: the West is now looking for the Kremlin's traces even in places where they may not exist. A very good example is Russia's interference in the American elections. It appears that it was not so widespread as decisively to affect the outcome (some $50,000 was spent on creating fake accounts on Facebook, which is a mere drop in the ocean when you consider that around $2.5 billion was spent on the election campaign); but the mere fact of interference by an outside power in the holy of holies of American politics, the elections, so enraged the American establishment that a witch hunt has been opened the like of which has not been seen since the days of McCarthyism, and the heads of the Internet giants, from Google to Twitter, have been lining up to take part in hearings in Congress so as to demonstrate their loyalty and uncover the traces of Russian agents. And, to be honest, the influence of the Kremlin's propaganda mouthpiece, the Russia Today (RT) television channel, was not so significant in America as to limit its activity there and, in so doing, place under threat of reprisals Western media in Russia. But the channel certainly deserves to be caught up in the storm that it has done so much to create. The toxicity of Russian influence is so great that the tiniest presence needs to be cleaned up. Any hint of even the most innocent contacts with Russians leads to scandal, and the 'Russian infection' could ultimately destroy Donald Trump, already weakened and embittered as he is.

All Russian sportsmen and women are also feeling this toxicity now, even those who were not named in the McLaren Report and who have nothing to do with the Sochi doping scam. Every Russian athlete is now, a priori, under suspicion; all Russian sportsmen and women are presumed to have taken drugs, and it is up to each one of them to prove their innocence. This is unfair and hurtful, but it's the result of that same radioactive special operation, that *Chekist* polonium, which has infected everyone's clothes. Russian holdings, capital, investments, businessmen, projects, real estate – all of these are now under suspicion, as the list of sanctions published by Washington in February 2018 illustrated. The world is now paranoid about Russian hackers, dopers, trolls or agents of influence. They are searching for Russians under the bed; and we will take with us this stigma, this radioactive background, wherever we go for many years hence, even after Putin is no longer in power.

Typically, the failure of various special operations all occurred simultaneously: in the same months in which 'Russiagate' broke in Washington, the Russian doping scandal happened in WADA and the IOC, as did the judgement on the shooting-down of MH17, which revealed even more evidence about Russia's participation. It may be that Russia's exclusion from the Winter Olympics is just the first alarm bell, and there may yet be the collapse of the whole system of Russian hybrid gains, from Crimea to Trump, from the Donbass to Assad.

And here we have the third fundamental weakness of the special operations: they are irrelevant in the modern world. Yes, it is complicated, mutually dependent and vulnerable; it is a 'risk society' over which it is easy to place the hybrid 'fog of war'. But it is also a society of radical transparency, a world of networks, video recordings and anonymous activists from Wikileaks to Bellingcat, where every step is tracked, every telephone call, every bank transfer; where you can no longer hide your account offshore, or your test-tubes, or your 'BUK' missiles, which, it is assumed, shot down MH17; where the special services are just as vulnerable, transparent and old-fashioned as the state they serve. Our *Chekists* operate as in days gone by: planning, operational development, recruitment, intimidation, disinformation – but in a global society of social networks and citizen control, they can be instantly found out by traces of polonium, urine samples and IP addresses, by tracking phone calls and selfies posted by soldiers on social media. And various observers rigorously point the finger of blame at their patron: the Russian state.

In exactly the same way, because of the interference of the special services, half a century ago, at the end of the 1960s, the Soviet Union lost its place in the developing information revolution. At that time, under Brezhnev, the fatal decision was taken to pass responsibility for the Soviet computing sector from the scientists to the *siloviki*. At that time, Soviet computer technology was at least on a par with the USA, perhaps even ahead: we had progressive programming languages such as 'Algol' and machines such as the BESM-1, which was a worthy competitor. But the *siloviki*, trying to minimize the risk to a strategic industry, turned this into a special operation, involving the theft of technology from the West, the reverse engineering of American examples (principally IBM) and their production in Soviet enterprises. But what had been done successfully with missile technology and nuclear weapons 'borrowed' from the West didn't work with computers, which were significantly more complicated and needed not secret constructors' bureaux but an open code, independent development, testing in production and on the market. The well-known sociologist and also historian of the Soviet computing sector, Manuel Castells, gives a humorous example: because the sizes of transistors and the width of the wires in the microsystems in the USA were given in Imperial measures (i.e., inches), while in the USSR they were metric, the *siloviki* decided to round up the American sizes to a convenient number – as a result of which the stolen chips didn't fit the Soviet connectors! Castells acknowledges that, because of this special operation, which lasted for several decades, the Soviet computer sector was about twenty years behind the USA by the time the USSR collapsed.

Today the special operations of the hybrid war are again throwing us decades back in our relations with the outside world, just as they did at the beginning of the 1980s and at the start of the 1950s. Once again, the world is afraid of Russia and is isolating it, but we can't capitalize on this fear and the consequences of it hurt us, like with our athletes and our sports fans. The lesson to be learnt from everything that's happened is simple and banal: everyone should mind their own business. Athletes should be coached by trainers, and not officers of the special services; relations with neighbouring countries should be worked out by diplomats and business people and not by Russian *spetsnaz* soldiers with no markings on their uniforms, as happened in Crimea; Russia's 'soft power' should be conveyed by artists and tourists, and not hackers, trolls and propagandists. And representatives of the special forces should carry out their own direct tasks, such as catching terrorists, and should not be substituting special operations for all the existing institutions and procedures. But in a country that chose, for the fourth time, to have as its President a *Chekist*, this all remains a utopian dream.

PART IV: THE WAR FOR MEMORY

HYSTERICAL REVISIONISM

Early in the evening on New Year's Eve, Moscow was blanketed by a huge snowstorm. The city ground to a halt in solid traffic jams. There stood buses with steamed-up windows, delivery vans carrying presents for the holiday, family saloons and official limousines, yellow cabs and nippy Smart cars. Also stuck were the sinister-looking black cars with their blue flashing lights flanked by four-by-fours carrying their guards, helpless before the raging elements. Pot-bellied policemen in their sheepskin coats froze at their posts on the crossroads, like memorials to time, while little mounds of snow grew on their winter hats. Pedestrians laden down with bags full of presents made their way along the pavements, trying to avoid the snowdrifts, and the fairy lights of the New Year markets continued to twinkle. The streetlights shone brightly on the Garden Ring Road, on Gogolevsky Boulevard children were throwing snowballs, and along Tverskaya Street someone had even made ski tracks.

Above all this New Year hustle and bustle, unseen by the pedestrians, by the drivers and even by the air defence radar, high up in a cloud of snow, Santa Claus raced along with his frisky reindeer. He was hurrying to Bolshaya Dmitrovka Street, where the grown-up children of the Federation Council, the upper chamber of the Parliament, were considering rewriting history. In his boundless sack, among the cuddly teddy bears and the Barbie dolls, Santa was bringing them a law that changed the 1954 Decree of the Presidium of the USSR Supreme Soviet about the transfer of Crimea from the Russian Federation to the Ukrainian Soviet Socialist Republic – a transfer from one Soviet republic to another. And Santa Claus also had to get to Okhotny Ryad, to visit the children of the State Duma, the lower chamber of the Parliament, who wanted to change the 1989 Decree of the Congress of Peoples' Deputies of the USSR, which condemned the USSR's war in Afghanistan.[1] Coming lower over the city, Santa's sleigh circled and Rudolf's red nose shone out like a landing light through the billowing gusts of the snowstorm ...

179

* * *

The Russian political elite was seized by an epidemic of historical revisionism. Desperate to change something in the gloomy present, suffering humiliation after humiliation (even the annexation of Crimea was to prove a foreign policy defeat, leaving Russia with a problem asset on its hands, placed under painful sanctions by the West and having alienated its closest allies and neighbours), Russia's politicians decided to play around with the past. The past wouldn't be able to answer back and they could rewrite their own history. The proposal was put forward to reconsider everything, from Russia's territorial losses – Crimea in 1954 and Alaska in 1867 (a petition to return Alaska was put by Russian activists on the website of the US White House, but failed to receive the 100,000 signatures it needed in order to be considered) – to colonial wars, such as that begun in Afghanistan in 1979. To justify Russia's claims, the boldest historical analogies were put forward. So as a basis for justifying taking back Crimea, Vladimir Putin quoted the annexation of Texas by America in 1845. If one follows this route, one could use the genocide of the American Indians in order to justify Russia's war in Chechnya. Or cite the Spanish Inquisition to show that chasing after 'foreign agents' in today's Russia is not so cruel. Indeed, even deeper historical arguments are possible: as is known, in their summing-up of the case against the art group Pussy Riot for singing a punk prayer in Moscow's Cathedral of Christ the Saviour, experts in all seriousness quoted the decrees of the Church Councils of the fourth and seventh centuries.

These initiatives by Russian law-makers fit in with the general tendency towards history in our country. History is simply the servant of the authorities, yet another resource at the disposal of the state, along with grain, furs, oil and a submissive population. As they say: 'Russia is a country with an unpredictable past.' Generation after generation, like some primitive magic, people believe in the ritual of rewriting history. So in Stalin's times, schoolchildren blotted out names in their text books and cut out photos of politicians and military leaders who had been declared enemies of the people. And in the late 1940s geographers carefully obliterated German names in what had been East Prussia and was now joined to the USSR, and Tatar place names in Crimea, from which all Tatars had been exiled. So it is now, when politicians naively believe, like children, that if they declare that Nikita Khrushchev (who was responsible for trans-ferring Crimea from Russia to Ukraine in 1954) was an enemy of the people, and if they rewrite the Supreme Soviet Decree, then Crimea will become ours and the international community will recognize this. Why not, then, call Yeltsin an enemy of the people and rewrite the Belovezha Accords of December 1991 about the dissolution of the Soviet Union, in order to re-establish the USSR, for which part of the population and the political elite have such nostalgia?

The fantasy of revisionism knows no bounds. We could look once again at the result of the 1986 World Cup Round of Sixteen match, when the USSR lost 3–4 in extra time to Belgium – I still feel in my heart the pain that this defeat brought. Why don't we also look again at the results of the Russo-Japanese War of 1904–5? Or the Crimean War of 1853–6? We could also reassess the 1572 St Bartholomew's Day massacre; and call an international tribunal in which Britain could be charged with putting down the Indian Rebellion of 1857 and the Boxer Rebellion of 1899–1901 in China. The wind of history blows through the heads of the revisionists like the crazy December snowstorm.

* * *

... After lunch on 31 December, the Federation Council, working at a great pace, passed the laws on changing the 1954 Decree on the transfer of Crimea to Ukraine, the 1989 Decree criticizing the invasion of Afghanistan, and the 1867 Agreement on the sale of Alaska. Warmed up by their very effective work and talking excitedly, the senators pulled on their coats and got out their cigarettes as they hurried to the exits and their cars, which should whisk them home to their heavily laden celebratory tables. But as they came out onto Bolshaya Dmitrovka Street, they felt that something in the air had changed. And on the ground, too – there were no cars waiting for them, no bodyguards, no colourful advertisements shining; on the cold, snow-laden street among the two-metre high snowdrifts stood gloomy, unlit houses with strange sloping roofs. The snowstorm had stopped, the frost had deepened, and the moon shone out from under the low dark clouds. In the distance they heard the sound of horses' hooves and wheezing, and further down the road they saw a patrol on horseback: horsemen in shaggy caps on squat horses were racing along Bolshaya Dmitrovka, sitting up in their saddles with long bows and arrows ...

It happened that after visiting Moscow, Santa Claus flew further to the East, to Kazan and Astrakhan, to Kzyl-Orda and Mongolia, to the source of the Onon River, where some other grown-up children, descendants of another great state of the steppe, had asked him to reassess the results of their own geopolitical catastrophe – the collapse of the Mongol Empire of the great Genghis Khan.

With whoops and laughter, the horsemen disappeared in a whirlwind of snow, much to the amazement of the stunned legislators. In their light cashmere overcoats and Italian shoes, and with their silent iPhones in their hands, the senators stood dumbfounded in the frost. Above their heads the twinkling stars of the boundless Eurasian night shone down with indifference.

THE HOLIDAY OF 5 MARCH

Every year at the beginning of March, Russia experiences a traditional folk amusement, as crazy as it is destructive: the burning of dry grass. Never mind the warnings of the authorities or the appeals of the ecologists, the grass-burning season is open. The coastal region is ablaze, soon the South of Russia will start to burn, then the flames will spread towards the Central Region, destroying tens of thousands of hectares of meadows and forests, whole villages and estates, even taking people's lives.

Also at the start of March, we give ourselves over to another national amusement, just as pointless and merciless: discussions about the role of Stalin in Russian history. What's more, the further we get away from the day of his death (5 March 1953) the louder grow the arguments, with explosions of emotion and people foaming at the mouth. Rather like the burning of the grass, arguments about Stalin are yet another variation of our peculiar Russian masochism, when people take pride in humiliation: it would be difficult to find a nation on this earth more ready to dance on the ashes of their own homeland.

This argument is absurd, endless and completely useless. It's absurd because discussing the role of Stalin is rather like arguing over whether it is worth washing one's hands before eating or whether you should steal the silver spoons when you're at someone's house. There are things one does not talk about in polite society, ethics that are axiomatic; this is not a question of morals, but of hygiene. The fact that we have not experienced de-Stalinization in the way in which Germany has gone through de-Nazification, and that we regularly return to the question of how we should relate to the figure of Stalin, merely bears witness to the archaic, pre-rational and mystical condition of our national consciousness.

The Russian philosopher, Pyotr Chaadaev, spoke about this in his 'Philosophical Letters' of the 1830s, asserting: 'We stand, as it were, outside of time, the universal education of mankind has not touched us.'[2] According to Chaadaev, Russia has no history, no 'wonderful memories' like other nations. Russia lives only in the present, its culture is imported and imitative, which is why there is no point of balance in the country. In Russia, Chaadaev writes, what rules is 'the pointlessness of life, without experience and vision'. And that is precisely why the arguments about Stalin are endless: they take place in a space where there is no historical memory, indeed, with no historical reflexion, just the absurd endlessness of total amnesia.

Finally, arguments about Stalin are absolutely useless, because they are based on a void. Stalin is a simulacrum, a sign without reference, the smoke of a long-extinguished pipe, empty boots standing on a pedestal. And all the different political forces pour their contents into this void: those who support the state talk about Stalin's modernization (economists have long ago exposed this myth for what it is, showing that Stalin's economics produced even worse results than would have been the case under the tsar, and much worse than the Japanese in the same period); and they talk also about the Great Victory of 1945 (another myth, this was achieved by the humongous human sacrifice of the Soviet people in order to cover up Stalin's strategic blunders). The Eurasians talk about Russia's 'special path', which Stalin embodied in the twentieth century. Liberals speak of the Russians' 'Stockholm Syndrome' (when hostages begin to identify their interests with the terrorists who are holding them captive). Each group concentrates on its own interests – but they use Stalin as the final argument. And both supporters and opponents end up using the same words, the very same appeal to 1937, the year that was the peak of Stalin's repressions. 'Are you an entrepreneur? In 1937 you would have been shot for that', say one group. 'You're stealing from the budget? They shot people for that in '37', retorts another. This discussion is not about Russia's past, it's about today's Russia; but the only arguments and language we have are '1937' and mass executions. The country thinks of itself in past categories: we are unable to tear ourselves away from the discourse of Stalinism – it remains our grammar, the language we use to describe everything. A country that is endlessly going round in circles judging Stalin has no future.

Way back in 1984, on the eve of *perestroika*, the film *Repentance* hit our cinema screens from the Georgian film director Tengiz Abuladze. Naive and honest, like all films of that period, the subject revolved around a single metaphor: the recently buried corpse of a dictator, bearing the characteristics of both Joseph Stalin and his powerful security minister Lavrentiy Beria, was dug up from its grave every night and taken to the home of his son. This is exactly what is happening to us now: for sixty-five years we have been digging up the corpse and dancing around it, with ritual curtsies, curses and declarations of love.

We ought to bury this corpse, drive a wooden stake through its heart, raise monuments to his victims over the whole of Russia, and declare 5 March as a national holiday, the Day of National Salvation. How many lives were spared because Stalin died? How many people were able to return from the camps? In mid-March 1953 the antisemitic 'Doctors' Plot' was due to start (it is rumoured that Stalin had already prepared a list of Jews who were to be sent to camps in the Far East). There was bound to be a new wave of repressions, a new twist in the Cold War, and the paranoia of the dictator who was rapidly losing his judgement could have resulted in nuclear catastrophe. What a joy it is for mankind that Stalin didn't live to see the thermo-nuclear bomb! And if a national idea is possible for the Russia of the future, then – albeit with a delay of seventy years – this should be de-Stalinization, just as de-Nazification became the idea of post-Hitler Germany.

THE OBLOMOV AND THE
STOLTZ OF SOVIET POWER[3]

Nothing stirs up passion in Russia more than the battle for our own past. Taking down and replacing memorials, renaming streets and towns, retouching photographs and wiping out names from history books: these are all part of the favourite national game. Here's a current example. In Moscow, on the famous House No. 26 on Kutuzovsky Prospekt, they have reinstated the memorial plaque to the General Secretary of the Central Committee of the Communist Party of the Soviet Union, Leonid Brezhnev, who was the leader of the Soviet Union from 1964 until his death in 1982. The plaque was up on the wall for ten years after the leader's death, but was taken down during the anti-Soviet 1990s, and for a long time all that remained was a dark patch and four holes, before the building was refurbished. Now it has been decided to smooth over this historical injustice.

At about the same time as this became known, we learnt that a group of left-wing activists had put forward a proposal to strip Mikhail Gorbachev of the Order of Andrei Pervozvanny, which he had been awarded by Prime Minister Dmitry Medvedev in honour of his eightieth birthday. Social media exploded with the usual abuse directed at Gorbachev, who 'sold out the country to the Americans'. Sociology confirms that the people have fond memories of Brezhnev, but they don't like Gorbachev. According to a poll conducted by the Levada Centre, Russians named Leonid Brezhnev as the best leader of Russia in the twentieth century (56 per cent replied positively, 28 per cent negatively). At the other end of the scale, Gorbachev came out top: 20 per cent considered him positively, 66 per cent negatively. It should be remembered, too, that when Gorbachev stood in the Russian presidential elections in 1996 he received only a humiliating 0.5 per cent of votes.

The reasons why the people love Brezhnev are clear. He falls into that archetype of the kindly old uncle, who lets you get away with mischief and gives you sweets. Brezhnev was the very embodiment of the Russia dream of *khalyava*:[4] living stress-free, changing nothing and not rocking the boat. That was how the country lived: we squandered the interest from the imperial inheritance and took out credit on the next generation (indeed, so generously, that to this day we are paying for the illusory well-being of the Brezhnev years), tearing off with a certain melancholy the pages of the calendar: Miners' Day, Militia Day, Day of the Paris Commune.[5]

Brezhnev's popularity in folklore, and even a certain sympathy brought out by jokes about his weaknesses, forgetfulness or slips of the tongue (for example, there is a joke that he once mistook Margaret Thatcher for Indira Gandhi because it said so in his speaking notes), bears witness to the deep resonance he had with the Russian folk element, with the inescapable entropy of the Russian character. Gorbachev, on the other hand, was very untypical for Russia. It is no surprise that Margaret Thatcher immediately liked him. He didn't drink, he was charming and loquacious (in Russia, people who speak well automatically make people suspect them of being insincere); and the main thing was that he was unusually alive, in contrast to the iron faces that we were used to seeing in the presidia and on the front pages of the newspapers. Gorbachev smashed the stereotypes and had an inexplicable – and for Russia a totally unusual – desire for change. He could simply have sat tight in his chair, perhaps remaining General Secretary to this very day, receiving delegations and awarding himself medals; but for some reason he felt the need to move this chair, and with it the whole power structure. Perhaps it was because he understood that this throne and the whole palace of Soviet power looked like a ridiculous anachronism in a world that was getting faster and more complex, where change was going to be the only way to survive.

In Ivan Goncharov's classic novel *Oblomov* (1859), there are two central characters: the dreamy and inactive landowner, Ilya Ilych Oblomov, and his friend, a German on his father's side, the practical, strong-willed and active Andrei Stoltz. Brezhnev and Gorbachev: here we have Oblomov and Stoltz, two faces of Russian power, the immovable-patriarchal, and the reform-minded, Peter-the-Great-like, clean-shaven, foreign face. Anthropologists confirm that there are two types of nations: those that adapt to their surroundings and those that change them. The first group includes most of the Asiatic countries and, clearly, Russia. The second type are cultures of the West – Faustian, predominantly Protestant, with a thirst for action and change. Brezhnev responded to the traditionalist aspirations of the population: let's just leave everything as it was. Gorbachev, like

187

many Russian modernizers, represented the second group, which was why he wasn't accepted by the people. They don't love Gorbachev because he was different, because he gave us freedom. But we hadn't known for such a long time what to do with it, and, as a result, we gave it back to the state.

Once again today we are living in Brezhnev's kingdom of simulation and self-deception, falling into insanity, allowing the years to slip by, years that have already turned into decades, calling up the ghosts of the Stalinist and late-Soviet eras. Putin the reformer, Putin the German, Putin like Stoltz, who presented himself not as a tsar but as a manager ('providing services to the people', as he described his role in the 2002 census): all this came to an end in 2003 when he arrested Khodorkovsky. A typical Russian timelessness settled over the country, with the round Botox face of the state above it, which reflects not even Oblomov's absent-mindedness, but the indifference of a Chinese Bogd Khan, with a desire to change nothing. As the political scientist, Stanislav Belkovsky, recognized: 'Putin is the ruler of inertia. You can never demand that such a person should move history onwards.' Under Putin, just like under Brezhnev, the country is simply standing still, while history moves on. How such a situation ends we know only too well.

Brezhnev probably deserves his plaque on the wall. A whole generation grew up under him, and you can't wipe out that memory. But Gorbachev also deserves a memorial, as a man who decided to make changes. He was the one who first threw open the windows in that great musty henhouse known as the Soviet Union. In the cold light of day, it turned out that the henhouse was built crookedly and awkwardly, and in the ensuing panic it collapsed. The fact that it fell apart was not Gorbachev's fault; it was the fault of those who planned and built the henhouse in the first place. But Gorbachev's merit is that this miserable project, which was not fit for purpose, was closed down, and collapsed into a multitude of national stories with the minimum of victims (if, for example, you compare it to the collapse of Yugoslavia), without major wars, uprisings, starvation or nuclear incidents.

Even more important still is that Gorbachev remained a democrat to the end. He didn't go down the route of authoritarian changes and didn't stage a Soviet Tiananmen (although a few individual cases of breaking up protest meetings in Vilnius in January 1991 and before that in Alma-Ata in December 1986 and in Tbilisi in April 1989 occurred during his rule). Tanks were brought onto the streets not by Gorbachev, but against him, in August 1991, but they turned out to be as fake and powerless as the dying system that had sent them. Gorbachev has passed into history not as a reformist dictator such as Pinochet or Park Chung-hee, but as a reform-minded idealist. His attempt to preserve the system, by building 'socialism with a human face' in the spirit of the Prague Spring of 1968, failed. But paradoxically, that failure cleared the way for the new institutions that followed and in which we live now; it allowed Russia to get in the last carriage on the train leaving for the twenty-first century. Without Gorbachev, there would have been no Yeltsin, no Putin, no post-Communist Russia. At some point, Russia will realize this and put up a monument to Gorbachev, and name streets, schools and airports after him. But that's not going to happen any time soon. For now, the majority of my fellow citizens prefer to live with the fairytales of kindly old uncle Brezhnev, under whose bushy eyebrows they slept so sweetly.

A BEAR OF A MAN

He was an awkward fellow. He was too big, too bulky, even the sweep of his arms was too wide. And he remains awkward, even in death: awkward for the current leadership (it's difficult to separate yourself from someone who personally put you in power), and awkward for the majority of the population, for whom (along with Gorbachev) he is seen as equally responsible for the collapse of the greatest country in the world, the mythical USSR. Boris Yeltsin died more than ten years ago, but he remains a figure who worries us, annoys us and bursts out of the frame. It's as if he's an illustration to the words of Dmitry in Fyodor Dostoevsky's *The Brothers Karamazov*: 'Yes, man is broad, too broad indeed. I'd have him narrower.'[6]

Yeltsin always had the capacity to surprise us, such as when he criticized Gorbachev at the Communist Party Central Committee Plenum in October 1987; or when he clambered up onto a tank outside the White House during the coup in August 1991; or when, with a weak heart, he danced on stage at a rock concert before the uncompromising presidential elections in 1996. He had a wide Russian nature the size of his personality, and to match it he had the broad scope of his gestures, the energy of a ram; he was sincere in his delusion – and just as sincere in his very Russian ability to forgive and to ask forgiveness, as he did in his final address to the nation on 31 December 1999, when he announced he was stepping down.

We shall probably never agree about Yeltsin, just as sensible Chinese people officially declare themselves about Mao: 70 percent right, 30 percent wrong. We can't give such a balanced assessment; we can't reach a consensus for the sake of calm in society and universal harmony. We don't know the proportions and the half-tones: Russia is a country with a binary, black-and-white way of thinking. In our social and political structures this binary nature inevitably leads to polarization and clashes, to revolution and explosions. That's why today we are living in a transformer box, in a humming electric field, where all ideas and historical personalities that come within the focus

190

of public discussion lead to instant polarization. We can't agree about Crimea, or about Ukraine, or about Lenin, or about Stalin, or about gays, or about migrants. Our arguments instantly divide society, splitting it into two irreconcilable camps; they cause splits in families and among friends and colleagues. 'The Yeltsin Test' is just such a marker of irreconcilability, a symptom of social schism.

A symbol of this eternal Russian binary nature is the memorial to Nikita Khrushchev in the Novodevichy Cemetery in Moscow. The work of the sculptor, Ernst Neizvestny, it has black tiles clashing with white tiles. This is exactly how we look at Yeltsin: black and white, no room for grey. For some, he is Judas and an agent of American imperialism; for others, the grave-digger of a rotten state that was ridiculed by the world. For some, like Vladimir Putin, the collapse of the USSR was 'the greatest geopolitical catastrophe of the twentieth century'; for others, it was the breakthrough to freedom. There is no middle view.

No one loves grave-diggers, but ultimately we can't avoid them. By the end of the 1980s an explosion was building up in the Soviet Union; the atmosphere was stifling and fraught with thunderstorms. The thunder roared and the turbulent flow of the nineties cleaned out the Soviet stables and threw us forward onto the banks of the twenty-first century. Yeltsin was that explosion of a man who broke the bounds of the possible. It is no coincidence that one of the nicknames that stuck with him from the time he was First Secretary of the Reginal Committee of the Communist Party in Sverdlovsk (as Yekaterinburg was then called) was 'the Bulldozer'. In reality, he reminded one more of a bear – not the caricature of the Russian bear, but a real beast from the Taiga, clever, threatening, but ultimately the eternally good hero of Russian folktales. There is an almost certainly apocryphal story about how, one summer, the fifteen-year-old Yeltsin became lost in the Taiga with a pair of younger schoolboys, how they wandered around lost for a month, living on berries and roots, before eventually Yeltsin brought them out to their people. He was a powerful beast with a natural instinct for survival, a true 'political animal', *zoon politikon*, in Aristotle's terms, a mythical totem of the Russian forests.

And even if the victory achieved by Yeltsin over the dying USSR in August 1991 turned out to be only temporary, it did at least give us a breathing space for almost two decades, when we could live with the air of freedom in our lungs. The atmosphere in Russia today is once more stuffy and fraught with thunder, like in the 1980s, but there's no new Yeltsin visible on the horizon ready to burst out like a ram and break this rotting system; there are no demonstrations of almost a million people on the streets of Moscow, as there were in 1990–1, no nationalist ferment on the edges of the empire. But even if Yeltsin's energy for change is largely forgotten, we can always remember two of his characteristics which can forgive much: his ability to ask for our pardon, and his ability to leave on time. These are, sadly, lacking among the present leadership.

MAIDAN IN MOSCOW

Unmentioned in official propaganda and half-forgotten by the people, yet another anniversary passed of the failed coup against Mikhail Gorbachev, which was carried out by the State Committee for the State of Emergency (GKChP in Russian, made up of certain members of the Soviet government) in August 1991. The only ones to remember it were the liberal media and a couple of dozen of the old democrats, who laid flowers at the monument to the three young men who died under an armoured personnel carrier on the Garden Ring Road in Moscow on the night of 20–21 August 1991. In fact, this event could have become the main holiday for modern Russia – the day of its founding and independence, our Fourth of July or Bastille Day, but the total oblivion surrounding it these days is no less significant.

According to the Constitution of the Russian Federation (Chapter 1, Article 3): 'The bearer of sovereignty and the sole source of power in the Russian Federation shall be its multinational people.' What happened in August 1991 was an act of people's sovereignty, when tens of thousands of people stood up to the tanks of the coup plotters, took the weakened power into their own hands and handed it to the nascent Russian state. The principal actors here were not those playing at being plotters in the GKChP, who were simply frightened men, nor was it Gorbachev or even Yeltsin. The most important participants were the people, who constituted the real power and legitimized its passing from Gorbachev to Yeltsin. It was the classic scenario of a national-liberation and bourgeois-democratic revolution.

The events of August 1991 and the collapse of the USSR became the basis for a new Russian statehood, and it is exactly from there that the current Russian elite have their beginnings, having received power and property in the post-Soviet collapse. If those August events hadn't taken place, Putin would now be a retired KGB colonel, living in his three-roomed flat with his dacha and 'Volga' car, and today's oligarchs would have lived out their time in state scientific research institutes, or would have spent long periods in prison for economic crimes. It's no coincidence that today they all stubbornly criticize the collapse of the USSR and the 1990s, the decade of changes, yet they all got everything thanks to that period, and they are all children of August 1991, products of the semi-collapse of empire.

That August I was in Moscow and spent three days and two nights on the barricades around the White House, the seat of the Russian Supreme Soviet (Parliament), which had become the centre of resistance to the coup. There are two feelings that remain with me from those incredible days. The first is the feeling of the implausibility of all that was going on; it was as if I was taking part in a huge dramatization. I remember feeling this from the first moments of the coup, when I heard the strains of *Swan Lake* playing on every TV channel (this classic performance by the Bolshoi Ballet was always broadcast at moments of crisis, instead of normal programming), and when I saw the tanks on Manezh Square near the Kremlin to where I hurried from home. The tanks stood around uncertainly, awaiting further orders, and here and there soldiers started to crawl out of the hatches, looking to bum a cigarette off passers-by. Already at that stage I began to feel that this wasn't for real. On the one hand, there was alarm, tanks, the Manezh, the silent Kremlin towers: in a word, a Soviet Tiananmen. On the other, the tankmen were curious to know what was going on, there was a holiday crowd, children climbing on the tanks: a typical family day out, a real carnival atmosphere.

Then there was the absurd press conference by the GKChP, where some of their leaders were clearly drunk –the Vice-President of the USSR, Gennady Yanayev, sat there with his hands shaking – and the *Vremya* news programme, where they slipped in a report about what world leaders were saying about the coup and the total confusion in the army and militia. The Soviet Union was falling apart like the cardboard decoration at the end of Vladimir Nabokov's novel, *Invitation to a Beheading*; like Tsarist Russia did in October 1917, which was described so exactly by the philosopher, Vasily Rozanov, in his diary, *The Apocalypse of Our Time*:

> Russia faded out in two days. At the most, in three. It would have been impossible to close down even *Novoye Vremya* as quickly as they closed down Russia. It was amazing how it all fell apart at once, into small particles, into little pieces. ... There was no longer an empire, no longer a church, army, or working class. And what remained? Strangely, nothing at all.[7]

It was made of cardboard, it was false; it didn't even frighten anyone any more – neither the Lithuanians nor the Americans. Standing on its sanctimonious morality and its cheap vodka, the Soviet Union was dying, just as it deserved, looking ridiculous and funny, in the end not even capable of carrying out a military coup. It was the end of the world as described by T S Eliot: 'Not with a bang but a whimper', and it left a sense of absurdity.

But there was another, even stronger feeling across those three days. It was a feeling of happiness, which I experienced in the human chains around the White House, the joy of freedom and recognition. Never again in my life would I come across so many people I knew all in one place: people I'd been at school and at university with; friends and relatives; neighbours and work colleagues; and not only from Moscow, either. It was an evening for meeting people, a gathering place for the Soviet middle class; for people who had grasped the idea of *perestroika* and who didn't want at the first shout to go back to *Sovok*,[8] as they contemptuously called the Soviet Union, back to ill-fitting Soviet suits and communal flats. We still didn't know at that point what we stood for or who we were with, but we had tasted freedom and we didn't want a return to the past.

Towards the end of the second night outside the White House, the carnival atmosphere disappeared and was replaced by a sense of alarm. Rumours began to spread that planes had landed at Kubinka military airfield, just outside Moscow, carrying the Pskov Airborne Division, and that they were on their way into Moscow to break up the defence of the White House. There was a call for volunteers to form a human shield across the Novy Arbat Bridge on the further approaches to the White House, and thirty men stepped forward. We stood on the bridge alongside the Ukraine Hotel. It was a chilly, starry night; a light mist rose from the river. We stood tensely looking down the empty Kutuzovsky Prospekt, expecting that any moment we would see the lights of the military trucks carrying the paratroopers. And it was at that moment on the bridge, in the area where I was born and where I grew up, just a hundred metres from my primary school, shivering from the damp or from something else, linked elbow to elbow with my fellows in the chain, that I felt myself to be a citizen of this country. The memory of the place and the feeling of the small Motherland came together with the sensation of history and human solidarity. In the years which have passed since I have never again had this feeling. People who stood on the Maidan, Independence Square, in Kiev in 2004 and 2014 have also spoken about this sensation. August 1991 was truly Russia's Maidan, where

Russian civil society was born, and which gave legitimacy to the authorities at that time.

Morning came. The paratroopers had been stopped by order on the outskirts of Moscow. The mist disappeared, the GKChP members were arrested. On Lubyanka Square, in front of the KGB Headquarters, they pulled down 'Iron Felix' – the statue of the founder of the Soviet repressive organizations, Felix Dzerzhinsky. The empty Soviet cartons were carried away by the wind and a real, tough, but free life began. More than a quarter of a century on, it all seems like some ancient fable. The spring of history, pressed down as far as it could be in those days, has sprung back and returned to its normal position. Today it seems that, as a result, it wasn't Yeltsin who triumphed, but the GKChP: all the democratic gains that were made in the country have been turned back. In effect, a one-party system has been reinstated with the lifelong rule of one man. The economy and society are being militarized, and the country is run by *Chekists*. All that remains for history to come full circle is to return the statue of Dzerzhinsky – which has been well preserved in the 'Muzeon' Moscow sculpture park – to its plinth on Lubyanka Square. Little has remained of that heady sense of freedom from those August days, apart from an internal freedom which it is difficult to take away. But even so, the sense of the absurd and of falsehood has only strengthened.

Falseness is the main thing produced by the actions of the authorities in August 1991 and today. Today's Russian state is, in essence, as empty and illusory as its hopeless predecessors in the GKChP, who couldn't even organize a *coup d'état*. Incapable of carrying out reforms, or even mass repression, all they can do is carry out media shows, like making nuclear threats to the West, simulacra, such as the pirate 'republics' of Donetsk and Lugansk, and lies, which they throw out onto social networks in the West.

From the point of view of the big picture of history, what is going on today is simply a continuation of August 1991, yet another stage in the long process of the end of empire, which is happening in a nonlinear fashion, through fevers, collapses, amputations and remissions. In the past, it happened by breaking up demonstrations in Alma-Ata in 1986, in Tbilisi in 1989, Vilnius and Riga in 1991 and by a peaceful rally around the White House in August 1991. Today, it is in South Ossetia, a part of Georgia that has been occupied by Russia, and Crimea, which has been annexed by Russia: the empire is dying, painfully and awkwardly. Eventually, a Russian national state should emerge from these transformations, which, like France and

Britain, has lived through its post-imperial trauma and is able to live at peace with its neighbours and remember its own roots, including how it was born on the barricades around the White House in August 1991.

A HOLIDAY WITHOUT TEARS

One of my earliest childhood memories is linked to 9 May: I'm drawing tiny leaves on a laurel branch. It was a card for my grandfather in honour of Victory Day. These were Brezhnev's times, when they started to set in bronze the cult of Victory Day, covering it with decorations, orders and laurel wreaths, hence the branch in my picture. I probably also drew the sun, a red star, and maybe a rather clumsy dove of peace – but I never drew a tank.

I remember marking Victory Day during my student life, the time of *perestroika*. After 1 May, the city was empty and clean, the lilac was in bloom, the trolleybuses seemed to smile and my feet carried me of their own accord to the Bolshoi Theatre, where they hadn't yet dug up the old square in front of the building and they were playing wartime music. You could wander among the people gathered there in their parade uniforms, some celebrating, some sad, who each year would get together in ever-diminishing groups beside a board bearing the name of their military unit. It was indeed the 'holiday with tears in their eyes', as Victory Day was painfully and accurately described in a well-known Soviet song; we all understood that this was nature passing on its way and we tried hard to preserve in our memory this place and this mood, like distant music, like the fading scent of the lilac.

Over the years the holiday grew bigger, yet there were fewer veterans and fewer tears; until there came a moment, some ten years ago, when I realized that 9 May had ceased to exist for me as a national holiday and had become simply a time for private reflection, of a tatty photograph of a young grandpa in his uniform as a Signals Major, and of his grave in the Khimki Cemetery, just outside Moscow; of a few nostalgic wartime songs by Mark Bernes and Klavdiya Shulzhenko[9] or the film *Come and See*, directed by Elem Klimov, about the shooting up of a Belarusian village by the fascists. Probably the point that caused my personal split with the holiday was the St George ribbon (the orange and black ribbon handed out to people on the streets on the eve of 9 May, in the colours of the medal ribbon of the Order of the St George Cross, a Russian military award); or, more accurately, it's not the ribbon itself but the cult surrounding it, poured out in a flood of banality and jingoism. So today I want to ask the question that the film director Michael Moore asked once of George Bush Jr: 'Dude, where's my country?' And I want to know: 'Where's my Victory?'

For Russia, 9 May is the fulcrum of the twentieth century. At one edge there was the War of 1914 and the year of revolutions, 1917, and at the other, 1991, the year the USSR collapsed. But the culmination of Russia's terrifying twentieth century, the huge sacrifice, the peak of the Soviet Union's might, from where it began its inexorable decline, was 1945. Victory Day is incontestably the single true memorial day in our modern calendar, as opposed to the newly invented Day of National Unity on 4 November, or Russia Day on 12 June. It is a day that was not invented by the propagandists, but came through suffering, and was paid for in blood. That is why the 9 May celebration is the most exact indicator of the age, the mirror that reflects the history of every postwar generation.

Over the course of seventy years, this holiday has changed radically, depending on the times. Stalin was afraid of the Victory, just as he was afraid of those who had served at the front, the victors. He was terrified that they would reveal his criminal cowardliness in June 1941 (after his faint-hearted disappearance for a week at the outbreak of war, when Politburo members Beria and Malenkov turned up at his dacha, Stalin was convinced that they had come to arrest him); his strategic failures; and the unacceptably high cost of victory. It is no coincidence that at the celebratory banquet on 24 May 1945, in a rush of unexpected openness, he turned down the eulogy being paid to him and instead proposed his famous toast, 'to the health of the Russian people', and to their patience, which allowed them to forgive the mistakes and mismanagement by the government and not to overthrow Soviet power. Eight million frontline soldiers, five million *Ostarbeiter* (Soviet people relocated for work in Germany) and almost seventy million people who lived in territory that had been occupied by the Germans were a dangerous and uncontrollable force for Stalin, especially the frontline soldiers, who feared neither the NKVD nor the Gestapo, and on whom the magic of Stalin's power – the magic of fear – had no effect. From 1947, 9 May was no longer a public holiday (they made the 1 January a holiday instead), and a new fierce wave of terror was rolled out across the country, from repeated arrests and deportations of whole peoples to a cultural reaction known as *zhdanovshchina*[10] and a battle against 'cosmopolitanism', which simply covered up a campaign of state-sponsored antisemitism. Many victorious frontline soldiers, partisans and people who had been in German prisoner-of-war camps were simply shipped off to the East without even the chance to catch their breath, sent to camps or deported. Once again, just as after the Polish invasion in 1612 and Napoleon's campaign of 1812, the Russian people had risen up and saved their pathetic leaders from defeat – and yet again, they submissively returned to the yoke of slavery.

During Khrushchev's 'thaw', many of these people returned, and with them a different, more human memory of the war developed. Moreover, Khrushchev himself was not particularly complimentary of the General Staff, starting with Marshal Zhukov. It is in this period that 'the Lieutenants' prose' appeared, by writers who had been at the front, such as Vasil Bykov, Daniil Granin, Grigory Baklanov and Viktor Astafiev; and the most perceptive films were made about the War, like Mikhail Kalatozov's *The Cranes are Flying* and Andrei Tarkovsky's *Ivan's Childhood* (winners, respectively, at the Cannes and Venice Film Festivals). A little later, at the start of the 1970s, the classic Soviet films about the war were made: *The Belorussian Station* and *The Dawns Here Are Quiet*. Along with Yevgeny Yevtushenko's poem, *Babiy Yar*, and everyone's favourite song, *Do the Russians Want War?*, based on the words of the same poet, these books and films created a new canon of understanding of the Great Patriotic War, in which two Soviet generations of the 1960s and the 1980s grew up: full of pride and bitterness, humane and peace-loving. For many decades, the Soviet people were repeating like a spell or a prayer: 'As long as there's no war.'

With the coming to power of Brezhnev, the 9 May holiday underwent yet another transformation. From the time of the twentieth anniversary in 1965, when for the first time since 1945 there was a military parade on Red Square and a reception in the Kremlin Palace, 9 May began to take on the trappings of a semi-official state cult. Once again, the day was declared a holiday. Memorials were unveiled (in 1967 Brezhnev opened the Tomb of the Unknown Soldier beside the Kremlin Wall); veterans found their place in the Party-Soviet system; multi-tome generals' memoirs began to be published (including those of Zhukov, having been brought back from disgrace); and epic films were made: the genre of memory moved from the lyrical to the epic. According to the historian, Nikita Sokolov, the idea to turn around the popular memory of the war and show it not so much as a victory for the people as a victory for the Soviet system, to show the effectiveness of socialism, came from the chief Communist Party ideologue, Mikhail Suslov. The living memory of the Victory was carefully painted in rosy hues, pouring on the balm of speeches and the concrete of monumental sculptures, such as the intimidating memorial complex at Malaya Zemlya near the city of Novorossisk on the Black Sea, where Brezhnev himself fought in 1943. The whole cult of Malaya Zemlya, puffed up in the 1970s and crowned by the General Secretary's book, is a good illustration of the talentless propaganda and the folk cynicism it provoked, such as in the well-known joke of the time: 'Where were you during the war? Did you fight at Malaya Zemlya, or were you just sitting around in the trenches at Stalingrad?'

This dualism of the people's memory and concrete officialdom carried on through the years of *perestroika* and into the 1990s. On the one hand, the time of *glasnost* revealed new facts about the carelessness and lack of talent of the Soviet military leadership. New evidence came to light about pointless sacrifices, and alternative interpretations appeared about the Second World War (such as by the revisionist writer, Viktor Suvorov), which cast doubts on the glittering image of the USSR as an innocent victim of fascism and a defender of peace. On the other hand, the bronze myth grew and strengthened, definitively formed in 1995 by the megalomaniacal and ridiculous Victory Memorial on Poklonnaya Hill in Moscow, for the sake of which the hill itself and the park already there had to be razed, thus destroying a legendary place of memory in the capital.

Then Putin's time began, in which the Victory has been well and truly taken over by the state. In the era of the redesigning of the vertical of power, the Victory has been employed to legitimize the ruling regime. Putin considers himself to be the direct descendant of Stalin's USSR *circa* 1945, which held a thirteen-million-strong army in Europe, redrew the map of the world and decided the fate of countries and peoples. The same myth becomes embedded in the consciousness of the population, which feels the burden of post-Soviet *ressentiment* and experiences the phantom pains of lost empire. The myth about the Victory gives them the opportunity to feel the illusion of greatness, to give themselves a merit to which today's Russia bears no relation. This is where the endless 'T-34' signs come from in honour of the legendary wartime tank, the order of Victory and the slogan in the windows of cars, 'On to Berlin!' These are magical runes, which call up the ghosts of the past and give an illusion of strength.

201

Despite Article 13 of the Constitution of the Russian Federation, which does not allow for any state ideology, the Victory has in reality become just such an ideology, the thought axis of the Putin regime. It is the universal lens that justifies any actions by the state, from repressive laws about 'the falsification of history' and 'insult to the memory', which block out any public discussion on the topic of the Second World War, to the granting of budgetary resources under the excuse of the anniversary. The seventieth anniversary of the Victory became a repressive mechanism for the state, a means of fighting anyone who has different opinions, a way of mobilizing and indoctrinating the population. This holiday has become its own logic of sovereignty in its higher, exclusive appearance: it is done not for the people but for the state; or, to be more accurate, for a solitary individual.

An even more surprising transformation of the holiday is that the Russian aggression in Ukraine is justified in the name of the Victory: the annexation of Crimea, the war in the Donbass, and now the Cold War with the West, right up to nuclear threats – in other words, everything against which the Soviet Union fought in 1945. From a symbol of sorrow and memory, the St George ribbon has become the symbol of a fratricidal war, the sign by which the separatists in the East of Ukraine can be recognized. Propaganda has created in peoples' minds a virtual continuation of the Great Patriotic War in the shape of the war in the Donbass, where the Ukrainians have been given the role of 'the fascists'; crooks like the field commander nicknamed 'Motorola' play the part of the hero-liberators wearing their medals; and the 'taking' of the town of Debaltsevo in the Donetsk Region in April 2015 is compared to military operations of the Second World War. Fighters in Donetsk now carry out their own victory parade. The Victory has changed its sign to the opposite side: now it brings not ploughshares but the sword; the incantation, 'As long as there's no war' no longer applies, and the answer to Yevtushenko's question, 'do the Russians want war?' is now affirmative: yes, they do, with Ukraine, America, the West – and to the finish. Thousands of cars are now driving around Russia with a sickening sticker in their rear windows, where the hammer and sickle is assaulting the swastika and with the slogan: '1941–1945: Let's repeat it.'

But behind all these rituals there is emptiness. The principal virtue of Putin's era is not even the vertical of power, it is not in the repressions or the corruption or the Orthodox renaissance; it is in the imitation of all the institutions, history, memory, power itself. It is in the symbolic order over reality and the individual. And the 9

May holiday has also become a victim of this gigantic falsification. False veterans with fake medals parade the streets – some of them are not war veterans, but veterans of the Communist Party or the NKVD-KGB. The average age of the 'veterans' who were invited to Moscow from all over Russia to celebrate the seventieth anniversary of the Victory was – seventy-three! False posters gaze down from the walls and the billboards, where ignorant designers have illustrated slogans marking Victory Day with pictures from photo collections showing American soldiers, Israeli tanks and even Luftwaffe pilots. On television, they showed coloured-in war films; on the radio, they played songs of the war years being sung under a recording of Russian pop music. The mincing-machine of Putin's postmodern society has ground down 9 May and produced a sad, half-finished product.

Even the main symbol of victory, the St George ribbon, has become a universal trade mark, which they stick on anything that comes to hand, from sandals to underpants, from bottles of vodka to German beer. The St George ribbon has today become something like New Year tinsel, which decorates everything you can think of in December because the soul simply wants a holiday. Now people also want a holiday, but all they get is an empty gesture, the place for memory becomes a place of contempt. This is probably the harshest accusation one can make against the current regime, which produces only simulations – of democracy, of modernization, of empire, and now a simulation of the Victory. We wanted a historical policy and an imperial myth, but we got banality and pop songs, the slogan 'On to Berlin' in the rear window of a Mercedes and 'veterans of the Donbass' on the TV screen.

But here's the paradox: my 9 May hasn't gone away; it's always with me. Behind the noise of the holiday, everything becomes clearer: that the Victory is greater than Stalin, Putin, the Kremlin, the Soviet Union; that this huge existential act of suffering and triumph cannot be privatized, neither by the state, nor by its lying propagandists. It belongs to the people, not the state; it's no wonder that Stalin was so scared of it. We should return the Victory to ourselves as a people's holiday, a secular Easter – a day of spring and freedom, of pride and dignity, a day to remember the victims and despise those who sent them to the slaughter. This is our day, which nobody has the right to take from us, nor spoil, because it takes place not on Red Square but in the hearts of the people.

WALTZ OF THE URALS *CHEKISTS*

The corporate New Year party was in full swing. The 'Soviet champagne' corks were popping, on the tables there were bottles of Georgian 'Saperavi' wine and vintage Armenian brandy, dishes of roast suckling pig and stuffed pike, red caviar in crystal bowls, bunches of grapes hung in baroque fashion over the sides of fruit bowls. From the gramophone came the voice of the legendary 1930s singer Pyotr Leshchenko, and couples swung round the floor in the pre-war dance, the Rio-Rita foxtrot. The Kronos-M creative agency was holding a retro 'New Year 1937' themed party in the club on Tverskaya Street in the centre of Moscow. On the invitation, printed on rough cardboard, there were portraits of Stalin and the Chairman of the Soviet government Mikhail Kalinin, a steam engine with a red star, the Spassky Tower in the Kremlin, and four skaters, each with one of four numbers emblazoned on their chest: 1, 9, 3 and 7.

The dress code matched the occasion: the women, with permed curly hair, were in tight-waisted dresses with puffed sleeves; the men had short haircuts, formal jackets and bell-bottom trousers with turn-ups, or they wore the stylized 1930s military uniform. The young account manager, Gennady, looked particularly dashing as an NKVD major: in navy blue jodhpurs with a maroon stripe, his soldier's shirt with its collar-tabs, and cap with navy blue cap-band, pulled down tightly on his shaven head. With his squeaky Sam Browne belt and his new box calf boots, Gena was the centre of attention. He proposed jokey toasts to 'vigilance' and sang in karaoke the popular song 'The Waltz of the Urals *Chekists*'; when he popped out for a smoke, he opened his cigarette case and offered everyone genuine 'Belomorkanal' *papirosi*, in a packet the design of which hadn't changed since the 1930s.

Throwing a rough army greatcoat over his shoulders, he stood in the porch of the club watching the flow of New Year's Eve revellers going along Tverskaya, lit up by the flashes of the lights from advertisements and traffic lights. Gena's head was spinning from the mix of brandy and champagne he had been drinking and from the unfamiliarly strong *papirosi*, and he wandered out onto the pavement under the large snowflakes. The pedestrians were not at all surprised by the sight of a man in jodhpurs, and hurried on their New Year way. A couple of times, taxis stopped, the drivers threw questioning glances at him and then drove off. Unexpectedly, a retro-automobile, a GAZ M-1, pulled over from the flow of traffic, a famous pre-war 'M-car', with grilles on the sides of the long bonnet. With a cursory gesture, the driver called him over and Gena, driven by curiosity, wandered over to the curb and sat in the back seat.

'Where to?' asked the driver.

'To see Father Christmas', Gena joked, 'in the High North.'

'As you wish,' replied the driver, and with a crunch put the car in gear.

Inside the car there was the sickly smell of cheap petrol, like in the country buses of Gena's childhood, and the young man became carsick. The driver remained silent as the car slowly made its way through the New Year's Eve traffic on Tverskaya, heading down towards Manezh Square, past the Moscow City Council building and the Central Telegraph. Gena closed his eyes and forgot where he was, but opened them when he heard the clanking of gates. The 'M-car' drove through the gates of the huge dark NKVD building on Lubyanka Square. 'What's going on?' he muttered in his half-awake state, but strong hands had already pulled open the door from outside, dragged him out of the car and pushed him into the entrance of the internal courtyard. In front of him, as if in a dream, there flashed past doors, bars, corridors, and featureless grey faces with fish-like eyes. A lieutenant of state security sitting in an office under portraits of Stalin and Dzerzhinsky indifferently wrote down his garbled explanation. On the tear-off calendar, Gena noticed the date: 29 December 1936. They started to search him. When they found his wallet and his documents, the lieutenant let out a whistle and called the captain. For a long time, the two of them examined his Russian passport with the two-headed eagle and the credit cards, the five-thousand-rouble banknote ('Tsarist money', said the captain knowingly), and, coming across the three one-hundred-dollar bills, muttered satisfyingly: 'A spy!' Next followed the degrading process of a strip search, the examination of the foreign labels on his shirt and underwear, and the first – not yet hard – punch in the face, which made Gena feel as if a salty wave had washed over him.

After thirty-five hours of endless interrogation, beaten, with a broken ring finger from having it shut in the door, sobbing, he signed a confession that he was an agent of a White emigrants' organization who had been sent into the USSR for the purpose of espionage and to carry out counterrevolutionary terrorist activity. He was sentenced under Article 58, Section 6, to ten years in a labour camp. And in the middle of January 1937, under a hard frost, he travelled in a cold, barred 'Stolypin' railway car[11] past Veliky Ustyug, the homeland of Father Christmas, through the Kotlass transit camp, and was handed over to the Ukhta-Pechora corrective labour camps in the Northern Urals.

When he arrived, he was put into a logging brigade. Unaccustomed as he was to physical labour, he was unable to fulfil his daily norm, for which he was regularly beaten by the brigade leader and other prisoners. His fashionable boots were taken from him by the criminals and in return he received 'seasonal footwear': foot-cloths and a scrap of a car tyre with a piece of wire to keep it attached to his foot. In the spring he went down with dystrophy and pellagra. He lay for a while in the hospital, and having survived through the summer with the help of vitamins from pine needles and wild onions, Gena returned to the barrack block. He turned into a classic camp 'wick' (as they were known, like in a candle), with an unshaven face, a mad look, with the padding falling out of his jacket – his appearance said, 'just light me now'. The criminals reckoned he had gone mad, so they left him alone. He found it difficult himself to think who he was and who he had been in the past and he simply lived the life of the camp from day to day: from his morning ration of bread with hot water, until his evening skilly, watery soup with soya; his daily bread ration was cut back from eight hundred grams to six hundred, because he didn't fulfil his norm.

Almost a year passed. It was December 1938. In the camp they prepared for the New Year by putting up a banner that read: 'In the USSR labour is a matter of honour, a matter of glory, a matter of valour and heroism.' In honour of the holiday, they turned the dining room into a club, decorating the doors with fir twigs and putting up a poster for a lecture, 'To the Victory of Communism! The USSR in Eighty Years' Time', which was to be delivered by a political officer from Ukhta. On the eve of the holiday, Gena was returning with a group of convicts to the camp through a pathway in the snow that they had cleared by logging; they were dragging through the forest brushwood and kindling for the stove in the barrack block. It was three o'clock in the afternoon, but it was already getting dark and the crimson sunset was burning low; as evening approached, the frost was biting sharper. Even after a year, Gena couldn't get used to the cold, but now to the usual shivering was added weakness and indifference. He looked around and sat down on a large spruce on the edge of the path. The convoy guard was still some way off and before he could run up and strike him with his rifle butt Gena could take a short break.

Gena looked up. Above the tops of the fir trees in the darkening sky shone the colourless, indifferent disc of the moon. He closed his eyes and suddenly he could imagine life under Communism eighty years hence. He saw a huge, well-lit city, spread out like an electric blot, towards which he was slowly descending, as if he were on a parachute. The city came closer and soon filled his whole field of vision. In its arteries there flowed an endless stream of cars, huge coloured billboards twinkled, there were clusters of tall towers with lit windows and, looking closely, he could see crowds of people on the streets and boulevards and strings of lights on the trees. The convoy guard must be close; any second now he would be hit in the stomach, and Gena curled up ever tighter.

'Get up!' He felt a careful hand on his shoulder. Gena remained still.

'Get up, you'll freeze to death!' repeated a woman's voice. Gena opened his eyes and saw two girls bending over him. He was sitting on a frozen bench on Tverskoi Boulevard, under an old lime tree. All around there were trees hung with lights. Gena looked around in amazement. The girls burst out laughing and ran off. All around there was a fairytale light, there were figures of angels and butterflies standing in the snow, Father Christmas and his reindeer, made of strings of lights and being lit up by the flashlights of cameras, as dozens of people were having their photos taken among these models. Gena scooped up a handful of fresh snow and swallowed a few fistfuls. His head was aching, the lights were swimming in front of his eyes, his broken ring finger was throbbing. He got up from the bench and slowly made his way along the boulevard in the direction of the square where the holiday music was playing, the huge numbers 2017 glowed, and it seemed as if Communism had finally arrived.

THE RETURN OF THE GHOSTS

Banknotes sometimes have hidden meanings. If you look at the Russian five-hundred-rouble bill, you'll see on it a picture of the famous Solovetsky Monastery, a prison monastery with a history going back over many centuries, situated on the Solovetsky Islands in the White Sea, in the North of Russia. And if it's an older banknote, issued before 2011, then you will see rising over the churches not cupolas but wooden boards. This indicates that it is not the monastery that is shown, but the Solovetsky Special Designation Prison Camp, one of the most terrifying Soviet labour camps, a predecessor of the GULAG[12] system and, indeed, of the Nazi concentration camps, where the inmates were ordered at the end of the 1920s to cover up the cupolas with wooden boards. These bills are still in circulation, knocking around in our hands, our pockets and our wallets, these symbols of the GULAG that hardly anyone recognizes, like ghosts come to visit us from a different reality, from the black hole of our history and our collective memory.

This image is shown in the book by the literary critic and historian Alexander Etkind, *Warped Mourning: Stories of the Undead in the Land of the Unburied*, translated into Russian from English. A psychologist, literary critic and cultural historian, and the author of such intellectual bestsellers as *Eros of the Impossible: The History of Psychoanalysis in Russia*; *Whip: Sects, Literature and Revolution*; and *Internal Colonization: Russia's Imperial Experience*, Etkind writes in *Warped Mourning* about the practice of collective memory and about the Stalinist repressions in the Soviet and post-Soviet consciousness. He poses what could be the key question for our political history and social psychology: why is the fundamental catastrophe of Stalin's terror, which befell Soviet society in the very heart of its history – for thirty years, from the mid-1920s until the mid-1950s, and accounting for tens of millions of victims – still not comprehended and conceptualized by our society and our politics? Why have we not rid ourselves of this trauma – named the victims, judged the executioners? And, what's more, why are the torturers justified in modern historical and political narratives by the self-appointed 'patriots'? In other words, why is Russian mourning so 'warped'?

Shortly before his death, the poet Joseph Brodsky expressed his surprise in an interview:

> It seemed to me that the greatest product of the Soviet system was that we all – or many of us, at least – considered ourselves to be victims of a terrible catastrophe, and even if this didn't create a brotherhood it did at least produce a feeling of compassion, of pity for each other. And I hoped that through all the changes this feeling of compassion would survive and live on. Because our monstrous experience, our terrifying past, unites people – the intelligentsia, at least. But this didn't happen.[13]

In actual fact, if in postwar Germany the memory of their catastrophe became a point of consensus and the nation united around the slogan, *nie wieder*, 'never again', then in Russia the memory of the repressions divided society into those who remembered and those who chose to forget – or even denied or justified the repressions: 'Those were difficult times'; 'But we won the War'; 'When you cut down trees, splinters fly.'

In Russia there are 'wars of memory' around the key events of our twentieth-century history: the revolution of 1917, the repressions of 1937, the Victory over Germany in 1945 and the collapse of the USSR in 1991; but far from uniting people in grief or pride, each of these dates drives wedges between friends, colleagues and family members. In reality, the Civil War in Russia has not let up for a single day but carries on in our collective memory. At the heart of our national consciousness, a black lacuna has formed, a sucking void, which the majority of people manage to skate around. But then occasionally bones rise to the surface, like on the bank of the Kolpashevo River near the Siberian city of Tomsk, where on 1 May 1979 the River Ob flooded and burst its banks, opening up a mass grave of victims who had been shot in 1937. Thousands of well-preserved corpses were washed out; and the local authorities ordered that they be chopped up by the propellers of the river tugs and washed away.

What is the source, what is the anamnesis of this 'anaesthesia dolorosa', the insensitivity of our nation to the fundamental trauma of the Stalinist terror? Why is it that Germany could acknowledge the catastrophe of Nazism and carry out the difficult task of self-cleansing, while Russia today is further than ever from comprehending

Stalinism? Etkind maintains that there are a few reasons. First, the sheer number of genocides and democides that were caused by Stalinism: from collectivization and the *Holodomor*[14] in Ukraine, to the deportation of whole peoples (the Chechens, the Kalmyks, the Crimean Tatars, and many others); from the Great Terror of 1937–8 to the antisemitic 'struggle with cosmopolitanism' in the last years of Stalin's life, from 1949–53. The Soviet terror struck at the most diverse ethnic, professional and territorial groups.

Second, there is the absurd suicidal nature of the repressions, the total madness and irrationality of turning the terror against the country. Much research has shown that the terror was ineffective economically (labour productivity in the camps was half what it was among free people), and destructive for the state and national security; the war was won against incredible odds *in spite of* the terror, not thanks to it. And here there is one more feeling that interferes with the memory: scepticism that such a thing could ever *really* happen. The historian of the Holocaust, Saul Friedländer, wrote that a deep disbelief – a refusal to believe in the reality of what had happened – was a typical reaction to the Nazi terror.[15] And this is exactly what happens with the victims and the witnesses of the GULAG. What's more, our contemporaries refuse to believe in the reality of Stalin's terror because it is so absurd and unimaginable. 'The human brain is simply not capable of imagining the crimes that were committed', said the writer Varlam Shalamov, who left us the most terrifying accounts of the GULAG in his work, *The Kolyma Tales*.[16]

The main difference, of course, was that in Germany the criminal regime suffered a military defeat, the country underwent occupation and enforced de-Nazification, which continued for decades. Nothing of the sort could have happened in the USSR, where victory seemed to justify the repressions, which began again with renewed vigour in 1946, and where the regime, with a few changes and modifications, has survived up to the present as the philosophy and practice of *chekism*, which is considered to be quite respectable these days. Etkind points out how incomplete was Khrushchev's de-Stalinization programme, because it basically left the ruling elite untouched, making Stalin the scapegoat and removing the question of the criminality of the regime itself. Mourning could never be fully expressed in the USSR and post-Soviet Russia in terms of the structural reasons while there are still people and institutions in power who are the direct descendants of Stalin's repressions.

As a result, Germany and Russia created completely different types of national memory. In Germany, that memory is 'hard' (as it is in

France and more generally in Europe), based on concrete objects: monuments, memorial camps and, more broadly, institutions that give a legal and material guarantee that the crimes of the past will not be repeated. But in Russia it is a 'soft' memory: personal memoirs, films, works of literature, popular and alternative histories. Most of Etkind's book is devoted to this 'soft' memory about the catastrophe of Stalin's terror, which is dispersed throughout Soviet and post-Soviet culture. In living, breathing and the polyphonic score of his book, the voices are intertwined with those of the writers Nadezhda Mandelstam and Yevgenia Ginzburg, Vasily Grossman and Andrei Sinyavsky; the philologists Dmitry Likhachev and Mikhail Bakhtin; the drawings from the camps by the artist Boris Sveshnikov and the 'barrack school' of art, which grew up in the postwar years in the Moscow suburb of Lianozovo. There is a separate chapter devoted to the films of the director Grigory Kozintsev – *Hamlet* (1964) and *King Lear* (1970). This is no coincidence; just as in his tragedies Shakespeare reinterpreted the traumatic experience of the Reformation, so Soviet culture looked to Shakespeare to reflect upon our national catastrophe.

Etkind compares memory to a saline solution: if you don't heat it and stir it, but gradually saturate it, then at some point it will start to crystallize and memory will solidify as monuments, institutions and moral norms. In Russia, memory is constantly being shaken up, so it's in a 'liquid' state and cannot crystallize. As the author points out, 'to continue the analogy of the temperature of the solution, a crucial condition for the crystallization of memory is social consensus; a low level of consensus crushes the crystallization of memorials, but strengthens the fermentation of memory among the minority who remember and reflect'. The inability of contemporary Russia to come to terms with its trauma and to work through the mourning for the victims of the GULAG speaks about the desperately low level of social trust, about the atomized society, the social anomie.

This unceasing fermentation of memory overflows in modern Russia in literary texts, oral legends and in narratives of mourning: in the 'magical realism' of Yury Mamleyev, Vladimir Sorokin, Viktor Pelevin and Vladimir Sharov, which Etkind compares with the magical realism of Latin American prose; in the 'magical historicism' of the Russian political technologists and propagandists and in the pop history of all kinds of re-enactors and of books about time travellers who turn up in different eras in order to change the course of history.

The ghostly visions of Russian writers, filmmakers, critics and even politicians extend the work of mourning into those spaces that defeat more rational ways of understanding the past. In a land where millions remain unburied, the dead return as the undead. They do so in novels, films and other forms of culture, that reflect, shape and possess people's memory.[17]

Back in 1993, the literary critic and, at the time, an adviser to President Yeltsin, Marietta Chudakova, suggested that the writings about the camps by Varlam Shalamov, Alexander Solzhenitsyn and Vasily Grossman will 'carry out the function of a Russian Nuremberg Process'.[18] But this didn't happen. Moreover, the large number of texts and cultural artefacts worked as an overflow valve, and let out the steam of a social discussion. In this sense, we can say that yet again Russia produced first-class culture but poor politics; instead of institutions, memorials or morality, it produced texts, but did not create any guarantees that the terror would not return. Here we have the essence of Russia's 'warped mourning': culturally productive, but politically destructive, producing pathological post-traumatic politics and a divided society.

Unfortunately, the author's narrative ends at the start of 2012, at the very peak of the 'Bolotnaya protests' and the hopes for political change. It would be interesting to continue it to the present and study the Russian politics of Vladimir Putin's third term in office in terms of post-catastrophic consciousness, to try to understand Putinism as a type of 'warped mourning'. In actual fact, this is a mimetic secondary policy, founded on a feeling of loss and resentment, trying to justify itself and resurrect outdated historical forms. It is not a new Stalinism (there are neither the economic nor the psychological resources in modern Russia for such a thing), but it is a type of post-traumatic reaction, which Freud called not nostalgia but melancholy, an unavoidable partner of mourning, which causes memory to turn into imagination. The work of the imagination and of 'magical historicism' in the rhetoric of Putin's regime is unusually strong: this is where lie the origins of the cult of the Victory and the battle with imaginary 'fascism' in Ukraine and in the West, the mimetic Stalinism of the conservative propagandists, the calling up of the ghosts of the past, from Ivan the Terrible to Marshal Zhukov. Herein lie, too, the reasons for the extraordinary resilience and popularity of this post-traumatic resentment among the masses: people begin to compensate for their own fears, humiliation, loss and lacunae in their memory with the melancholic worry about 'loss of empire', and they replace the memory of the repressions with the illusion of geopolitical greatness. In this sense, Putin's regime, with its unprecedented popular support, is the consequence of unprocessed mourning.

In his conclusion, Etkind quotes Freud: writing after the First World War, he said that if suffering is not remembered, then it will be repeated. 'If we do not cry for the dead, like ghosts they will continue to haunt the living. If we do not acknowledge our loss, it threatens to return in strange forms; this particular combination of the old and the strange is particularly eerie.'[19] Looking at the post-traumatic landscape of modern Russian politics and culture, we observe exactly that appearance of the eerie, 'post-Soviet haunting' – a parade of ghosts, from children in Tyumen in Siberia, wearing the uniforms of the NKVD and standing guard at the new monument to the founder of the Soviet machine of repression, Felix Dzerzhinsky; to the veterans of the *Cheka* carrying out 'lessons of courage' in schools. The neo-Stalinists and the 'historical revisionists' create pirate republics in Eastern Ukraine, where they hold trials and shoot deserters and looters, based on Stalin's actual orders from the time of the Great Patriotic War. The ghost of Stalin appears in films, on posters, tee-shirts, the covers of school exercise books and iPhone covers; columns of Stalinists, like zombies, plod to the grave of their idol on 5 March, the anniversary of his death. You can dismiss this as being mere confusion and delusion; but the bite of a zombie can be fatal.

If there is some way out of this eternal return of the dead, then it is in that very 'crystallization of memory', making it concrete in the form of monuments, state decisions and constitutional verdicts. The cancerous tumour of Stalinism, with all its metastases, must be cut out from all the organs of state control; the crimes of the past should be reflected in our history books, in declarations by our political leaders, decisions of the courts, national memorials and labour camp museums. The programme of de-Stalinization and the perpetuation of the memory of the GULAG are contenders for the role of that very national idea that the authorities are constantly going on about.

Without this, our dead will remain unburied, our catastrophe go unnoticed and the Solovetsky camp will slip past unrecognized on the creased five-hundred-rouble notes gradually going out of circulation.

213

TYRANTS DESTROYED

On a frosty day in Moscow, 26 January 2018, two events took place that should never have happened, but did, nonetheless. In one of the city's registry offices, an official legalized a marriage between two men, Yevgeny Voitsekhovsky and Pavel Stotsko. They had married in Copenhagen, where same-sex marriage is allowed, and now the official had put a stamp in their passports to say they were married. On the same day, in the Pioneer cinema in Moscow, in front of a full house, they put on the Russian premiere of the British comedy film, *The Death of Stalin*, despite the fact that the Ministry of Culture had revoked the screening licence. And even though these two events were not connected, for a split second it seemed as if the system had crashed and treacherous cracks had appeared in it.

Sitting in the packed hall of the Pioneer, I realized that cinema really is art for the masses, and no downloads or DVDs can compare with watching a film with a live audience. There was laughter in the hall from the very first scene, in which the pianist Maria Yudina (played by Olga Kurilenko) plays Mozart's twenty-third piano concerto, accompanied by an orchestra. In the film, the audience have already started to leave when Stalin demands a recording of the concert – and it transpires that they haven't made one. The terrified sound director chases the audience back to their seats to try to ensure that the music and the applause sound exactly the same as in the original concert. Even given the absurdity of the situation, who can vouch for such an event not happening in those times, when heads would roll for a misplaced comma in a text or the wrong note in a music score? And when the conductor is knocked out after banging his head on a fire bucket and another conductor is sent for (looking for all the world like Gennady Rozhdestvensky), the second conductor, hearing the nighttime knock at the door, resignedly gets up, bids farewell to his wife, in passing, instructing her to disown him during interrogation, and makes his way towards the staircase in his dressing gown. Is this a black comedy? Or is it a reflection of reality? Especially in the light of Julian Barnes's novel, *The Noise of Time*, where, after a crushing article in *Pravda*, Shostakovich is expecting to be arrested at any moment, and so every evening he shaves, gathers his belongings in a small suitcase, and goes out to the stairwell, so that his arrest won't bother the family.

The whole film is like this: it isn't just buffoonery, but a higher form of comedy, à la Chaplin, probing, where behind all the jokes and the gags we can see the black abyss of being. The director, Armando Iannucci, is well known for his political satires, such as *The Thick of It*, or the mockumentary based on it, *In the Loop*, and he doesn't try to hide that he is filming a farce: there is no point in trying to find absolute historical accuracy in *The Death of Stalin* (deliberately, the crowds on the streets are caricatures – grandmothers in headscarves, bearded *muzhiks*; the Commissar of State Security, Lavrentiy Beria, indulges in pleasures with schoolgirls in the basement of the Lubyanka, amidst the sound of shots and shouts of, 'Long live Comrade Stalin') – and the facts were not exactly as presented (for example, Marshal Zhukov wasn't in Moscow at the moment when Stalin died). But the film is loyal to a different, deeper, truth: it mercilessly reflects the spirit of the times, where fear was mixed with the absurd, and laughter with death. The film is not realistic, but it is truthful, in the same way, for example, that Shakespeare is truthful. *The Death of Stalin* is very accurate in its assessments: again and again, it is clear that humour can reveal the essence of the era and the characters much more accurately than a historical reconstruction or a costume drama. Perhaps the best example of this was Charlie Chaplin in *The Great Dictator*, which was banned not only in the Axis powers[20] but in the USSR, too, because Stalin didn't like it.

For all the grotesque, operetta-like qualities of the characters, they have been drawn with deadly accuracy: the weak-willed Chairman of the Council of Ministers, Georgy Malenkov; the Jesuitical People's Commissar for Foreign Affairs, Vyacheslav Molotov, betraying his wife, Polina Zhemchuzhina, seven times in one day; the maniacal Commissar for State Security, Lavrentiy Beria; the conceited Marshal Georgy Zhukov; Stalin's heir, Nikita Khrushchev, who, under the mask of being a country bumpkin is really a cunning schemer. Then there's the rude, mistrustful, cruel and lonely Stalin, suffering a ridiculous and ugly death, lying in a pool of his own urine. Each of the masks has its own authenticity and depth, but above all they are hopeless, incorrigibly ridiculous, confusedly turning in a ritual dance around the corpse in their baggy trousers, trying to hide with party slogans their Darwinian struggle for power and for their lives.

And it is in this sense that this film probably presents the greatest threat to our current leadership. It's not just that it's a funny film; it's because we are used to our leaders being portrayed as great, frightening, even helpless (as in Alexander Sokurov's film, *Taurus*, where the dying Lenin was shown) or abhorrent (like in Alexei German's picture, *Khrustalyov, My Car!*, about the last days of Stalin's life) – but never funny. The myth of Stalin in all its parts – apologetic, critical, statist, liberal – can't cope with coming up against British humour. It flies into a tantrum before *Monty Python*. In Russia we're not used to speaking in this way about those in power. We've never had a television series such as *Yes, Minister!* or *Absolute Power* with Stephen Fry, or Iannucci's other comedies. The legendary show *Kukly* ('Puppets' – a clone of the British satirical programme *Spitting Image*), remained as a programme of the Yeltsin era, having run aground with the series *Little Zaches: The Story of Putin from Beginning to End*; Putin found it insulting.[21] Laughter takes apart the very foundations of power, removing its sacred nature and its secret; it shows up human weakness, chance and meaninglessness. Laughter is the Achilles heel of power, which Vladimir Nabokov understood well in his pamphlet *Tyrants Destroyed*: 'Having experienced all the degrees of hatred and despair, I achieved those heights from which one obtains a bird's-eye view of the ludicrous.'[22]

The present leadership's fear of Iannucci's comedy is twofold. On the one hand, Stalin's myth lies at the base of Russian power as an indulgence, as the state's ultimate monopoly of violence, deeply ingrained in the collective subconscious; however anyone in the ruling elite relates to Stalin, they know instinctively that laughing at Stalin is the most painful spot for the authorities. But on the other hand – and this is even more important – in the depth of their souls they suspect that they are just as grotesque and just as funny, and when the inevitable change of leadership happens in the Kremlin there will be exactly the same scampering around like cockroaches and tragicomic scenes. Just as it was sixty-five years ago, so now the only political institution is the body of the leader, and the question of succession is spontaneous, not predestined, and there will be just such a furious 'bulldog fight under the rug', as Churchill allegedly described it so accurately.

Incidentally, the local failure of the system that took place on 26 January was quickly put right. The police turned up in the Pioneer cinema and the film was hurriedly stopped. As for the young men who had had the stamps put in their passports at the registry office confirming their gay marriage: the police paid a visit to their flat.

216

When they didn't open the door, the director of communal services shut off their electricity and Internet, and the Interior Ministry cancelled their passports and fined the men for 'spoiling' them. When journalists turned up at their flat, they found miserable policemen on the staircase, who complained that they had had to sit in ambush all night, and in the morning they were having to go off and break up an opposition rally ... The absurdity of these events is even stronger than the films of Armando Iannucci; and we watch these farcical comedies about ourselves every day of the week.

RUSSIAN RESENTMENT

Ukraine Mania

One of the more surprising metamorphoses of the mass Russian consciousness in recent years has been the pathological fixation with Ukraine. The average Russian knows all about the confectionery business of the Ukrainian President, Petro Poroshenko, and about the hairstyles of the politician, Yulia Timoshenko; they are better informed about the results of the parliamentary elections in Ukraine than they are about the elections for their own Duma. And they can go on for hours about 'the Ukrainian fascists' and 'the Banderovites' (followers of Stepan Bandera, a Ukrainian nationalist in the first half of the twentieth century), which they've heard all about on Russian TV. People talk about how, after watching news on Russian television about Ukraine, the middle-aged and older generations are so wound up that they rush about the house spewing out curses about 'the Kiev junta'. It is now a sort of 'Ukraine mania', a mass psychosis among Russians, brought on by watching propaganda on television. Ukraine has become the mental training ground of the post-Soviet consciousness, where people work up their hate speech, techniques for making an image of 'the Other', and ways for mass mobilization of the population.

Such an unhealthy fixation with a neighbouring country bears witness to a deep post-imperial trauma. Ukrainians were too close to us, too much like us, for Russia to allow them simply to slip away quietly. For a quarter of a century Ukrainian independence was looked on as some sort of mistake, a bit of a joke – the very word *nezalezhnost*, Ukrainian for 'independence', was usually said in Russia with an ironic accent. Russians accept Moldovan, Tajik, even Belarusian independence perfectly calmly; but they can't accept Ukrainian independence. And we're not talking here about imperialists or nationalists, but about the vast bulk of the educated classes, who look on Ukraine as some sort of banana republic, while trying to conceal a deep resentment against this stupid 'little brother' who brazenly tore up their blood ties. Even the poet, Joseph Brodsky, failed 'the Ukraine test', cursing our neighbour in his famous poem, *On the Independence of Ukraine*. Rather like Alexander Pushkin in the nineteenth century, with his anti-Polish ode, *To the Slanderers of Russia*, Brodsky, the dissident and idol of the liberal intelligentsia, revealed the depth of his wounded great-power consciousness, which he took with him to America from Russia, along with his memories about the imperial greatness of St Petersburg.[23]

The Slave Revolt

Nevertheless, there is more to this jealous Russian attention towards Ukraine than simply nostalgia for the empire. Britain and France also experienced post-imperial phantom pains, but in these countries no one compared themselves to their former colonies. In Russia's case we can talk about a much deeper psychological mechanism – about symbolic compensation, the transfer and projection of our own complexes and frustrations onto the symbolic figure of 'the Other'. The well-known Russian sociologist, Boris Dubin, spoke about this in April 2014, just after the annexation of Crimea:

This is a very peculiar mechanism, when you transfer onto someone else your own problems and your inability to deal with them, by humiliating the other. Everything that was said in Russia about what was going on in Ukraine was not really about Ukraine but about Russia itself – that's the whole point![24]

Boris Dubin described here a classic condition of resentment, without actually using the word. In a state of resentment, it is usual to have a feeling of enmity towards the one whom you consider to be the cause of your misfortune ('the enemy'), a helpless envy, an awareness of the futility of trying to improve one's status in society. This is a continuation of an inferiority complex, which by way of compensation forms its own moral system, refusing to accept the enemy's values and placing on him all the blame for your own misfortunes.

The understanding of resentment was first raised by Friedrich Nietzsche in his work, *On the Genealogy of Morality*. According to this German philosopher, *ressentiment* (resentment) is the defining characteristic of the morals of slaves, who are a lower race and incapable of historical activity or of altering the conditions of their own lives. According to Nietzsche, *ressentiment* reveals itself in the slave revolt:

> The beginning of the slaves' revolt in morality occurs when *ressentiment* itself turns creative and gives birth to values ... slave morality first has to have an opposing, external world, it needs, physiologically speaking, external stimuli in order to act at all, – its action is basically a reaction.[25]

In other words, resentment is the slave's hatred for everything that looks to him like freedom.

Nietzsche was writing about *ressentiment* in 1887, but the word came up again a quarter of a century later, shortly before the First World War, in 1912, when Max Scheler, a German Lutheran who was converting to Catholicism, wrote a monograph about it. A man with a tragic outlook on life who committed suicide in 1928, he had a foreboding of the approaching disaster and effectively predicted the 'Weimar *ressentiment*' in postwar Germany, which produced a figure like the unsuccessful architect and artist, Adolf Hitler. Hitler (like the unsuccessful seminarian, Stalin) is a figure from Dostoevsky, an angry and vengeful 'underground man' straight out of *Notes from Underground*, or the lackey Smerdyakov from *The Brothers Karamazov*, who falls greedily upon the heights of power. It is no coincidence that in his essay Scheler refers to examples from Russian literature:

> No other literature is as full of *ressentiment* as the young Russian literature. The books of Dostoevsky, Gogol and Tolstoi teem with *ressentiment*-laden heroes. This is a result of the long autocratic oppression of the people, with no parliament or freedom of press through which the affects [sic] caused by authority could find release.[26]

Russia is a country which displays classic resentment. On the one hand, century after century it has witnessed various forms of class slavery, from serfdom to the Soviet *propiska* (permission to live in a particular city). This state slavery affected not only the tax-paying population, but even the privileged classes, including the nobility, who were obliged to the state through titles, estates and their very lives, not to mention those engaged in industry and trade, whose ownership of property was always relative, dependent on the whims of the state. In such conditions, people begin to feel offended, they sense that they are unwanted and their talent unappreciated, and figures such as the 'superfluous man' emerge, like Eugene Onegin in Pushkin's poem of the same name, and 'the underground man' from Dostoevsky's tale, thumbing his nose at the crystal palace of the rational world order. And it's only a small step from here to the terrorists and bombers, to the frightening Pyotr Verkhovensky from Dostoevsky's *The Demons*.

On the other hand, for more than three hundred years, if we count from the time of Peter the Great (or almost five hundred, if we start with Russia's first encounter with the technology of the gunpowder revolution at the time of Ivan IV, 'the Terrible'), Russia has jealously copied the West, from time to time rebelling against this imitation. This phenomenon of constantly trying to catch up with modernization while continually lagging behind the world leaders in the basic socioeconomic indicators (Britain in the eighteenth and nineteenth centuries, the USA in the twentieth and twenty-first) is a fertile breeding ground for resentment in the foreign policy sphere. Russia either sees itself as Cinderella, unfairly forgotten by the evil stepmother and the ugly sisters, or presents itself as a nation sacrificed, which puts itself on the line to save the world from destruction, be it from the Mongol hordes or the fascist tanks.

The early twentieth-century Russian philosopher, Vasily Rozanov, pointed out on a number of occasions this sense of Russians as being victims. He compared them to the Jews, who also have a strong sense of being a people sacrificed. It is no coincidence that conspiracy theories are so developed in Russia, as are fantasies about 'worldwide behind-the-scenes deals', which have been hatching plots against our country for centuries. But all this amounts to nothing more than variations on the theme of resentment, which all comes from the inability to change the external conditions of our existence, and from our inability to catch up with the West and overcome our own provinciality. This impotence expresses itself in the demonization of the opponent and in the creation of a dreamt-up reality, where Russia stands alone in opposing the rest of the world.

Putin's Resentment

Russia in the first decade of the twenty-first century is a classic example of where resentment has become state policy. One of the main propaganda myths of the Putin era that began to spread almost in the first few months after Putin came to power was the 'theory of Russia's defeat', beginning with the lamentation about the collapse of the USSR as 'the greatest geopolitical catastrophe of the twentieth century', going right through to the similar meme about the 'evil nineties'. A sensible way of looking at it was that the peaceful dissolution of the Soviet Union (in contrast, for example, to the explosive collapse of Yugoslavia) was not a defeat for Russia but a new opportunity for it: it had retained its principal territory, its population, its nuclear potential and it was considered as the successor state to the USSR. Yet it had thrown off the costly ballast of empire, it could complete the transition to the post-industrial state, and it could align itself with the Northern Hemisphere's richest nations. Strictly speaking, the active part of the Russian population, including all the ruling elite and President Putin himself, used this opportunity successfully. In the early 2000s, Russia came to terms with the crisis of 1998,[27] and, capitalizing on the windfall created by the weak rouble and rising oil prices, doubled its GDP, joined the World Trade Organization and cooperated with the USA in the war on terror. However, at the same time the myth was constantly repeated for domestic consumption about the geopolitical defeat, the humiliation and plundering of Russia by global liberalism and its henchmen: President Boris Yeltsin and the architects of the economic reforms, the Prime Minister Yegor Gaidar, and the Deputy Prime Minister Anatoly Chubais.

The idea about defeat and the feeling of offence against the reformers and the world outside became a convenient excuse for the lack of social progress and the parasitism of the Putin era, and it tied in well with the deep Russian tendency towards resentment. As the modern Russo-American philosopher Mikhail Iampolski has remarked:

> The whole of Russian society, from Putin to the humblest worker, carries with him the same amount of resentment. For Putin the source of this resentment is that on the world stage neither he nor Russia is treated as an equal, respected player. For the worker, it is because of his helplessness in the face of the police, the bureaucrats, the courts and the crooks … The resentful fantasies of the authorities at some moment struck a curious resonance with the resentment fantasies of the ordinary people.[28]

Modern Russian resentment divides into two levels. On one level, political commentators and analysts who support the state have skilfully constructed the idea of 'the humiliation' of Russia by the West: the political scientist, Sergei Karaganov, talks about 'the creeping military and economic and political expansion that has been going on for almost a quarter of a century into the areas of Russia's vital interests, which is in effect a "Versailles policy in kid gloves", which has brought out in a significant part of the elite and the population of the country a sense of humiliation and a desire for revenge'.[29] In fact it seems that a totally contradictory process has taken place: over the course of twenty-five years the West tried to integrate Russia into its institutions, proposing privileged conditions for partnership with both NATO and the European Union, at the same time as this 'humiliated' elite was rushing to spend its oil dollars on Western real estate, citizenship for their families and education for their children. But Russia as a whole didn't make use of the open window of opportunity, instead chanting the mantra about being offended and humiliated and inflating NATO's war in Kosovo in 1999 to the level of a universal catastrophe. Operation 'Allied Force' (the NATO codename for the military operation in Kosovo) was indeed a rushed, poorly thought-out and not legally justified action; but it wasn't aimed directly at Russia, and, what's more, this mistake by the West certainly does not give Russia the right the build a foreign policy on the principle, 'The West can do it, so why can't we?'

Vladimir Putin's thinking on foreign policy, judging by his speech at a session of the Valdai Club in Sochi on 24 October 2014, is constructed totally on the paradigm of respect and humiliation:

> You may remember the wonderful saying: Whatever Jupiter is allowed, the Ox is not. We cannot agree with such an approach. The ox may not be allowed something, but the bear will not even bother to ask permission. Here we consider it the master of the taiga, and I know for sure that it does not intend to move to any other climatic zones – it will not be comfortable there. However, it will not let anyone have its taiga either. ... True, the Soviet Union was referred to as 'the Upper Volta with missiles'. Maybe so, and there were loads of missiles. Besides, we had such brilliant politicians like Nikita Khrushchev, who hammered the desk with his shoe at the UN. And the whole world, primarily the United States, and NATO thought: this Nikita is best left alone, he might just go and fire a missile, they have lots of them, we should better show some respect for them.[30]

The expressive string of words such as 'taiga', 'bear', 'shoe' and 'missile' indicate how important for the Russian president are such 'male' concepts as 'respect' and 'authority'. According to this logic, the West did not show the necessary respect; it failed to answer

Russia's openness to cooperation after 9/11, when Vladimir Putin was the first world leader to declare his support for George Bush and offered him a global partnership in the war against terror. As Igor Yurgens, an economist, lobbyist and a man with many years' experience observing the life of the Kremlin, noted: 'Both Putin and his close circle had a feeling of humiliation and betrayal on the part of the West (at least, that's how it looked to them).'

The breaking point, it seems, was in autumn 2004: first there was the terrorist action in Beslan, where Chechen fighters seized a school, taking around a thousand children hostage, for which President Putin unexpectedly blamed certain forces behind the terrorists who wanted to snatch Russia's 'juicy morsels', clearly meaning the West. Then there was the 'Orange Revolution' in Ukraine in the winter of 2004, when the Kremlin directly blamed the USA for apparently aiming to weaken Russia by tearing away from it its key partner. Putin's stubborn reluctance to see the real forces and processes that had led to Beslan and to the Maidan (the collapse of the neopatrimonial regimes in the Caucasus and in Kiev, which Moscow supported), and his desire to blame everything on the intrigues of the USA, is typical resentment: an attempt to transfer his own misfortune onto the figure of an external enemy.

On the other level, there is enormous resentment on the part of wide sections of the population who have been unable to adapt to the new reality of the market economy, or to the global flows of finance, information, images, migrants or technology, and who take out their anger on the Russian liberals and reformers. Many political parties expressed the views of these layers of society, from the Communists to 'A Just Russia' (a political party), but most of all over the past twenty-five years they have been represented by Vladimir Zhirinovsky's Liberal Democratic Party, which captured this Russian resentment precisely, with its slogan, 'For the Russians, for the Poor!'[31] In this catchy slogan, postulated as an axiom, no one stops to explain why the Russians are poor and how they are poorer than, say, the Tajiks, the Moldovans and all the other fellow partners in the post-Soviet transit. Before our very eyes the discourse of offence becomes the dominant one in the social sphere and it becomes a particular genre of Russian politics.

The Offended and the Insulted

In Brezhnev's times, a joke did the rounds about Soviet man's sixth sense: 'the sense of deep satisfaction', a cliché used in the propaganda, which he was supposed to experience when he became familiar with the details of a regular congress of the Communist Party. Now it seems that the basic instinct of post-Soviet man is a sense of the opposite kind: deep offence at the outside world.

In the public discourse, there are special groups in whose name offence is created, such as, for example, veterans. It appears that veterans (and not only war veterans, of whom there are very few left, but veterans of labour, the Communist Party or the KGB) form a group with particular reactions, in whose name it is convenient to label and to judge everything. Another offended group is the 'Orthodox community', which sees its role as calling out blasphemy in shows, be it Oscar Wilde's *An Ideal Husband* in Konstantin Bogomolov's production in the Moscow Arts Theatre, or *Jesus Christ Superstar* in Rostov. This choir of victims was recently joined by representatives of the *siloviki*: the security guards at the Cathedral of Christ the Saviour experienced 'moral suffering' when they witnessed Pussy Riot's performance.

Soviet speech practices have returned with a vengeance. The authorities have recreated the Soviet practice of orchestrating outraged public opinion: 'Inhabitants of Tolyatti Against a Memorial to Alexander Solzhenitsyn'; 'Veterans of Novgorod Offended by the Programmes of the *Dozhd*[32] television channel.' This is typical collectivization of speech, the creation of a collective body with its sacramental phrase, 'I haven't read Pasternak, but I'm outraged!', which comes from the times when meetings were held attended by thousands of Soviet citizens to judge the author of *Doctor Zhivago*, even though they hadn't actually read the book. This is the body of society that speaks through the mouths of veterans, guards, loyal representatives of the arts and trained journalists at President Putin's press conferences. A whole class of professional offended people has emerged, which under the impression of 'speaking for the people', transmits the will of the 'owners of the discourse' and, in doing so, becomes an effective instrument of repression, the pervasive censor of the collective unconscious.

Spreading the discourse of offence, in practice the state cleans the public arena; like a virus, resentment is self-perpetuating in society and produces new prohibitions, taboo subjects and groups of offended citizens. Officially, the regime is not involved; it simply formulates 'the will of the people', expressed in various ways through hysteria, denunciations and collective letters – but in reality it moulds this will then goes on to manipulate it.

The March of the Losers

The myth about Ukrainian fascism grew out of the state's teenage complexes, the elite's childish disappointment with the West and the social infantilism of the population. The resentment demanded an object for symbolic revenge: after twenty years of having a go at Gaidar and Chubais, people had already tired of that; the opposition protests on Bolotnaya Square in 2011–12 had already been broken up; America was a long way off; and then suddenly there was the Ukrainian Maidan, the mass protests on the Maidan (Independence Square in Kiev; 'Maidan' means 'square' in Ukrainian) in the winter of 2013–14. For the second time in ten years, Ukraine was daring to ignore its big brother and was trying to tear itself away from the paternalistic paradigm on the way to a bourgeois-democratic revolution and European development. The answer was consolidated Russian resentment, in which the frustrated ambitions of the Kremlin merged with the jealousy of the Russians. Ukraine was declared a traitor, and its treachery was even more offensive because the Ukrainians were supposed to be the Russians' blood brothers, the closest of all in the Slav family. In accusing Ukraine of treachery, there were clear echoes of the *ressentiment* of the Weimar Republic and the *Dolchstoss im Rücken* ('stab in the back' theory),[33] which was popular in Germany in the 1920s and 1930s; this time it was a European 'stab in the back'.

The invention of 'Ukrainian fascism' was a diabolical triumph for the political technologists, who managed to create the myth about the 'Banderovites' and the 'punishers' (a reference to the German squads that carried out reprisals following Ukrainian partisan activity during the Second World War) and suggest it to the government and the vast majority of the population through television. For some years now, the whole of Russia, including President Putin, has tended to live as if in an endless TV serial, a parallel reality, where fascists march around Kiev, where Ukrainians, not Donbass rebels, shoot down MH17, and where the West sponsors the 'Maidan' revolution, planning to bring Ukraine into NATO and to position the US Sixth Fleet in the Black Sea.

Typically, the use by Russian propaganda of the image of fascism as a synonym for absolute and final evil is the ultimate dehumanization of the enemy. In the Russian discourse, fascism represents the universal value of 'the Other'; a whole new Russian identity is built on the ideology of the victory over Nazism. An ontologization

226

of the conflict with Ukraine is taking place, making it the struggle of absolute good against absolute evil. And according to Nietzsche, here is where *ressentiment* creates its own system of values, 'the moral of the slaves', which says 'no' to everything external and foreign. Mikhail Iampolski remembers the French political philosopher, Étienne Balibar, who described *ressentiment* as 'anti-politics': 'Anti-politics is not just the result of the crisis of statehood, it is also the product of Nietzschean *ressentiment*, which has its roots in the inability to act positively. As Nietzsche believed, everywhere we have only pure negativity, a reaction to the resistance of the outside world.'[34]

Russia's war in Ukraine is an example of anti-politics, of pure negativity, based on a feeling of personal loss; compensation both for the elite's inferiority complex in relation to the West, and the people's loss concerning the conditions of their own life. The state can't change Russia's role on the international stage with the help of 'soft power' or quality economic growth, and it cannot achieve respect or recognition from its partners. The vast majority of the population, trapped within the framework of the class system that Putin has restored, is also unable to break out from the bounds of state paternalism (in reality, class slavery) and social parasitism, a syndrome of trained helplessness. The symbolic compensation was the creation of a dreamt-up enemy in the image of Ukraine and dreamt-up victories: the annexation of Crimea and the creation of the pirate republics of Donetsk and Lugansk. But from the broader point of view, the popular slogan 'Crimea is ours!' and the actual seizure of southeast Ukraine became 'the march of the losers'. This is the final parade of the forces that have suffered an historical defeat in the battle with globalization. They have lost in the clash with the open society and with the mobilization of citizens, with the Internet and with the European Union, with modern art and the financial markets, with 'soft power' and with complex structures. Crimean resentment is a contract of the state with a critical mass of people who are unable to adapt; it is an apology for weakness, the defensive reaction of a fading nature, an historical dead-end.

The irony of the situation is that these dreamt-up resentful offences become real. Russia called up the ghosts of confrontation so zealously that, as a result, it was put under sanctions, which are having a negative effect on the economy and the standard of living. Russia's geopolitical specialists scared us so wonderfully with fairytales about NATO expanding into Ukraine that, as a result of their paranoid politics, they turned Ukraine into a hostile country and obtained a decision by NATO to widen its military presence and set up permanent bases in the Baltic States. And Putin took offence against the West over such a long period and so demonstratively that the West eventually answered him in kind, turning Russia into a pariah state. Resentment is a vicious circle, which gives rise to hostility all around: as the saying goes, 'one who takes offence hurts only himself'.

The only prospect is of Russia's inevitable collision with reality, healing itself of its empty ambitions, imagined offence and its inferiority complex, and coming to terms with its status as a mediocre country of average income. Lord Skidelsky described these perspectives in an article, explaining the idea that there will be no world war with the West for resources, and that the West's only wish is to see a stable and non-aggressive Russia, even if it has an authoritarian government. All that remains is to hope that Russia's recovery from its post-Soviet resentment does not prove to be as tortuous and bloody as was Germany's healing process to recover from its Weimar *ressentiment*.

THE FLOWER REVOLUTION

A strong wind is blowing across the Bolshoi Moskvoretsky Bridge and a snowstorm is swirling all around. Spring is a month late coming to Moscow, as if agreeing with the authorities' decision to switch Russia to 'permanent Winter time': in October 2014, President Putin ended the practice of the country changing over to summer time. In March, the frosts set in, it snowed again, and this April night it's as cold as winter. Heavy snowflakes are swirling around in the spotlights above the walls of the Kremlin, over the Spassky Tower – which is covered in scaffolding as it is being restored, and looks like a grim gigantic ziggurat – and over Red Square, beyond which, like a phantom, the shining lights of the GUM shopping arcade are visible. At one o'clock at night the bridge is empty, there are neither cars nor people, and only around the improvised memorial at the spot where Boris Nemtsov was murdered is there a group of volunteers, protecting the memorial from hooligans and vandals. This people's memorial made out of fresh flowers has already been destroyed a few times by unidentified workers wearing plain clothes, from the city's street-cleaning department, and by hooligan pro-government activists – but every time that has happened the memorial has sprung up again and people have continued to bring flowers, posters, portraits of Nemtsov and Russian flags, which have once again become the symbol of the opposition movement, just as it was when the USSR was collapsing in 1991.

The opposition politician, Boris Nemtsov, was shot on the bridge by Chechen killers on the night of 27 February 2015; the motive for the assassination, according to the ruling of the court, was because he had insulted Islam. But most people in Russia are in no doubt that this was not a religious but a political murder, linked to Nemtsov's opposition activity and his harsh criticism of Putin. Today the memorial to Nemtsov is a genuine *Via Dolorosa*, a road of grief, covered in a carpet of carnations, which runs along the last route walked by the politician, from the start of the bridge to the spot where he was murdered; here a pyramid of flowers stands. Day and night people bring bouquets, some even order large baskets to be delivered by the florists: the bridge is covered in baskets with hundreds of roses. On these cold spring days, the flowers on the bridge have become a citizens' protest, and it's no joke that they have frightened the authorities, who don't know what to do with this spontaneous memorial. Right in the centre of Moscow, underneath the walls of the Kremlin, a symbolic war with flowers is taking place: a war between winter and spring; between fear and hope; between the state, ashamedly hiding away behind the backs of the street-cleaners, and the buoyant urban class.

Why is the state so afraid of these flowers? There's a number of reasons. The first and most obvious one is that they are a ghost of the 'colour revolutions', which started in the 'Carnation Revolution' in Portugal in April 1974. According to the legend, it began when one woman from Lisbon placed a carnation in the barrel of the rifle of a soldier standing in front of her. It was the season for carnations, and people started handing out flowers to the soldiers. An almost bloodless military coup successfully took place on 25 April 1974, which put an end to one of the last dictatorships in Europe. After that, within a year, the Franco regime in Spain had ended, as had the Colonels' Junta in Greece. Thirty years later, flowers returned to politics: in the wake of the 'Rose Revolution' in Georgia (2003) came the 'Orange Revolution' in Ukraine (2004) and the 'Tulip Revolution' in Kyrgyzstan (2005). Recent years have witnessed attempts at 'colour revolutions' in Belarus, Uzbekistan and Armenia. It's more than likely that these have been exaggerated by journalists, but fear opens eyes wide, and 'flower paranoia' has firmly settled into the souls of post-Soviet autocrats.

Second, the history of spontaneous memorials is a battle for the city's space: who does it belong to, the state or the citizens? The whole of late-Soviet and post-Soviet history can be presented as a process whereby civil protest has taken over areas in Moscow, from the demonstrations attended by hundreds of thousands on Manezh Square and at the Luzhniki Stadium in 1990–1, and from the protests and scuffles around the White House (at the time the home of the Russian Parliament) in 1991 and 1993, to the years-long battle with the 'Strategy-31' opposition movement behind the Mayakovsky statue on Triumphal Square on Tverskaya Street. The 'Strategy' movement was rallying for the right to demonstrate seven times a year, on the thirty-first day of each month of that length, thus carrying out the freedom of assembly guaranteed by Article 31 of the Russian

Constitution. Demonstrations in 2011–13 widened the geography of the battle: now it included Chistoprudny Boulevard, Bolotnaya Square and Sakharov Prospekt, as well as the Garden Ring Road, which, in February 2012, protestors turned into 'the White Ring', creating along it a living chain made from white ribbons, the symbol of the opposition. In moving around the city, these protests have been creeping ever closer to the Kremlin, and the murder of Nemtsov on 27 February 2015 unexpectedly and visibly placed a bloody spot and created a place of memory right alongside the walls of the Kremlin. The fifty thousand people who went in procession to the place three days later in the March of Remembrance didn't just pay their final respects to the murdered politician; they also threw down a challenge to the people behind these walls, whom they considered to be either directly or indirectly linked to the killing.

And third, the story with the flowers on the bridge is a battle for memory, which in recent times has become the scene of the sharpest political confrontations. 'The Memorial Era', the arrival of which was declared by the French historian Pierre Nora, turned out in Russia to be an unprecedented attack by the state on the historic memory of the nation, a vociferous battle with 'falsifiers' and 'vilification', the censoring of intellectual discussion. The country is presented with an edited version of Russian history, which is simply a chronicle of victories and accomplishments in praise of the state, in which there is no place for victims, human suffering or the question of responsibility for the crimes of the regime – from the Stalinist repressions of 1937 to the shooting of the Polish officers at Katyn in the spring of 1940; from the invasion of Prague in 1968 to the invasion of Afghanistan in 1979. In exactly the same way, the propaganda wipes out the memory of the newest victims of hatred, the political murders of the past thirty years: the journalists Dmitry Kholodov and Vladislav Listyev, Yury Shchekochikhin and Anna Politkovskaya; politicians Sergei Yushenkov and Galina Starovoitova; the editor-in-chief of Russian *Forbes* magazine Paul Khlebnikov, and the Chechen human rights' defender Natalia Estemirova; the secret service agent Alexander Litvinenko, and the lawyer Sergei Magnitsky. This roll-call of martyrs can be continued, and Boris Nemtsov is simply the latest, and perhaps the best-known, victim on the list. But each of these cases has in common the state's desire not to allow any public reaction.

They started to trample on Nemtsov's memory within the first few hours after the tragedy: in the words of President Putin's press secretary, Dmitry Peskov, Nemtsov was 'little more than an average citizen, and he didn't represent any political threat'; the Duma demonstratively refused to honour the memory of Nemtsov with a minute's silence (only the deputies Dmitry Gudkov and Valery Zubov stood up); no member of the leadership, or any high-ranking city official, attended the memorial service or the funeral. In the same way, the sweeping away of the flower memorial on the bridge by anonymous cleaning staff and hooligans from the patriotic movement SERB[35] (they are the ones who vandalized Nemtsov's grave in the Troekurovsky Cemetery, throwing away all the flowers and portraits that had been placed there) bears witness to the fact that the state is afraid of the people's memory. That fear also led to pressure being put on the largest clubs and open spaces in Moscow so that they would refuse to hold a concert with some of the biggest names in Russian rock music in Boris Nemtsov's memory on the fortieth day after his death.

The story of the flower memorial continues. And if the ghost of the 'colour revolutions' lives on only in the frightened heads of the inhabitants of the Kremlin, or still stalks places far away from Russia, if the authorities can win the battle for the city only by administrative bans and police barriers, then they have already hopelessly lost the battle for memory. The meme 'Nemtsov bridge' went viral on the Internet, a memorial plaque was put up on the house where Nemtsov lived, a movement is growing to name a street in Moscow after the murdered politician, and the memorial on the bridge has already been firmly established in the Moscow topography of protest. They can ban it and put a permanent police guard on the bridge – but if they do, people will simply take their flowers elsewhere, or to a third place: there are many places in Moscow linked to Boris Nemtsov. Perhaps they could ban the sale of flowers in the city (which, incidentally, the Russian authorities are more than capable of doing ...). The paranoia surrounding the clearing away of the flowers and prevention of the concert from taking place, and the agreement of the leading figures in the state to remain silent, all indicate that Nemtsov was far from being 'an average citizen'. The state fears him more after his death than they did when he was alive – which only goes to show the size of his personality and the significance of Nemtsov as a figurehead.

WHO'S AFRAID OF
SVETLANA ALEXIEVICH?

The inventor of dynamite, Alfred Nobel, simply couldn't have imagined what sort of bomb he was placing under the Russian mass consciousness when he introduced his Nobel Prize for Literature. Of the five Russian language laureates of the twentieth century – Ivan Bunin in 1933, Boris Pasternak in 1958, Mikhail Sholokhov in 1965, Alexander Solzhenitsyn in 1970 and Joseph Brodsky in 1987 – four of them were persecuted in their motherland. 'White Guard' Bunin;[36] 'Anti-Soviet' Pasternak; 'Traitor' Solzhenitsyn; and 'Parasite' Brodsky: their Nobel Prizes were seen in the USSR as a political provocation, leading to them being defamed in the press and judged by the masses (Brodsky was slightly less affected by this than the others, since the Soviet era was already ending). If we add in the Nobel Peace Prizes awarded to the dissident Andrei Sakharov in 1975 and Mikhail Gorbachev in 1990, a year before the collapse of the USSR, then we see a very clinical picture: instead of being proud of its laureates, on each occasion Russia rejected them, united not by joy in the country's achievements, but by hatred for the West. Or, more precisely, by an eternal paranoia, a conviction that the outside world is doing this simply because it is plotting against us.

In this sense, the Nobel Laureate for 2015, Svetlana Alexievich, is in worthy company with authors who are recognized by the world but indignantly rejected by their own country. Yes, she's actually a Belarusian writer born in Ukraine, but her books tell of our general Soviet and post-Soviet experience, about the merciless millstones of the empire, so therefore she belongs also in equal measure to Ukrainian and Russian history and culture – and the offended attitude towards her in Russia shows that she is considered to be one of our own, but an apostate who is washing our dirty linen in public.

Why do the indignant Russian 'patriots' denounce Svetlana Alexievich? On the whole, there are three objections: first, they say, she is hardly known in Russia; second, they attack her because, they say, what she writes 'is not literature' (it's documentary prose); and, third, their main objection, is that she is a 'Russophobe', who plays up our problems and 'does PR on someone else's grief'. All three of these accusations indicate one thing: Russia does not like, is unable and is simply afraid to talk about its traumas. And it is, namely, the trauma and memory that cannot be expunged of the tragedy of Russia's terrifying twentieth century that comprise the overriding theme of Alexievich's books, and she has chosen the cruellest and most uncomfortable genre: documentary prose, where you can't hide your pain behind fiction. If Flaubert called himself 'the pen-man', then Alexievich calls herself 'the ear-woman': she listens to the noise of the street and picks out the voices of people and their personal stories. Her mission is to testify (in the high, biblical sense); she is here in order to speak about the trials and tribulations of the individual. Alexievich herself spoke about this in an interview she gave to the magazine *Ogonyok*:

> Our principal capital is suffering. This is the only thing which we constantly mine. Not oil, not gas, but suffering. I suspect that this is what all at once attracts, and repels and surprises the Western reader of my books. It is that courage to go on living, no matter what.[37]

Alexievich's gift for compassion is indicative of her Belarusian roots. 'I was traumatized from childhood by the subject of evil and death', she acknowledges, 'because I grew up in a postwar Belarusian village where this was all anyone talked about. We constantly thought about it.' Lying as it does at the crossroads of wars, and suffering from the wheels of history more than anywhere else, Belarus created its own particular culture of memory, encapsulated in the books of the writers Vasil Bykov and Ales Adamovich: as the Belarusian poet, Vladimir Neklyaev, noted, if all of Russian literature came out of Gogol's *Overcoat*, then Alexievich's art comes from the documentary book by Ales Adamovich, Yanka Bryl and Vladimir Kolesnik, *Out of the Fire*. The Belarusian gaze of Alexievich is the anti-imperial vaccination of humanity for our common culture, the best representatives of which, from Pushkin to Brodsky, were often blinded by the temptation of empire.

Her works are a catalogue of the tragedies of Soviet and post-Soviet history: the Great Patriotic War (the books *War Does Not Have a Woman's Face* and *The Last Witnesses*, respectively about women and children in war); the war in Afghanistan (*Boys in Zinc*); the Chernobyl disaster (*Chernobyl Prayer*); suicides in the transition period of the 1990s (*Enchanted with Death*); and the problem of post-Soviet refugees (*Second-Hand Time*). Her books are uncomfortable, her observations ruthless and passionless, like the tale about the single mother from the Stalinist year of 1937 who, when arrested, asked her childless girlfriend to look after her daughter. The friend brought the girl up, and when the mother returned from the camps after seventeen years and asked to see how her daughter had turned out, it emerged that it was the friend who had denounced her, because she dreamt of having the daughter for herself; unable to cope with the reality of this, the mother went and hanged herself. Alexievich has hundreds of similar stories, which she pushes, like needles, into the most painful spots – areas not normally talked about in Russia.

The 'Alexievich problem' for Russia is not political, nor psychological; and it certainly is not because of her imagined 'Russophobia', or the political preferences of the Nobel Prize committee. It's in the deep complexes of the Russian consciousness, which cannot talk about pain and cannot cope with the experience of trauma. On the whole, the subject of pain is taboo in Russia. Suffering is something internalized, which people try to deal with inside themselves or possibly in a very narrow family circle, but it is never brought out for public viewing. It is not normal in Russia to talk openly about pain. Often, if people happen to hear by chance about an illness from someone they're talking to, they'll wave them away, as if they are afraid of being infected: 'Oh, don't offload your problems onto me!' Topics such as cancer, disability or deformity are as taboo as they always have been. People will collect money to help, but often that is simply a way of buying one's way out of someone else's pain, a magic spell. The Russian mass consciousness is archaic and superstitious. We hear, so frequently: 'Don't demonstrate other people's illnesses on yourself!', or 'Don't talk about illness or you'll go down with it!'

Because of this superstitious horror in Russia, the experience of the collective trauma of the twentieth century has never been openly discussed: the Revolution, famine, the GULAG, the war, evacuations, deprivation. In many families, younger generations learn about the repression of their relatives only by hearsay; at first people kept quiet out of fear, then this became habit: the less we talk about frightening things, the sooner we'll forget about them. Eighty years on, this experience has not been assimilated into our culture or the mass consciousness, nor have the witnesses – conversations about the repressions, incredible in their moral blindness, go round in circles: people seriously argue about whether they were justified or whether the evidence of them has been exaggerated. Varlam Shalamov's books, with their terrifying accounts of what went on in the camps in Kolyma, stand like a solitary monument to the side of these discussions: people are too scared even to come close to them.[38] In the same way, people are afraid to touch on the subject of the famine in the Volga Region in the 1920s and 1930s and the *Holodomor* in Ukraine in 1932–3, or the siege of Leningrad – there was hysterical reaction in the media after a single question (which wasn't even approved!) on the *Dozhd* television channel as to whether it was worth the cost of one and a half million lives to hold onto the city.[39] Any attempt to discuss the victims or the human cost of the victory is cut short by the strict internal censor of the Russian mass consciousness.

In exactly the same way, the experience of Russia's colonial wars in the twentieth century hasn't been brought out, from Budapest in 1956 and Prague in 1968, to Afghanistan in the 1980s and Chechnya in the 1990s. Compared to the way in which the Americans have agonized over Vietnam – with thousands of books, films, eye-witness accounts – Russia hasn't even begun to pick over the bones (in 1992 in Minsk, veterans of the Afghan War even brought a political court case against Alexievich for debunking the heroic myth about the war in her book, *Boys in Zinc*). The Russian philosopher, Pyotr Chaadaev, was right when he wrote two hundred years ago that Russia is a country without a memory, a space of total amnesia, a virgin understanding of criticism, rationality and reflexes. All our state narrative, family histories and individual experiences are built around a huge emptiness, a lacuna, a minefield. We prefer to tread safe paths with pat phrases and generalities: 'Those were difficult times'; 'It was tough for everyone.' The Second World War, Afghanistan, Chernobyl, people's broken destinies – they all flare up briefly in the newspapers and are instantly forgotten by society, pushed off into the silt at the bottom of pain. The same is happening today in the conflict in Ukraine: it seems that the fate of the paratroopers from Pskov, the tankmen from Buryatia or the special forces troops who have disappeared in the anonymous battles of the nonexistent war concerns only the opposition newspaper, *Novaya Gazeta*; society has already forgotten about this war and now watches with fascination the clips produced by the General Staff about the bombings in Syria.

This inability to accept, discuss and comprehend trauma leads Russia to an endless cycle of loss. In the same interview with *Ogonyok*, Alexievich asks the eternal question:

What is the point of this suffering which we all go through? What does it teach us if we just keep repeating it? I am constantly asking myself this question. For many people suffering has become a value in itself. It is their main task in life. But freedom does not grow out of it. I simply have no answer to this.[40]

And here she is stating one of Russia's deep secrets: all too often, sacrifices are simply pointless. For what did tens of thousands die from cold, hunger and beatings in the now abandoned coal-mines of Vorkuta, or lie buried beneath the sleepers of the useless 'railway of death' from Salekhard to Igarka in the Far North? Why did tens of thousands of civilians perish in the first Chechen campaign in 1994–6, which was so ineptly lost by Russia; or in the equally senseless and helpless war in the Donbass today? The people remain silent, the state refuses to comment – and the victims are merely a footnote.

Suffering in Russia is supposed to have its own value, which fits in with the Orthodox line ('Christ suffered and so should we', as the Russian saying goes), and with the centuries-old tradition of slavery, reverence before the Leviathan of the state, disdain for the life of a single person, and the endless patience that has been elevated to a state-approved virtue: remember Stalin's famous toast at the Victory banquet on 24 May 1945: 'To the patience of the Russian people!' The experience of this state-sanctioned suffering does not carry across into social action, but does come out in certain cultural forms: in the well-known Russian sense of longing (toska), in the boundless Russian song and in the depths of Russian drunkenness (usually, all three at once). But there is also the endless Russian self-irony: as the writer, Viktor Pelevin, puts it, 'the cosmic significance of Russian civilization is in transforming solar energy into people's grief'.[41]

Svetlana Alexievich breaks this cultural convention of violence by the state and suffering by the people, and the sanctification of the victim. She violates what is taboo as well as the etiquette of our speech; she is the awkward witness who spoils the blissful picture in the courtroom, which has already been agreed by the judges, the prosecutor, the accused and the victims themselves. This is why the 'patriots' and the guardians of the state myth are so afraid of her books. And it's why Alexievich's Nobel Prize is so essential for Russia – it's not politics and it's not literature: it's a therapy session, an attempt to teach society to listen and to speak about pain. Like the impassive witness, John, in the Book of the Apocalypse, Alexievich says to her readers: 'Come and see.'[42]

THE PRIVATE NUREMBERG
OF DENIS KARAGODIN

Russian state propaganda has found yet another enemy. It is thirty-four-year-old Denis Karagodin, a philosophy postgraduate student at Tomsk University, who undertook a private investigation into the shooting by the *Chekists* in 1938 of his great-grandfather, a peasant called Stepan Ivanovich Karagodin, with the aim of naming and condemning those responsible for the murder. One might think that there would be nothing special in Karagodin publishing the names of all those responsible for his great-grandfather's murder, since all of them are dead and the case has been long closed on the time principle. Surely the information would have only academic and archival interest, and no legal consequences? However, the haste with which the regime's propagandists set about hounding Karagodin illustrates that his action struck a painful chord and scratched a weak link in the machine of violence.

The peculiarity of our situation is that violence is anonymous, an inherent part of the state, accepted in society like some kind of constant in Russian life; it's inescapable, like the cold winter. The names of the members of each *troika* were anonymous ('people's courts' of three people); and the names of everyone who took part in the firing squads, the names of the investigators and the snitches (*stukachy*, as they call in Russian those who denounce others, from the verb *stuchat*, 'to knock'), are all hidden away in the KGB archives. In the USSR after 1956 there was an unwritten agreement according to which the victims of Stalinism were rehabilitated in exchange for anonymity for those who carried out the terror. The KGB carefully censored any information about the repressions; the names of the investigators and denouncers were removed from all the personal details of the victims; relatives received the files with pages either glued together or torn out. They considered that the very act of rehabilitation was sufficient for a person to be satisfied: you were still alive (or had been shot but had had your good name returned), so thank God; could you expect anything more from our state? In conditions of a permanent borderline situation, of a choice between life and death, the state not having shot you began to look like the greatest good.

'I'd like to name you all by name', wrote Anna Akhmatova, in her poem *Requiem*, a powerful witness of the Stalinist repressions, but her dream was merely to name all the victims; Akhmatova wasn't talking about those who carried out the repressions.[43] During the period of rehabilitation of the victims of the Stalinist repressions under Khrushchev, the NKVD investigators were called to account; but in practice only a few individuals were punished. On the whole it was limited to administrative responsibility – being fired from their posts or losing their pension or their rank. According to the evidence uncovered by the historian Nikita Petrov, under Khrushchev no more than a hundred people were declared responsible. Under Brezhnev and Gorbachev, the whole process was stopped. There were a few cases when incriminating evidence against individuals was published, such as about the investigator Alexander Khvat, who tortured the geneticist Nikolai Vavilov, or about the Head of the NKVD *Komendatura* (Commandant's office), Lieutenant-General Vasily Blokhin, who personally shot between ten and fifteen thousand people, but these were individual cases and there were no legal consequences. The executioners and the investigators and their victims continued to live side by side; they would bump into each other on the street or in queues and sometimes even went drinking together (there is the famous case of the writer Yury Dombrovsky, who spent ten years in the camps doing just that with his investigator). In the space of anonymity which was 'the Soviet people', there was a yawning great black hole right in the centre named 'repressions'; but everyone carefully went around the edge of this lacuna, from official government reports to private family histories, where this matter was diligently covered up.

Moreover, this conspiracy of silence became a guarantee that the terror would continue. In the same way that the flywheel of the Stalinist repressions worked anonymously, so the pursuit of dissidents continued anonymously in Brezhnev's USSR, using the machine of 'punitive psychiatry'. Nowadays we come across the anonymous violence of the law enforcement system, where torture has become the norm. But only isolated cases come to light thanks to social networks, like the tortures that took place in the 'Dalny' police station in Kazan, where a man arrested for being drunk on the street was raped to death with a champagne bottle; or the case of the lawyer, Sergei Magnitsky, who died while in a detention centre because he was refused medical help. But hundreds of other police stations, detention centres and prison camps remain places of totally depersonalized violence, just like thousands of Russian homes, in which daily – hourly – women become the victims of domestic violence. (Officially, up to forty women die every day in Russia from being beaten, but no one knows how many deaths are covered up by medical staff and police putting them down to other reasons.) But this violence is considered normal; it remains unnamed and anonymous, it's not usual to talk about it or tell the police, and now, in any case, it's been decriminalized: according to a law passed by the State Duma in 2017, beating people close to you when it's inflicted for the first time is not considered a crime. But cases do become known through social media, such as one recently in the city of Oryol, where the police refused to help a girl but promised 'to register her corpse' when she was killed – within half an hour the man she lived with had beaten her to death.

In Russia, violence is the socially acknowledged norm, the way to solve problems and define relations, the way to act between the authorities and the people, between men and women, parents and children, teachers and pupils. This is precisely why we need to prevent violence from being automatic and anonymous – it should be called what it is, attributed and judged. Our society is growing up and is beginning to speak about violence. Not so long ago the flash mob 'I'm not afraid to speak out' appeared, when Russian women for the first time in their lives spoke about the sexual violence and humiliation they have suffered. Then there was the scandal of the elite School No. 57 in Moscow, when the names were revealed of the teachers who, over the course of many years, had been sleeping with their female pupils. And finally we had the fearless philosopher from Tomsk, Denis Karagodin, who, having spent four years digging in the archives of the KGB to find the names of those responsible for sentencing and shooting his great-grandfather in 1938, received all the names and established the name of each member of this criminal group who took part in the murder, from the driver of the car that went to pick him up when he was arrested, to the NKVD typists and all the way up to the People's Commissar (minister) of Internal Affairs, Nikolai Yezhov, and Stalin himself. The names are declared, the chain of silence is broken and the Mafia *omertà* (code of silence) is removed from society.

The Russian culture of violence stands on two pillars: the right of the strong and the silence of the weak, and the second is no less important than the first. Remember how everyone pounced on the women who spoke out about rape and harassment: they themselves were the guilty ones! They shouldn't have provoked their attackers! In the same way, for years a conspiracy of silence was woven around the prestigious Moscow school, for fear of spoiling the corporate etiquette of the capital's intelligentsia. And even more important for understanding the complexes and fears of modern Russian society is 'the silence of the lambs' before the executioners, the lack of desire to raise and discuss the issue of the Stalinist terror. Immediately after Denis Karagodin's posts on the Internet with the names of the killers, there followed replies saying that there was no need to stir up the past and rock the boat. The former Duma deputy, Alexander Khinshtein, who had links with the *siloviki*, wrote in the newspaper *Moskovsky Komsomolets* that he had only good words for the NKVD forces and he poured criticism on those 'who wish to divide our recent past into black and white'.[44] The journalist Natalya Osipova, writing in *Izvestiya* in a column under the typical title of 'I fear justice', also seemed to be afraid of disclosure, repeating the favourite thesis of the Russian propagandists of the postmodern era: everyone has their own truth, their own version of reality, their own list of who's guilty and their own list of martyrs. She concluded that 'a bad peace is better than a good civil war'.[45]

The call for forgiveness and reconciliation between the descendants of the executioners and their victims is a typical Russian way of solving a problem not by a law but by an agreement, taking away the responsibility for finding a judicial solution and moving it into the murky world of political expediency. Terror in Russia has been smeared in a sticky layer across society and across history in such a way that it appears that everyone has taken part in it and everyone is at one and the same time both guilty and not guilty. Karagodin translates the question into a straightforward judicial one: if the state killed people for its own diabolical quasi-legal reasons, then now it should answer for it before the law. From the amorphousness and subjectlessness of Russian life, he highlights the names of those who carried out or took part in the terror – and for this reason he is dangerous for the system, which rests on the anonymity of terror and the silence of the victims.

The guardians of the system understand only too well that once the names of the long-dead executioners start to be exposed, the living participants in terror will no longer be able to retain their anonymity – and suddenly 'the Magnitsky list' rises up in the public space and hits the ruling elite in a sensitive place (it is no coincidence that removing this list was one of the first demands made by Putin to Donald Trump's administration). And then the European Parliament

241

is calling for the acceptance of 'the Dadin list', with specific names included on it of people who are linked to the torture of the civil rights activist Ildar Dadin, in the correctional colony in Karelia; he's managed to inform people about this via his lawyers. As is the case with the Stalinist executioners, simply rehabilitating the victim is insufficient: it is essential to specify the criminal act of a particular person responsible for the repression and, if possible, punish them for it. But, following this logic, risks start to appear on the horizon for the Russian authorities associated with the annexation of Crimea, and with the shooting down of MH17, and with the war in Eastern Ukraine, and with many other aspects of new Russian history, each of which is fraught with legal consequences for many officials, right up to the highest people in the state – exactly the same as Denis Karagodin did by showing that Joseph Stalin was a participant in the murder of his great-grandfather.

It is precisely by pulling on the thread of just one story about a peasant who was murdered by the *Chekists* in 1938 that can one gradually unravel the whole spider's web of anonymity and lies; and that's exactly why the state so fears the 'Karagodin effect', and has let loose on him its propaganda dogs. But Russia has no road into the future other than the legal one. The country has lived for too long under the shameful agreement between the victims and the executioners. The time has come to live according to the law and give a precise judicial assessment of the Stalinist terror and those who carried it out, and make justifying it a criminal offence – as justifying the Holocaust is now in most Western countries. Without this legal clarity regarding Stalinism in the past and the political terror taking place now in Russia, civil peace will be impossible, either with the current regime, or after it.

THE BATTLE AT THE RIVER ISET

There's yet another battle for memory raging in Russia. This time in the firing line for the propaganda barrage is the Yeltsin Centre in Yekaterinburg, a memorial museum, complete with library and multimedia centre, dedicated to the first Russian President, Boris Yeltsin, who hailed from the region. Specifically, objections were raised to an eight-minute-long cartoon film about Russian history, which they show to visitors. Speaking out against it were the film director, Nikita Mikhalkov, and the Culture Minister, Vladimir Medinsky; and the Mufti of the North Caucasus, Ismail Berdiev, declared that the Centre should be 'blown sky-high'.

The critics were answered by President Yeltsin's widow, Naina, and the local leadership, the Governor of the Sverdlovsk Oblast, Yevgeny Kuivashev, and the Mayor of Yekaterinburg, Yevgeny Royzman. Royzman replied to Medinsky and the Prime Minister, Dmitry Medvedev, saying that the ministers 'should be very careful about what they say'. It was they who, along with Vladimir Putin, opened the Centre in 2015, underlining the role of Russia's first president.

The row about the museum reflects the schizophrenia of the Russian leadership towards the figure of Yeltsin and to the 1990s in general. On the one hand, nearly all of them, politicians and oligarchs, grew up in Yeltsin's shadow, as they say – from Vladimir Putin, who served as the faithful bag-carrier of Yeltsin's comrade-in-arms, the charismatic Mayor of St Petersburg, Anatoly Sobchak; to Vladimir Medinsky, who was a pro-Yeltsin activist during the coup in Moscow in 1991; to Nikita Mikhalkov, who appeared during the presidential election campaign in 1996 as a trusted supporter of Boris Yeltsin. On the other hand, in the new political consensus of Putin's 2000s, the 1990s have become a target for abuse, they are seen as the original sin, stigmatized; and the new identity of power is being built on denying anything positive about that decade. Observing how the current elite tries to extricate itself from its links with that period

243

and with Yeltsin is a truly Freudian spectacle, reminding one of the Oedipus Complex and patricide.

However, this is not merely a case of the shadow of Yeltsin, which still makes the ruling class uncomfortable; it's a lot bigger than that. It's about Boris Yeltsin, and the Centre named after him, and his local region, the Urals, and in particular the film clip that is shown in the museum, which presents an alternative view of the generally accepted line of Russian history, which is authoritarian, imperial and Moscow-centred: it's this that has particularly upset the guardians of power. By the very fact of its existence, the Yeltsin Centre demonstrates the possibility of there being a different Russia: nonimperial, free and federal, which could have happened in the 1990s but which was torn up on 31 December 1999, that very New Year's night when Boris Yeltsin appeared on television and announced that he was stepping down, effectively naming Vladimir Putin as his successor.

The exterior of the museum is rather unusual. It was an unfinished and crudely constructed shopping centre, just like hundreds of others that sprang up in Russian cities in the 1990s. It was redesigned by the architect Boris Bernasconi, and turned into an open exhibition space with an enormous atrium, inside which there rises a spiral staircase, rather like in the Guggenheim Museum in New York. Huge windows look out onto a wide city pond, fed by waters from a dam on the Iset River, an industrial river that flows between Yekaterinburg's factory buildings and the pre-revolutionary merchants' houses. But the most outstanding feature of the building is the façade made of perforated aluminium. Most of all, this reminds one of a rusty iron curtain; light shines through the holes in it. In no sense could the building be described as pompous or even looking like a 'memorial'; rather, it looks like the rethinking of a cult object from the 1990s, a shopping centre, in technocratic and political terms, a redevelopment of commercial real estate for the public and human space.

This is what was turned into the Yeltsin Centre, which has become the focus of the cultural and social life of Yekaterinburg. As well as the museum and the library, there is an educational centre, a conference hall, a bookshop called 'Piotrovsky', which is probably the best one east of the Urals, and the '1991' café, where they sell burgers, Soviet-era cuisine, locally brewed craft beer and a bird-cherry cake made to Naina Yeltsina's special recipe. Dozens of conferences, concerts and exhibitions take place in the Centre, and the museum has become the most visited in the region, with up to a thousand people a day passing through its doors.

244

A real indication of the genuine popularity of the Centre is that it has become a stopping point for wedding parties; dozens of them can turn up on an autumn day.[46] Along with the statues of Lenin and the Bolshevik leader Yakov Sverdlov (after whom the city was re-named 'Sverdlovsk' in Soviet times, before reverting to its original name in 1991, although the region remains Sverdlovsk Oblast), the statue of Yeltsin – an imposing figure, carved out of a block of marble by the sculptor Georgy Frangulyan, and giving the impression that Yeltsin is stepping out of it – has also become a part of the traditional route for newlyweds as they tour the city's 'places of memory'. And on the bronze statue of Yeltsin, where he has apparently sat down on a bench to relax in the foyer of the Centre, the nose is shiny – it has become the norm to rub it for good luck. Here, Yeltsin is one of their own, a man from the Urals, an ambassador for the industrial population who conquered Moscow and changed Russia, and the people of the Urals stand shoulder to shoulder in his defence – as they did after Vladimir Medinsky and Nikita Mikhalkov denounced the Yeltsin Centre.

The Urals is a region with a very strong and deep sense of local identity. It represents an anti-imperialist alternative, and is an independent centre of power; it was no coincidence that in his speech against the Yeltsin Centre Mikhalkov mentioned the talk of Urals separatism which occurred in the 1990s. And independent politicians like the Mayor of Yekaterinburg, Yevgeny Royzman, simply strengthen the feeling that this is a special place. The siting of the museum in Yekaterinburg, one of Russia's cultural and industrial centres, was a strong step on the road to the decentralization that our country so badly needs, and the hysteria that erupted in Moscow because of the Yeltsin Centre was partly caused by the instinctive fear of regionalism.

But the main apple of discord is the eight-minute-long film clip of Russian history, which is shown on a constant loop in the small cinema at the start of the museum's exposition. It shows an unorthodox version of Russian history: as a series of attempts to break out to freedom. It doesn't show the Battle on the Ice of 1242, when the Prince of Novgorod, Alexander Nevsky, defeated the knights of the Livonian Order on Lake Chudskoe; but it does talk about the Novgorod *Veche*, the free city assembly, which elected its own princes and twice forced out Alexander Nevsky because he infringed the city's liberties, in contravention of their agreement. There is no mention of the capture of Kazan, the capital of the Kazan Khanate, by Ivan the Terrible in 1552; but there is 'the elected council', the informal government called by the young Tsar Ivan when he planned to reform the monarchy. The film talks about the enlightened dreams of Empress Catherine II at the end of the eighteenth century, which changed the word 'slave' to 'subject' in official documents; and about the draft constitution drawn up by Mikhail Speransky under Emperor Alexander I at the start of the nineteenth century; about the Decembrist uprising in 1825; and about the great reforms of Emperor Alexander II in the 1860s and the emancipation of the serfs. It tells how, in the twentieth century, the people were not broken by fear or Stalin's machine of repression, and were able to carry out industrialization and build 'the Magnetic Mountain', the largest metallurgical plant in the world in Magnitogorsk; achieve victory in the Second World War; conquer the Arctic and Space; it tells of Khrushchev's thaw and Gorbachev's *perestroika*. The film ends with the election of Boris Yeltsin, who completes the series of reforming leaders and becomes President, relying not on his personal power but on the independent choice of the people.

The film clip shows not the standard 'History of the Russian State', as written by all Russian historians, starting with Nikolai Karamzin and Vasily Klyuchevsky in the nineteenth century, but the history of Russian freedom. The video is full of respect for the people, their choice and their sovereignty. As the philosopher, Kirill Martynov, put it, it is 'a republican history, seen through the eyes of the downtrodden, who are excluded from the corrupt state food chain';[47] and this is what has upset the critics most of all, who demand from historians a dutiful list of rulers and victories, an encyclopaedia of the state's greatness.

The row about the Yeltsin Centre is not a discussion about Yeltsin or even about the 1990s; it's a row about Russian freedom and about the alternatives, the different paths of Russian history. The film shows how, century after century, Russia stood before the choice of freedom – but ended up choosing autocracy. In reality, the same thing happened with us in the nineties, and the main exposition in the museum illustrates this brilliantly. It was thought up by the film director Pavel Lungin, as a biblical seven days of creation – seven days that turned out to be turning points of the era, from the Plenum of the Central Committee of the Communist Party in October 1987, when Yeltsin declared that he didn't agree with the course being taken by Gorbachev, through the barricades of the coup of August 1991 and the ruins of Grozny, destroyed by the war in Chechnya from 1994 to 1996, to the presidential elections of 1996 and Yeltsin's heart operation later the same year.

The concept of the museum was created by the American company, Ralph Appelbaum Associates, famous for the Holocaust Museum in Washington, the Queen Elizabeth Olympic Park in London and the Jewish Museum and Tolerance Centre in Moscow. In the gallery devoted to 19 August 1991, visitors find themselves in an ordinary Moscow flat of those times: there's a divan, a rug, and a sideboard containing books and photographs (genuine items that belonged to the three young men who died during the defence of the White House); on the small cabinet there stands an old-style telephone, which suddenly starts to ring – and when you pick it up you can hear actual conversations from that time, with worried Muscovites telling each other about seeing tanks on the streets. This room leads straight onto the barricades, with metal barriers and the Russian tricolour, and from there visitors enter the empty void of a food shop in the autumn of 1991. On the counter lie scattered useless food vouchers, and on the shelves there are tins of seaweed, the only thing you could buy in the shops in those days of food shortages ...

'... And on the seventh day He rested, after His work of creation.' The journey through the nineties ends up in the President's office, the artefacts for which were all taken from the Kremlin and set up in Yekaterinburg. Beyond the fake windows there is a frosty December day in 1999, an accurate pile of documents stands on the desk, along with a malachite writing set and a steaming cup of tea; a jacket hangs on the back of the chair as if the owner had just popped out for a minute. In one corner the lights flash on the Christmas Tree, and in front of the desk there stand a television camera from Russian Television Channel One and a TV monitor, on which Yeltsin, sitting in that very chair, repeats his farewell address to the nation.

Leaving the office, visitors are now in an empty room called 'The Freedom Gallery'. On the wall there hangs a picture by the conceptual artist Erik Bulatov, where the word 'freedom' becomes lost in the clouds; on the window frames there are screens, on which famous people speak lovely yet unreliable words about freedom; in the windows there is the view of the dam on the Iset River, with the factories in the distance, a low sky, blackened by the smoke from the factory chimneys.

And a little to the right of the river, you can see the rich golden cupolas of The Church on the Blood, built on Yeltsin's personal instructions: as a sign of repentance, they say, for taking the decision when he was First Secretary of the Sverdlovsk Region Committee of the Communist Party to knock down the Ipatiev House, the place where the Royal Family was murdered.[48]

This exit into emptiness says no less about the era than do the 'seven days' of its creation. The era ends on that winter's day, when, under the gaze of the television camera, the heavy and puffy Boris Yeltsin handed over his office and the nuclear briefcase to the young Vladimir Putin, who was confused and couldn't believe his luck, while Yeltsin, wiping away a tear, said to him, 'Look after Russia'. At that moment, Russia once again – as in the stories of the Novgorod *Veche*, Catherine's reformist projects and Speransky's dreams of a constitution – chose authoritarianism. Yet another attempt to break through to freedom slowly died as the nineties wore on and, as a result, produced Putin. And as the visitor looks round this empty gallery, he or she simply cannot but think about the pattern of what happened and about Russia's path through history, which each time tries to set out on the path to freedom, but inevitably slides down into slavery.

Nevertheless, the Yeltsin Centre is dangerous for the guardians of the state and the obscurantists, who see it as an alternative space, as an image of a different Russia – nonimperial and not run by Moscow. They see it as epitomizing the freemen of the Urals and regional autonomy, as a mechanism for remembering the gatherings of millions of people on the Manezh Square in Moscow and that period when the state, the eternal Russian Leviathan, stepped aside and shrunk back under the pressure of space, the people, history and freedom. It's like the bulky stone version of Yeltsin at the entrance: this bear of a man, the representative of that same rebellious element of the people which so frightens Nikita Mikhalkov, behaving like the typical Russian *barin*, the landlord, in the times of serfdom. Instead of the Yeltsin Centre, they would rather build across the country a chain of Stalin Centres and military-patriotic parks with tanks. But they are quite incapable of seeing a very simple truth: genuine patriotism means freedom. And the museum on the River Iset preserves this idea as a memory, as nostalgia – and as hope.

CONSTITUTION DAY

On a cold morning in mid-December 2015, a grey-haired old man stepped onto the platform of the Yaroslavl Station in Moscow from a third-class carriage of the fast train No. 43 from Khabarovsk to Moscow, carrying a knapsack in his hands. He was of shortish height, broad-shouldered and stocky, wearing an old sheepskin coat, fur hat and mittens, and with felt *valenki* boots on his feet. He stopped, looking around in wonder, but was immediately shoved in the back by passengers exiting with their luggage, and was cursed by a porter with a trolley. 'What're you standing there for gawping, grandad! Get a move on! You've arrived!'

The old man picked up his bag and moved off along the platform with the crowd. The policemen with a dog by the exit were busy checking the documents of two Chinese people and paid him no attention. As he drew closer, the dog gave a quiet growl, but then whined and tucked in its tail. The old man went past the stalls selling icons and the kebab kiosks, squeezed past the crush to get into the metro and found himself on Three Stations Square, with its clusters of taxis, ringing of tram bells and smoke-blackened railway bridge, beyond which he could see tall towers. Large snowflakes began to fall from a leaden sky. The old man pulled his belt tighter around himself, threw his knapsack over his shoulder, and set off on foot into the throbbing winter city.

This old man was none other than the Decembrist, Alexander Nikolaevich Lutsky, a junker of the Moscow Life-Guards Regiment, who was charged with taking part in the uprising on Senate Square in St Petersburg on 14 December 1825 and who was known also as 'the forgotten Decembrist'. He was born in 1804 in Borovichi, into the family of Senior Officer Nikolai Andreevich Lutsky, who belonged to the old noble family from the Lutsk District in Volhynia. Alexander did not actually take part in the Decembrist Uprising, but in defending the crowd he wounded a police horse, for which he was arrested and incarcerated in the Peter and Paul Fortress on an island on the Neva.

The investigation lasted over a year, and in January 1827, a military court decreed that 'Lutsky be relieved of his Junior Officer rank and under the terms of military rule 137 he be hung.' Three months later the death sentence was commuted to permanent exile 'with hard labour', and he was sent off to Siberia. He didn't go with the other Decembrists, but was sent on 'the bar' with the ordinary criminals. They spent the whole journey in foot shackles, and by day were handcuffed and attached to an iron rail known as 'the bar'. They walked between twenty to twenty-five *versts*[49] each day, through heat and frost, and when they came to villages they sang the mournful 'Lord have mercy' in order to beg alms from the peasants. On the way, Lutsky frequently fell ill; he ended up spending two months in the infirmary in Kazan, and five months in Perm.

Lutsky was relieved of hard labour down a silver mine only after twenty years, during which time he had married the daughter of the mine's barber, Martha Portnova, and had four children. An amnesty was declared in August 1856, but this news didn't reached Lutsky until 1857, which is why he has gone down in history as 'the forgotten Decembrist'. He settled in the town of Nerchinsk, in the Trans-Baikal Region, where he taught at the Nerchinsk Parish school. The last record of 'the nobleman teacher Alexander Nikolaevich Lutsky', found in the archive in Chita, is dated 8 December 1870.

Further details about his life are sporadic. It's known that Lutsky liked to go hunting and would head off alone into the taiga with his rifle and his dog; he could be gone for several days. Despite his advanced years, he enjoyed excellent health and was remarkably strong; it seems that the hard labour had toughened him up and given him a rare will to live. It is generally thought that he disappeared in the taiga during a fierce snowstorm on 22 February 1882, aged seventy-eight, having lived through the reigns of three emperors; but in fact, having lost his dog, he took refuge from the storm in the empty shelter of a Buryat shaman. There he found dried biscuits, yak's fat and herbal tea, and, having brewed this and drunk it he fell into a wonderful sleep – for 133 years.

When he awoke in the autumn of 2015, he emerged from the taiga and wandered in amazement along the streets of Nerchinsk, craning his neck to look up at the tall buildings and dodging the cars. His natural intelligence and his experience as a prisoner helped him to adapt to his new surroundings; and the collection of squirrel skins which he brought out of the taiga helped him to avoid being sent to a psychiatric hospital and even enabled him to obtain a new passport 'to replace the lost one'. In the police station they just laughed, having concluded that they were dealing with just another 'pest', an unlucky prospector who had found his way out of the taiga just before the winter set in. At the start of December, Lutsky made his way to Shilkia, and from there to Chita, where he boarded the train from Khabarovsk and arrived in Moscow on the morning of 12 December – Constitution Day and on the eve of the one hundred and ninetieth anniversary of the Decembrist Uprising, which his old new Motherland had almost forgotten about ...

* * *

The Decembrists occupy a special place in our national pantheon, but opinions about them are split in two. Some see them as irreproachable heroes, the seventeen-year-old generals who went through the Napoleonic campaign and the allurement of Paris, and who created the first and only 'revolution of dignity' in Russia. Others, though, consider them to have been inept conspirators, whose plan for an uprising failed miserably: Pyotr Kakhovsky failed to shoot the Tsar; the 'dictator', Prince Sergei Trubetskoi, went and hid at his relatives' place; Captain Alexander Yakubovich didn't lead the Guards to attack the Winter Palace; Colonel Alexander Bulatov was unable to seize the Peter and Paul Fortress; and four thousand soldiers and rebellious officers were left standing in the cold all day not knowing what to do, just five hundred paces from the Winter Palace, until, as the sun was going down, they were fired upon with buckshot. From one side it is seen as an attempt to plant the first green shoots of the French Enlightenment in their native soil; from the other, it is perceived as the complete collapse of their ideas, leading to all hope of change in Russia being frozen for the next thirty years until the Crimean War finally bankrupted the system of serfdom. On the one hand, they were canonized by the Soviet system, caressed by the propaganda and official histories: streets and steamboats were named after them, local historians and schoolchildren trod in their footsteps and more than twenty thousand academic works were written about them. On the other hand, the authorities today clearly don't love them: they see the Decembrists as rioters and Voltaireans, as freemasons (literally: a recent film, *The Order of the Russian Knights*, accuses the Rosicrucian Order of organizing the uprising) and even as agents of influence from the West – another recent film, *The Mirage of Enchanting Happiness*, tells how British intelligence used the Decembrists as a way of getting their hands on the gold in the Urals.

And if Yemelyan Pugachev[50] is a metaphor for the senseless Russian riot,[51] then the Decembrists are a metaphor for the doomed Russian uprising. Alexander Herzen created the sacrificial myth about the Decembrists, which was taken up by tens of thousands of people, from members of 'the People's Will'[52] to the Bolsheviks, who created, in the words of the modern historian Sergei Erlikh, 'a sacrificial class' of the Russian intelligentsia. This myth encouraged the 'sixties generations' of both the nineteenth and twentieth centuries, including the writer Natan Eidelman, with his books about the Decembrists, and the poet Alexander Galich, with his *Petersburg Romances*: 'Dare you go out to the Square / At the appointed hour?'[53] The Decembrists' myth has even encouraged the opposition today: at his trial, Mikhail Khodorkovsky called his wife, Inna, 'a Decembrist' (referring to the historical fact that almost all the Decembrists' wives voluntarily followed their husbands to Siberian exile), and in his first message from prison in Chita, in the Trans-Baikal region, he wrote that he was 'in the land of the Decembrists'. The protests in Moscow in December 2011 and the entire 'White Protest Movement' that winter also followed the Decembrist myth, both with its pride and its elite character, and the fact that it was doomed to failure: it was unable to excite the crowd and persuade them to march from Bolotnaya Square to Revolution Square by the Kremlin. That was exactly the 'Decembrists' syndrome': individual dignity yet collective defeat. On the evening of 30 December 2014, when there was a 'people's assembly' on Manezh Square in Moscow (discussing the sentence passed on the Navalny brothers, which had been fabricated by the state), a few thousand people stood in the frost along the pavements on nearby Tverskaya Street and Okhotny Ryad, unsure about chanting slogans, or going onto the Square or stopping the traffic – just like the Decembrists, two hundred years ago.

* * *

... By one o'clock in the afternoon, Alexander Lutsky had reached the Kremlin. He stood on Red Square, crossed himself in front of the Cathedral of Our Lady of Kazan and the Resurrection Gates, was amazed by the clumsy equine statue of Marshal Zhukov, underneath whom the horse appeared to be striding forth with an outlandish gait, and wandered on up Tverskaya Street, past the bright shop windows and through the crowds, lively with the New Year approaching. Reaching Pushkin Square, he saw the statue of the poet, whose work he used to read in his youth, but whom he had never met. It was busy around the monument. Workmen had erected a huge artificial Christmas tree and fairytale plywood towers, and alongside them buses had pulled up, and out of them were emerging dozens of men in black uniforms and protective vests bearing the word 'Police'.

The construction of the Christmas tree was being directed by a chubby man holding a folder, who was giving instructions to the workers, and saying something to the actors who had just turned up. Seeing Lutsky with his knapsack on his back he called out: 'What's this then, Santa Claus, why are you late? And what's with the sheepskin coat? No one said anything about that.'

Much to the surprise of the Decembrist, they plonked a fake red hat decorated with silver on his head, placed in his hand a heavy staff with a twisted handle and told him to go and wait by the stage, which the workmen were hurriedly putting together. By now the snow was falling much more heavily; a veritable snowstorm was brewing. At that moment, Lutsky noticed a group of people who had gathered on the other side of Pushkin's statue. Standing a little way apart from each other, they began to unfurl homemade banners, which read, 'Observe the Constitution'. Some of them were holding little booklets of the Russian Constitution in their hands. The policemen started to run towards these people, ripping their banners out of their hands, pushing their arms behind their backs and marching them off, barely resisting, to other buses standing there, which had bars on the windows. At the same time, some of the others in black formed a line. People were coming up a staircase out of the ground and the men in black started to push them back down, as their commander began to say into a loudspeaker: 'Citizens, disperse! There's a Christmas tree being put together here! Don't stop, move into the metro!'

A little way off to the side of this pandemonium, Lutsky noticed an elderly lady standing on her own, holding a banner which said, 'Down with the power of the *Chekists*!' One of the men in black raced over to her and started to snatch the banner, but the woman resisted and wouldn't give it up. The man hit her. At this, beside himself with anger, Lutsky rushed over and clouted the policeman on the back with his staff. Surprised by this assault, the policeman let go of the woman and fell down in the snow, at which four hefty lads in black pounced on the Decembrist and started to beat him with their truncheons and their fists, seized his arms, put him in handcuffs and threw him into the bus with the barred windows, deliberately hitting his head on the door as they did so. 'And this bloody protestor dressed up as Santa Claus!'

Breathing heavily, the Decembrist collapsed on the bench, and spat out blood. There was only one other detainee in the bus, a young man who looked at Lutsky with curiosity. Waiting until he had got his breath back, the young man asked him:

'So they got you then, grandad?'

'Ah, it's nothing, I'm used to it ... They used to beat us with cudgels that were much worse. And our handcuffs were heavier.'

'You've been in prison, then?'

'Twenty years down a mine.'

'Twenty years!' drawled the young man with respect. 'Were you a political?'[54]

'Yes, a political.'

'And what were you after?'

'A constitution.'

'*We* want a constitution, too', said the young man, excitedly. 'Today's Constitution Day, and they bang us up for it.'

''T'was ever thus,' said the Decembrist. They were silent for a while.

'So what else were you after?' the young man asked.

'The abolition of estates', Lutsky began to reminisce; 'equality for all before the law, freedom of speech, freedom of association ...'

'That's exactly what we want! Nothing ever changes in this country ...'

Outside the bus, New Year music started to play: a group of balalaikas struck up, and in a high voice, rising and falling, a woman was singing folk couplets. Her singing was mixed in with weak cries of, 'The Constitution!' and orders from the police colonel: 'Clear the square! Don't hang around, into the metro!'

Lutsky smirked: 'We called for a constitution, too. We told the soldiers that "Constitution" was the name of the wife of the Grand Prince Constantine, so that we would get them to shout her name: "We want Constantine and Constitution!" You should find a woman's name, too.'

'I know, we'll say that "Constitution" is the name of Putin's new dog!'

'Caligula made his horse a member of the Senate', said Lutsky. 'It's all been done before.'

The gearstick of the bus crunched, the vehicle shook and set off. The jolly music and the shouts of the demonstrators faded, only bits of the exhortations of the colonel drifted to them: 'Citizens ... don't obstruct the path ... into the metro ... .' The snow-covered trees of Strastnoy Boulevard swam past, with the crows cawing above them. It was beginning to get dark, it had stopped snowing; a turquoise sky with pink clouds appeared. The van turned right onto Petrovka Street, and through the bars on the windows they could see the red-brick walls of the Higher Petrovsky Monastery.

'Chaadaev was right,' muttered Lutsky to himself. 'Time stands still, and this is a country where everything changes every year and nothing changes for centuries.'

'Don't worry, grandad', said the young man, getting out a flask with brandy. 'We'll celebrate the New Year in the detention prison, then there'll be the court case, and eventually we'll be sent to Chita. Article 318, attacking an officer of the law when he is on duty, part one, without risk to life, up to five years. But you're used to it, anyway. Well, here's to the New Year!'

'Here's to the New Year,' said Lutsky and swallowed the brandy. The paddy wagon, its engine buzzing, continued along the eternal route of Russian history.

GLOSSARY AND ABBREVIATIONS

Chaadaev, Pyotr – Russian philosopher who wrote eight *Philosophical Letters* between 1826 and 1831, the main thesis being that Russia had always lagged behind the West and had contributed nothing to progress. The letters were considered unsound and were banned by the Russian imperial authorities. Chaadaev was declared insane and put under constant medical supervision.

Cheka, Chekist – The first Soviet secret police force formed after the Bolshevik Revolution of November 1917 was called the 'All-Russian Extraordinary Commission' (Russian: *Vserossiiskaya Chrezvychainaya Komissiya*), abbreviated to VChK (Russian: *Ve-Che-Ka*) and commonly known as *Cheka* (from the initialism ChK). The word 'Extraordinary' in the title suggested that it would have extraordinary powers. Throughout subsequent Soviet and Russian history, although the name has changed on a number of occasions (the last Soviet version being the KGB and, post-Soviet, the FSB), the organization became an essential part of the state apparatus. A member of the first organization hence became a *Chekist*, a nickname by which members of the successor organizations have always referred to themselves. A system run by *Chekists* may be referred to as *Chekism*.

Decembrists – Army officers who staged an unsuccessful uprising in 1825 in support of greater freedoms. Some of the ringleaders were executed, most were imprisoned or sent into exile in Siberia.

Disinformation – 'Disinformation' is one of the few words to have come into English from Russian. It means the use of false, misleading or partially true information with the *deliberate* intention of misleading the recipient. It should not be confused

256

with 'misinformation', which is the passing on of inaccurate or wrong information in the mistaken belief that it its true.

DPR – Donetsk People's Republic, *Donetskaya Narodnaya Respublika* or *DNR*; one of the two self-proclaimed areas in Eastern Ukraine to have called themselves *Novorossiya* after the Russian-backed war broke out in 2014; see **LPR**.

Federal Assembly of the Russian Federation – The Russian Parliament, created by the post-Soviet Constitution of 1993. The Federal Assembly comprises the **Federation Council** (the upper house, sometimes referred to as 'the Senate') and the **State Duma** (the lower house).

FSB – *Federalnaya Sluzhba Bezopasnosti*, Federal Security Service; the post-Soviet successor to the **KGB** (see below).

Glasnost – 'Openness', a part of Mikhail Gorbachev's plan to reform the USSR. He realized that his plan to restructure the country – *perestroika* (see below) – would not work if people did not finally admit openly to problems and shortcomings. *Glasnost* encouraged people to do this.

GULAG – The system of prison camps established across the Soviet Union under Stalin in 1929. It is an acronym for *Glavnoe uprav-lenie lagerei*, the Main Directorate of Camps. It became known in English especially with the English-language publication of Alexander Solzhenitsyn's major work, *The GULAG Archipelago*, in 1974. The fact of its publication abroad was the main reason why, that year, Solzhenitsyn was exiled from the USSR.

KGB – *Komitet Gosudarstvennoi Bezopasnosti*, Committee for State Security; the last name of the Soviet era for the secret police, initially established by the Bolsheviks in 1917 as the *Cheka*.

LPR – Lugansk People's Republic, *Luganskaya Narodnaya Respublika* or *LNR*; one of the two self-proclaimed areas in Eastern Ukraine to have called themselves *Novorossiya* after the Russian-backed war broke out in 2014; see **DPR**.

Muzhik – 'A bloke'; originally meaning a peasant man, it is now used either to suggest a common or uncouth fellow, or, in a male company, 'one of the guys'.

NGO – Nongovernmental organization, such as charities. This can also (in Russian) be used to signify not-for-profit organizations.

OMON – *Otryad militsii osobogo naznacheniya*. Special police squads, used particularly for crowd control or as riot police. They were first introduced in the late 1980s, shortly before the break-up of the USSR. Since then the Russian police have renamed themselves 'police' instead of 'militia' but the acronym 'OMON' has remained the same.

Oprichnik – The term given to a member of the *Oprichnina*, an organization of praetorian guards established by Tsar Ivan the Terrible to govern a division of Russia from 1565 to 1572.

Papirosi – Cheap Russian cigarettes which, instead of a filter, have a cardboard tube that is pinched twice before the tobacco is lit at the other end.

Patsan, (pl. patsany) – 'Lad', as in the idea of being 'one of the lads', a word commonly used in the criminal subculture. This is very much a part of Putin's view of himself and why he feels he can connect with the male part of the Russian population.

Perestroika – Mikhail Gorbachev's plan to reform the Soviet Union when he was General Secretary of the Communist Party (and thus, leader of the country) between 1985 and 1991. *Perestroika* literally means 'restructuring'; but the Soviet system proved incapable of restructuring and in 1991 collapsed. See also **Glasnost**.

Potemkin Village – Something put on purely for show, with no substance behind it. The term comes from stories of a fake portable village built solely to impress Empress Catherine II by her minister and lover, Grigory Potemkin, during her journey to Crimea in 1787. As the Empress rode past, she saw what appeared to be smart dwellings and happy peasants; but the 'dwellings' were no more than stage sets.

Propiska – Soviet-era registration, which allows the bearer to live in a particular city, introduced to prevent mass migration to the big cities. This is considered by the Council of Europe to be a violation of human rights, and when Russia joined the Council in 1996 it agreed to do away with the *propiska*.

Samogon – Homemade vodka, particularly produced in the Russian countryside. Russians can be very inventive in making *samogon*, using all kinds of grain, fruit and vegetables.

Siloviki – Literally, the men from the 'power ministries'. But this is not referring to energy; it means 'power' in the sense of strength (Russian: *sila*), and refers to the security forces (such as the KGB/FSB), Ministry of Defence and Ministry of the Interior (which as well as being responsible for the police also has thousands of its own troops) as well as for numerous other uniformed services: the National Guard (*Rosgvardia*), the Prosecutor General's Office (*General'naya prokuratura*), The Investigative Committee (*Sledstvennyi komitet*), the Federal Guards Service (FSO), the Federal Prison Service (FSIN), the Federal Emergency Committee (*Emercom*), etc.

Sovok – A slang term, which came in towards the end of the Soviet Union to mean either the old-fashioned Soviet way of doing things, or someone whose mentality was still stuck in those outdated ways. The added irony is that it is also the Russian word for a dustpan.

Stukach, (pl. stukachy) – Commonly used slang term for someone who denounces other people, especially (but not exclusively) in Stalinist times. It is derived from the verb *stuchat*, 'to knock'.

SVR – *Sluzhba Vneshnei Razvedki*, the External Intelligence Service; the part of the former **KGB** (see above) responsible for intelligence gathering outside Russia.

Toska – 'Longing', 'yearning' or even 'melancholy'. Russians can be very emotional; and when abroad (either by choice or, even worse, because of exile), '*toska po rodine*', 'yearning for the Motherland', can be a very powerful emotion, greater than is conveyed by the term 'homesick'.

Valenki – Winter boots made of felt, looking like oversized wellingtons. They tend to be worn by peasants or labourers.

VKontakte (VK) – Russian social media network, rather like Facebook.

VTsIOM – *Vserossissky tsentr izucheniya obshchestvennogo mneniya*, Russian Public Opinion Research Centre: founded in 1987, this is the oldest polling centre in Russia.

Vysotsky, Vladimir – Vladimir Vysotsky was a popular singer of ballads in the 1960s and 1970s, whose often humorous songs were regarded as being on the edge of what was acceptable to the Communist leadership. He died in 1980 aged just forty-two, which helped contribute to his cult status.

White House – In Soviet times, the White House was the seat of the Russian Supreme Soviet (Parliament). It was at the heart of the opposition to the failed coup against the Soviet President, Mikhail Gorbachev, in August 1991; and then the scene of the stand-off against the Russian President, Boris Yeltsin, in October 1993, which ended when Yeltsin ordered tanks to fire on the building. It is now the seat of the Russian government.

NOTES

Part I: The War for Space

1 'Space' here should be understood in the sense of everything around us, not what is beyond the planet.
2 Victory Day – 9 May – the anniversary of the end of the Second World War in Europe, is still celebrated as a national holiday in Russia. The peace treaty with Germany was signed late on 8 May, by which time it was already the 9th in Moscow.
3 https://www.facebook.com/mgorskih/posts/864591610296259.
4 https://ru.wikisource.org/wiki/%D0%A3%D0%BC%D0%B5%D1%80_%D0%90%D0%BB%D0%B5%D0%BA%D1%81%D0%B0%D0%BD%D0%B4%D1%80_%D0%91%D0%BB%D0%BE%D0%BA_(%D0%9C%D0%B0%D1%8F%D0%BA%D0%BE%D0%B2%D1%81%D0%BA%D0%B8%D0%B9) (in Russian). In 1914, following the outbreak of the First World War, St Petersburg was renamed 'Petrograd', as the original name sounded too German and was thought inappropriate given that Russia was at war with Germany. In 1924, the city was once more renamed. As the place where the Bolshevik Revolution of October 1917 had begun, and following the death of the leader of the Revolution, Lenin, the city was given Lenin's name: Leningrad. In 1991 it reverted to its original name, St Petersburg.
5 http://pelevin.nov.ru/romans/pe-genp/1.html (para. 8).
6 This is a phrase that has been used to signify a short conflict aimed at distracting the public's attention from problems in society. It was first used to describe the war against Japan in 1904–5, which went horribly wrong for Russia and ended in defeat. The need for a 'small victorious war' was said to be one of the reasons why President Boris Yeltsin started the ultimately humiliating conflict in Chechnya in December 1994, which ended in June 1996 with the Russian Army forced to retreat in shame and disarray.
7 Putin and many in his circle come from the secret police (FSB or its Soviet predecessor, the KGB); the Ministry of Defence; the Armed Forces; or the Ministry of the Interior. Collectively, these are known as 'the power ministries', 'power' in the sense of strength – *sila* – not energy. Those who exercise this *sila* are known as *siloviki*.

8 The 'Cat Stomping Law' was introduced in January 2013 by the St Petersburg City Council. It levies a fine against anyone making too much noise between the hours of 2300 and 0700, by 'shouting, whistling, moving furniture, singing, playing a musical instrument or other actions which would disturb the peace and quiet of citizens'. There were proposals put forward that the list should include, 'loud snoring, loud sex, moving a refrigerator and a cat stomping'. These suggestions were left out of the law, but nevertheless gave it its nickname.

9 Gerhard Schroeder, former German Chancellor, and Silvio Berlusconi, former Italian Prime Minister, each of whom has forged close links with Putin.

10 The first Soviet secret police force was called the *Cheka*, and those who served in it, *Chekists*. The KGB and its successor, the FSB, still pride themselves on their connection with the *Cheka*. The author is here using the term disparagingly, linking it with religion – which the *Cheka* persecuted mercilessly – to describe Vladimir Putin.

11 https://www.colta.ru/articles/society/2477-konservativnaya-revolyutsiya-smysl-kryma. 'The Conservative Revolution. The Meaning of Crimea' (in Russian), 17 March 2014.

12 A number of cities in the USSR were given the title of 'hero-city' because of the battles that took place there during the Second World War (or 'Great Patriotic War', as Russians call that part which involved the Soviet Union). Sevastopol is one such city.

13 The favourite of Empress Catherine the Great, Grigory Potemkin, is credited with conquering the southern territories and incorporating them into the Russian Empire, including Crimea and a region therein called Taurida. As a result, he was given the name 'Potemkin-Taurida'. Prokhanov believes that Putin should have similar recognition for seizing back Crimea from Ukraine.

14 Samuel Huntington was an American political scientist, best known for his 1993 theory, the 'Clash of Civilizations'. He argued that post-Cold War, future wars would be fought not between countries, but between cultures, and that Islamic extremism would become the biggest threat to world peace.

15 The Young Pioneers organization educated children between the ages of nine and fifteen to be loyal to the dictates of the Communist Party and the Soviet motherland. Most children belonged to the Pioneers.

16 The euphemism, 'the final charge to the south', was used by the nationalist politician, Vladimir Zhirinovsky, as the title of his book on the invasion of Afghanistan, which began at the end of 1979, and which he foresaw as ending with Soviet soldiers 'washing their boots in the Indian Ocean'. In fact, it ended with the Soviet Army pulling out of Afghanistan in February 1989 with its tail between its legs and a legacy of disillusion and discontent, which contributed to the collapse of the USSR a little over two years later. See note 17 for a reference to Zhirinovsky.

17 The Liberal Democratic Party of Russia was the first political party to register after the Communist Party's monopoly on power was removed from the Soviet Constitution in February 1990. Led by Vladimir Zhirinovsky, a fanatical Russian nationalist, the party was reportedly created by the secret police, the KGB, with the express aim of discrediting in the eyes of the Russian people the terms 'liberal' and 'democratic'. The party was and remains neither liberal nor democratic.

18 http://www.kph.npu.edu.ua/!e-book/clasik/data/mmk/cathedra.html.
19 'Pulling up their pants and chasing the Komsomol' is a line from the Russian poet, Sergei Yesenin, as he tried to reconcile himself with the new Soviet life in the early 1920s.The Komsomol – the Young Communist League – was the next stage after the Pioneers. It encouraged social activism and further indoctrinated Soviet youth.
20 Sometimes known as the DNR, from the Russian original, *Donetskaya Narodnaya Respublika*. It should be noted that neither this designation nor the Lugansk People's Republic (LPR/LNR) are recognized internationally as separate republics.
21 8 March was always marked in the USSR as International Women's Day. It is now celebrated more widely around the world. It was one of the dates of the 'Red Calendar', introduced by the Bolsheviks after the Revolution as a replacement for the church calendar, with its feast days and saints' days. The Red Calendar devoted specific days to workers in different areas of society, such as 'Miners' Day', referred to a little later.
22 https://www.colta.ru/articles/society/5329-22-dnya-v-dnr. '22 Days in the DNR' (in Russian), 11 November 2014.
23 Stepan Razin and Yemelyan Pugachev led peasant revolts. In Soviet times these were idealized into early examples of uprisings of the common people.
24 Nestor Makhno was commander of the Revolutionary Insurrectionary Army of Ukraine, which fought for an independent Ukraine during the Civil War. Alexander Antonov led an insurrection in the Tambov Province in Russia against the Bolsheviks.
25 Pavlov was assassinated in 2016.
26 'Kofemaniya' is a popular chain of coffee shops in Russia.
27 https://www.vedomosti.ru/newspaper/articles/2013/10/29/obschestvo-ne-spravlyaetsya-s-pritokom-migrantov. 'Integration: Society Can't Cope with the Flow of Immigrants' (in Russian), 29 October 2013.
28 Vladimir Nabokov, *The Gift* (Panther Books, St Albans, 1966; trans. Michael Scammell, pp. 148–9).
29 The Belovezha Accords were so called because, on 8 December 1991, the Presidents of Russia, Ukraine and Belarus, meeting in the Belovezha Forest Reserve in Belarus, signed the deal setting up the Commonwealth of Independent States (CIS). The establishment of this organization signalled the end of the USSR, although it was only seventeen days later, on 25 December, that Mikhail Gorbachev formally resigned as Soviet President.
30 The Maidan – Freedom Square – as the main square in Kiev was named after the break-up of the Soviet Union, was the centre of the protest movement that eventually brought about the fall of the regime of the pro-Russian President, Viktor Yanukovych, in February 2014.
31 In April 1986, an explosion at the Chernobyl nuclear power plant in Ukraine caused an ecological disaster in the surrounding areas of Ukraine and Belarus. It remains the world's worst nuclear disaster.
32 In the classic Russian bath-house – the *banya* – while in the steam room people beat each other with eucalyptus or birch branches to stimulate circulation. Eucalyptus is supposed to be a sign of better quality.
33 Places in Pokémon Go that allow players to collect items such as eggs and more Poke Balls to capture more Pokémon.
34 The State Duma is the lower house of the Russian Parliament. The upper

house is the Federation Council, members of which are referred to as 'senators'. The two houses together are called the Federal Assembly.

35 https://www.interfax.ru/russia/519453. 'Medinsky says computer games are evil' (in Russian), 19 July 2016.

36 The Customs Union gives customs-free travel for citizens of the member states of the Eurasian Economic Union: Armenia, Belarus, Kazakhstan, Kyrgyzstan and Russia.

37 Following allegations of rigged elections for the State Duma in December 2011, there were mass demonstrations in Moscow, the like of which had not been seen since the last days of the Soviet Union. These demonstrations seemed to convince President Putin that he needed to have a stronger grip on society.

38 https://www.svoboda.org/a/27686926.html Radio Liberty, 'Kremlin Firewall' (in Russian), 20 April 2016.

39 The vast majority of the territory of the Soviet Union was 'closed' to foreigners: they were not allowed to go there. There were also numerous 'closed towns' – sometimes large cities – where even Soviet citizens needed a special pass to live or visit. For foreigners there was no such thing as a visa for the Soviet Union. The visa stipulated the places to be visited and was valid for travel only within a twenty-five-kilometre radius of the centre of that place – provided no 'closed' areas fell within it.

40 In 2009 it was announced that the Russian government was to create a place of technological advancement and innovation at Skolkovo, just to the west of Moscow.

41 *Oprichnik* was the term given to a member of the *Oprichnina*, an organization established by Tsar Ivan the Terrible to govern a division of Russia from 1565 to 1572. The *Telluria* of the third title is an imagined republic with large deposits of 'tellurium' peacefully snuggled in the Altai Mountains.

42 Stephen D. Krasner, *Sovereignty: Organized Hypocrisy* (Princeton University Press, 1999).

43 The *Zemsky Sobor* was a type of feudal parliament, first called by Ivan the Terrible in 1549. In 1613 it elected Mikhail Romanov to the throne, beginning a dynasty which lasted until Nicholas II was removed by the Revolution of February 1917.

Part II: The War for Symbols

1 Moscow-City is the business district of the Russian capital, where the skyscrapers have gone up since the collapse of the USSR. The name was chosen as a direct reference to 'the City of London', the British capital's business district.

2 Stalin ordered the building of seven imposing skyscrapers of similar design, nicknamed 'wedding cakes', including Moscow State University, the Ukraina Hotel and the Foreign Ministry. In the post-Soviet period an eighth has been built.

3 A line from the untitled poem, which begins, 'Now I am dead in my grave with my lips moving'. http://writing.upenn.edu/epc/library/Mandelstam_Poems_Ilya-Bernstein.pdf. 'The Poems of Osip Mandelstam', trans Ilya Bernstein (EPC Digital Edition, 2014, p. 40).

263

4 Peter the Great brutally put down a rebellion by his soldiers known as the *streltsy* – from the verb, *strelyat*, meaning 'to shoot' – who were protesting about their conditions. Some were publicly executed on Red Square.

5 Within a few months of the Revolution in November 1917, the Bolsheviks moved the Russian capital back to Moscow from Petrograd (formerly St Petersburg, later Leningrad; now once again St Petersburg).

6 https://www.vedomosti.ru/opinion/articles/2008/03/14/stalinskij-proekt-u-stola-vlasti. 'The Stalinist Project: At the Table of Power' (in Russian), 14 March 2008.

7 In 1722, Tsar Peter the Great introduced the Table of Ranks, which carefully delineated the standing of everyone in the military, government and court. 'Feudalism' in Russia effectively lasted until the emancipation of the serfs in 1861.

8 This is what the peasants had to do in tsarist times if the Tsar's carriage went past.

9 A cargo cult is a belief system among members of a relatively undeveloped society in which adherents practice superstitious rituals hoping to bring modern goods supplied by a more technologically advanced society.

10 https://texty-pesen.ru/zato-my-delaem-rakety.html. Yuri Vizbor, 'But we build missiles', words and music (in Russian).

11 In August 1991, hard-liners in the Communist leadership tried to seize power to prevent the President, Mikhail Gorbachev, from signing an agreement with the constituent republics of the USSR, which, they believed, would lead to the break-up of the country. Their so-called coup lasted less than three days and had the effect of speeding up the process of the disintegration of the Soviet Union. In 1993, there was a stand-off between the Russian President, Boris Yeltsin, and his opponents in Parliament. After fighting on the streets of Moscow had left dozens dead, Yeltsin took the decision to send in the tanks and bombard the Parliament building, where his opponents had barricaded themselves in.

12 The Russian (and before that, Soviet) Army used to be staffed by professional officers and conscript soldiers. Under President Putin a category has been introduced of 'contract' soldiers, who sign up for a specific period and who are paid, unlike conscripts.

13 https://ria.ru/20150619/1079035580.html. 'Russian Defence Ministry Orders Research on 'Colour Revolutions' (in Russian), 19 June 2015.

14 http://www.strana-oz.ru/2013/2/klassifikaciya-i-ranzhirovanie-ugroz (in Russian).

15 Vladimir Vysotsky was a popular singer of ballads in the 1960s and 1970s whose often humorous songs were regarded as being on the edge of what was acceptable to the Communist leadership. http://vysotskiy-lit.ru/vysotskiy/stihi-varianty/317.htm. Letter to the Editor (in Russian).

16 *The Observer*, 17 March 1985.

17 https://tass.ru/politika/2536355 (in Russian), 17 December 2015.

18 Alexei Yurchak, *Everything Was Forever, Until It Was No More: The Last Soviet Generation* (Princeton University Press, 2005).

19 Khatyn is a Belarusian village where the entire population of more than 150 people was slaughtered, mostly burned alive, by the Nazis in retaliation for an attack by Soviet partisans. Eight people managed to survive. Babiy Yar is the site of the mass extermination of the Jews and other residents of Kiev by

the Germans in 1941. It is believed that nearly 34,000 Jews were massacred in less than forty-eight hours.

20 Alexander Pushkin, Letter to Pyotr Vyazemsky (8 June 1827).

21 The Russian term is '*okolofutbol*', literally meaning 'around football'. It suggests that the hooligan movement is based on football without really being a part of it. 'The thugs' game' conveys the idea, without, perhaps, the irony of the Russian.

22 The Communist International (Comintern), known also as the Third International (1919–43), was an international organization led by the Communist Party of the Soviet Union that advocated world communism and carried out subversive acts to try to bring this about.

23 Walter Benjamin (1892–1940) was a German Jewish philosopher, cultural critic and essayist; Jürgen Habermas (b. 1929) is a German philosopher and sociologist in the tradition of critical theory and pragmatism; Giorgio Agamben (b. 1942) is an Italian philosopher best known for his work investigating the concepts of the state of exception, 'bare life' and *homo sacer*. The concept of biopolitics (see below) informs many of his writings; Slavoj Žižek (b. 1949) is a Slovenian philosopher. His subjects include continental philosophy, political theory, cultural studies, psychoanalysis, film criticism, Marxism, Hegelianism and theology.

24 A phrase uttered by Putin during a press conference in September 1999, commenting on the Russian air force bombing of the Chechen capital Grozny.

25 https://pora-valit.livejournal.com/1258484.html. 'Time to call a halt? Everything you need to know about emigration' (in Russian), Voice of Russia radio station, 21 March 2013.

26 Lubyanka Square is where the KGB/FSB headquarters is; behind this large building is the infamous Lubyanka Prison, to which thousands of political prisoners and innocent people were taken in Stalin's time and later. The memorial – a large stone brought from the Solovetsky Islands, the scene of a notorious prison camp – was deliberately placed on this spot and unveiled in a ceremony in the more liberal period of Mikhail Gorbachev's leadership in 1990.

Part III: The War for the Body

1 The later years of Leonid Brezhnev's time as General Secretary of the Party, and thus ruler of the Soviet Union, were marked by a lack of economic and political progress. As a result, this period was dubbed 'the era of stagnation'. Little changed after Brezhnev died in November 1982 and was replaced by Yury Andropov; nor when Andropov died and was replaced by Chernenko in February 1984. It took the arrival of Mikhail Gorbachev in March 1985 for the era of stagnation to end.

2 http://1libertaire.free.fr/MFoucault219.html (in French).

3 In June 1996, after the first round of the Russian presidential election and before the decisive run-off vote between Yeltsin and the Communist candidate Gennady Zyuganov, Yeltsin suffered a heart attack. This was kept from public knowledge. After Yeltsin won the second round, it was announced that he had had a heart attack and he subsequently underwent a

quintuple heart by-pass operation. Political life in Russia remained in limbo for months.

4 https://themoscowtimes.com/articles/no-putin-no-russia-says-kremlin-deputy-chief-of-staff-40702. '"No Putin, No Russia", Says Kremlin Deputy Chief of Staff', *The Moscow Times*, 23 October 2014.

5 The branch of science that deals with death.

6 This title is a play on the name of the infamous Russian forgery, first published in 1903, *The Protocols of the Elders of Zion*. The fake document is supposed to describe a Jewish plan for global domination. It was translated into multiple languages, and disseminated internationally. The publishers claimed that these were the minutes of a meeting where Jewish leaders discussed their goal of global Jewish hegemony by subverting the morals of Gentiles, and by controlling the press and the world's economies. In 1921 it was exposed as a fraud by *The Times*.

7 The Synod of the Eastern Orthodox Church of 1666–7 introduced reforms that were then adopted by the Russian Church. Those who refused to accept the changes became known as the 'Old Believers' and were persecuted. Some fled abroad, others set up communities in Russia's vast wastelands, some of which were discovered only in Soviet times.

8 Harvey Milk was an American politician and the first openly gay elected official in the history of California, when he served on the San Francisco Board of Supervisors in 1977–8.

9 Bertrand Delanoë was Mayor of Paris 2001–14; Klaus Wowereit was Mayor of Berlin 2011–14; Ole von Beust was Mayor of Hamburg 2001–10; Glen Murray was Mayor of Winnipeg 1998–2004.

10 In 1966, Andrei Sinyavsky was sentenced to seven years in a labour camp for 'anti-Soviet activity', because of the opinions voiced by some of the characters in his novels, which had been published in the West. His trial, along with fellow writer Yuli Daniel, was seen as marking the end of the period of liberalization under Nikita Khrushchev (who had been ousted in 1964) and the start of the dissident movement.

11 The dock in Russian courts is usually inside a cage. This is ostensibly to protect those in the courtroom from violent defendants, but in practice is more usually simply a way of denigrating the accused. The principle of 'innocent until proven guilty' is often not adhered to in Russian courts.

12 *Dedovshchina* is institutionalized violence against the new conscripts by the older ones – 'the grandfathers' or '*dedy*' (hence the term). Every year, hundreds of young conscripts suffer permanent injury or even death as a result of this treatment.

13 Vladimir Sorokin, 'Day of the *Oprichnik*' (Penguin Books, 2018; trans. Jamey Gambrell, p. 129).

14 A day's unpaid work demanded of a vassal by his overlord.

15 'Comment voulez-vous gouverner un pays qui a deux cent quarante-six variétés de fromage?' 'Les Mots du Général', Ernest Mignon, 1962.

16 The Magnitsky List includes officials shown to have profited from corruption or been guilty of human rights abuses, and prevents them from travelling to countries where this is enforced. It is named after Sergei Magnitsky, a Russian lawyer for the Anglo-American businessman Bill Browder, who, after uncovering a multimillion-dollar fraud by senior Russian officials, was arrested on false charges and then murdered while in prison. Browder has

made it his mission to try to have a Magnitsky Law adopted in as many countries as possible, thus preventing corrupt officials from travelling abroad to take advantage of their ill-gotten gains.

17 A popular Russian soft drink.

Part IV: The War for Memory

1 In 1954, Crimea was transferred from Russian jurisdiction to Ukrainian jurisdiction, as a gesture to mark three hundred years of unity between Russia and Ukraine. As both republics were part of the Soviet Union, at the time the gesture was largely symbolic. In 1989, following the withdrawal in February of that year of the last Soviet troops which had been conducting a military campaign in Afghanistan since late 1979, the Congress of People's Deputies declared that the campaign had been a political mistake, ordered by a small group within the Communist Party's ruling Politburo.

2 http://www.vehi.net/chaadaev/filpisma.html (Letter 1, para. 8) (in Russian).

3 Ilya Oblomov and Andrei Stoltz are the two main characters in the nineteenth-century Russian novel *Oblomov*, by Ivan Goncharov, which is one of the classics of Russian literature of the period. Although the two characters in the novel are friends, they are completely different: the typical Russian landowner (*pomeshchik*), Oblomov, is lazy and a dreamy character, while Stoltz, of German origin, is energetic and wilful. In Russia, they are usually seen as epitomes of Russian (and Asian) laziness and Western practicality.

4 *Khalyava* is a peculiarly Russian concept. Basically, it means getting something free, especially if it comes from the state, misusing state funds, having a sinecure job, etc.

5 For a description of 'The Red Calendar' and the special days, see Part I, note 21. The type of calendar referred to is printed as a block on cheap paper, with each day being torn off as you go through the year.

6 English language version, Andrews UK Ltd, 2012, p. 266.

7 Vasily Rozanov, *The Apocalypse of Our Time* (Praeger Publishers, New York, 1977; trans. Robert Payne and Nikita Romanoff, pp. 228–9).

8 *Sovok* is a derogatory name for all things Soviet, and is also the Russian word for a dustpan.

9 Famous Soviet singers of the 1930s–60s.

10 Named after Andrei Zhdanov, who was responsible for that round of purges.

11 Reforms introduced by Petr Stolypin (prime minister, 1906–11) led to a massive deportation of peasants and prisoners to Siberia. A special type of carriage was introduced for these settlers, consisting of two parts: a standard passenger compartment for a peasant and his family and a large zone for their livestock and agricultural tools. After the Revolution, the *Cheka*/NKVD found these carriages convenient for transporting convicts and exiles: the passenger part was used for prison guards, the cattle part for prisoners.

12 The system of prison camps established across the Soviet Union under Stalin. GULAG is an acronym for *Glavnoe upravlenie lagerei*, the Main Directorate of Camps.

13 https://www.krugozormagazine.com/show/Brodskiy.2107.html. *Krugozor* magazine (in Russian), February 2014.

14 In 1932–3, Stalin ordered the deliberate creation of a manmade famine in Ukraine, which wiped out millions of Ukrainians. The word *Holodomor* is the Ukrainian (and Russian) word for famine.

15 https://www.theguardian.com/books/2007/sep/16/historybooks.features.

16 Varlam Shalamov, *The Kolyma Tales*, (Penguin Books, Harmondsworth, 1994; Trans John Glad).

17 Alexander Etkind, *Warped Mourning: Stories of the Undead in the Land of the Unburied* (Stanford University Press, 2013, p. 245).

18 As cited in *The Ashgate Research Companion to Memory Studies*, edited by Siobhan Kattago (Routledge, 2016, p. 255).

19 Etkind, *Warped Mourning*, p. 245.

20 The Axis Powers before and during the Second World War were Germany, Italy and Japan. Despite formally signing the Tripartite Pact in 1940, they were united by little more than their common enemies. Bulgaria, Hungary and Romania later joined, as did Yugoslavia – for two days.

21 Like *Spitting Image*, *Kukly* parodied the politicians of the day. The programme was extremely popular in Russia in the 1990s, and President Yeltsin apparently found his own puppet very funny. Putin, however, was unable to laugh at seeing himself portrayed satirically by a puppet, and the show was closed in 2002. In time, the channel that had shown it, NTV, was also shut down.

22 Vladimir Nabokov, *Tyrants Destroyed and Other Stories* (Weidenfeld & Nicholson, 1975, p. 36).

23 Brodsky was expelled from the USSR in 1972 for 'anti-Soviet activity'. He never published the poem, *On the Independence of Ukraine*, but he did deliver it on a few occasions at poetry readings.

24 https://www.vedomosti.ru/opinion/articles/2015/07/03/599078-rossiiskoe-obschestvo-ne-vidit-sebya. *Russian Society Can't See Itself* (in Russian), 2 July 2015.

25 http://www.inp.uw.edu.pl/mdsie/Political_Thought/GeneologyofMorals.pdf. Friedrich Nietzsche, *On the Genealogy of Morality*, (Cambridge Texts in the History of Political Thought, trans. Carol Diethe, First Essay, Section 10, p. 20).

26 https://mercaba.org/SANLUIS/Filosofia/autores/Contempor%C3%A1nea/Scheller/Ressentiment.pdf. Max Scheler, *Ressentiment: Das Ressentiment im Aufbau Der Moralen*, p. 101, n. 26; translation into English by Louis A. Coser from the text of 1915.

27 In August 1998 Russia defaulted on its debts and almost overnight the rouble crashed to about a quarter of its value. This made imported goods very expensive, and it acted as a stimulus for Russian industry.

28 https://www.colta.ru/articles/specials/4887-v-strane-pobedivshego-resenti-menta. *In the Country Where Resentment Has Triumphed* (in Russian), 6 October 2014.

29 https://www.vedomosti.ru/opinion/articles/2014/07/28/izbezhat-afgani-stana-2. *Sergei Karaganov: Avoid Afghanistan-2* (in Russian), 28 July 2014.

30 http://en.kremlin.ru/events/president/news/46860.

31 For more on Zhirinovsky and his Party, see Part I, notes 16 and 17.

32 *Dozhd* is the only TV station in Russia not controlled by the government. It broadcasts online.

33 The *Dolchstoss im Rücken* ('stab in the back' theory) was that in the First

World War the German Army was 'undefeated in the field' and had been 'stabbed in the back' – i.e., had been denied support at the crucial moment by a weary and defeatist civilian population and their leaders. This idea gained popularity in Germany in the difficult postwar years of the 1920s and '30s.

34 Iampolski, *In the Country Where Resentment Has Triumphed.*

35 The extremist 'South East Radical Bloc' (SERB), which started up in Eastern Ukraine when the war began in March 2014, and has since been active in parts of Russia.

36 'White Guard' refers to the Russian Civil War of 1917–22, when 'the Reds' – the Bolsheviks, who had carried out the Revolution in November 1917 – defeated the supporters of the former Tsarist system and anyone else who opposed them. Collectively, they were known as 'the Whites' or 'the White Guards'. Bunin hated Bolshevism and left Russia in 1920, never to return. He lived most of the remainder of his life in France, until his death in 1953.

37 https://www.kommersant.ru/doc/2827530. *Why Do We Cry and Pray So Bitterly?* (In Russian), 12 October 2015.

38 The camps in Kolyma, situated in the far northeastern corner of Russia, were considered the most notorious in the whole GULAG system.

39 Re *Holodomor*, see above. The siege of Leningrad by the German Army in the Second World War lasted from 8 September 1941 to 27 January 1944, and cost the lives of one and a half million of the city's inhabitants. Re *Dozhd* TV, see note 32.

40 Alexievich, *Why Do We Cry and Pray So Bitterly?.*

41 http://pelevin.nov.ru/texts/pe-t.html (in Russian).

42 *Come and See* is a Soviet war tragedy film made in 1985 by Elem Klimov, based on the book *Out of Fire* (referred to in the text) about the Belarusian villages burnt to the ground with their inhabitants by the Nazis.

43 https://www.poemhunter.com/poem/requiem/.

44 https://www.mk.ru/politics/2016/11/22/nenakazuemoe-proshloe-nuzhno-li-iskat-palachey-nkvd.html. *The Unpunished Past: The NKVD Executioners Should be Sought Out* (in Russian), 22 November 2016.

45 https://iz.ru/news/646830. *I Fear Justice* (in Russian), 23 November 2016.

46 There is a tradition in Russia for wedding parties on the way from the registry office to the wedding breakfast to stop off at various sites of historical or local interest. If it is a war memorial, the bride may even lay her bouquet there. A separate superstition is to rub or touch a part of a bronze statue for luck.

47 https://www.novayagazeta.ru/articles/2016/12/12/70870-utomlennye-eltsinym. *Burnt by Yeltsin* (in Russian), 12 December 2016.

48 The Church on the Blood was built in 2000–3 on the site where the Ipatiev House stood. Fearing that the House could become a focus for royalist sentiment, in 1977 the Soviet Communist Party ordered it to be knocked down. As First Secretary of the local Party Committee, Yeltsin saw to it that the order was carried out.

49 An obsolete Russian unit of measurement, equivalent to a little over a kilometre.

50 In 1773–4, the Cossack, Yemelyan Pugachev, led a peasant revolt to try to seize the throne from the Empress Catherine II.

51 This is an oft-cited quote from <u>Alexander Pushkin's</u> *History of the Pugachev Rebellion*, 'God save us from seeing a Russian riot, senseless and merciless'.

52 'The People's Will' (Russ: *Narodnaya Volya*) was a nineteenth-century revolutionary political organization that used terrorism in an attempt to promote reforms in the country. It is best known for killing Tsar Alexander II in 1881.

53 https://books.google.co.uk/books?id=2X7GAAAAQBAJ&pg=PA148&lp g=PA148&dq=Alexander+Galich+Petersburg+Romances&source=bl&ots =ZkFcrVONSO&sig=ACfU3U2fcpvMPYlbXVNhm4G4tx2DwPOS2Q&- hl=en&sa=X&ved=2ahUKEwi-k_bxuIvgAhWJXhUIHeirCpYQ6AEwDn oECAMQAQ#v=onepage&q=Alexander%20Galich%20Petersburg%20 Romances&f=false.

54 In both Tsarist and Soviet times prisoners were divided into two groups: criminals (who had broken the law) and 'politicals', who were arrested for their political views. This is also a feature of Putin's regime.

INDEX